THE PAS
UNDERGROUND
GUIDE
to the
REVISED
COMMON
LECTIONARY
Year A

THE PASTOR'S UNDERGROUND GUIDE

to the

REVISED COMMON LECTIONARY

Year A

by

Shelley E. Cochran

Chalice Press
St. Louis, Missouri

Cover design: David Nassar
Art Director: Michael Domínguez

10 9 8 7 6 5 4 3 2 1   95 96 97 98 99

Library of Congress Cataloging–in–Publication Data
(pending)

Printed in the United States of America

CONTENTS

ACKNOWLEDGMENTS

Many people have helped contribute to this work and I would be remiss if I did not acknowledge them. I am grateful to Dr. Darrell Doughty, Dr. Charles Rice, and Dr. Janet Fishburn, who, each in his or her own way, helped bring this book to birth. I am also grateful for contributions made to my work by Dr. Horton Davies. I am thankful for the invaluable editorial work given to me by Dr. Carol A. Kitchen and by Dr. Megan Simpson of the Drew University Writing Center. I thank folks I worked with at the Drew University Library, who not only assisted me in doing research but also gave the support of their friendship. I also am grateful for the forbearance and support of my friends who encouraged me when the writing got rough, and for the help of the Drew University Academic Computer Center Staff, who more than once rescued large parts this book from the mysterious black holes of my computer disks.

INTRODUCTION

Liturgical Hermeneutics:
Worship and Lectionary as Interpreters
of Scripture

This book is about the *Revised Common Lectionary*. It is not like most books about the lectionary, though, which is why I've called it an "underground guide." It will not give you liturgical helps based on the lectionary. It will not give you biblical commentary on the various lectionary texts. It will not introduce you to the themes characteristic of the various seasons of the church year as they appear in the lectionary texts. It will not even introduce you to the basics of using the lectionary. Those books are readily available and I highly recommend their use.

Instead, this book is about *the lectionary as an interpreter of the Bible*. It is about the ways the lectionary shapes and influences our experience of the Bible in public worship. It is, in a sense, an inside look at the inner workings of the lectionary and how those inner workings affect our knowledge and understanding of the scriptures.

In order to truly understand the lectionary and the subtle yet powerful influence it has on the way we view the Bible, we must begin with an even more fundamental issue: the relationship between the Bible and Christian worship in general. This is, of course, a much larger question, but it is an important starting place because in many respects the lectionary is the primary point of intersection between the Bible and the

1

worship of the church. In fact, with the possible exception of the sermon, the lectionary is the most direct place where scripture and liturgy come together.

Let us begin then with the Bible. That is where Christian tradition, especially the Protestant tradition, usually begins— and for good reason. The Bible has held a central place in Christian liturgy for centuries. It has served as the authoritative guide for worship. It has been the primary source for liturgical symbolism, imagery, and language. And it has acted as one of the most, if not *the* most, important shapers of the liturgical tradition.

However, while the Bible definitely influences Christian worship, I maintain that the opposite is also true. The way in which we understand the Bible is likewise shaped by the fact that we hear it read and interpreted most often in worship. The hymns, the prayers, the ceremonies of worship all add an additional twist to the way we are likely to hear the Bible when it appears in the sermon.

To get a picture of the degree to which worship colors our understanding of the Bible, imagine for a moment the numerous times you may have heard Handel's *Messiah*. Think of all those moving arias and stirring choruses. All the words are straight out of the Bible, and yet they are not the Bible. A disproportionate number of the passages, for instance, are taken from the prophets and the epistles. Most are not in biblical order. Some passages in the *Messiah* do not even contain the complete biblical sentence from which they were taken. But even more important for our understanding of those passages is the way they have been put together. As one highly regarded biblical scholar has noted,

> Few people have any idea who produced the libretto for the [*Messiah*], and fewer still have any sense of the principles of selection operative in its combination of various biblical texts. Yet those who listen to the great choruses are convinced by a special form of argument that a whole variety of scriptural passages are "messianic." Students of Isaiah may offer whatever arguments they like about the original setting of the lines "For unto us a child is born, unto us a son is given"....People know such passages are "messianic"—simply because they are part of Handel's *Messiah*.[1]

---

[1] Donald Juel, *Messianic Exegesis: Christological Interpretation of the Old Testament in Early Christianity* (Philadelphia: Fortress, 1988), p. 16.

The liturgy's powerful influence on our knowledge and understanding of the Bible is quite understandable, though, given that much of the Bible itself was written for or came out of the context of public worship. In fact, some such as William Willimon, have even argued that worship is the Bible's "native habitat."[2]

Traditionally, then, the church has been inclined to see the influence of worship on our knowledge and understanding of the Bible in a positive light. The liturgy has long been regarded as a wise and benevolent teacher, a perfect, almost indispensable guide through the intricacies of scripture. And in many respects, this is true. Worship can, and often does, provide the community of faith with a helpful lens by which to view the Bible.

This is, of course, not the only way to look at it. The influence of the liturgy also has its "shadow side," which preachers cannot afford to ignore if we are to fulfill our calling as faithful interpreters of the Word. As is the case with Handel's *Messiah*, the liturgy is sometimes not so helpful. At times it can even mislead people into erroneous assumptions about the Bible, particularly if the only time such people ever hear the Bible is in the context of worship.

As an example, John Barton asks us to consider the popular liturgical formula, "This is the word of the Lord." It is a powerful statement, he says, taken right from the writings of the prophets. When used after each biblical reading indiscriminately, however, it presupposes a prophetic paradigm for interpreting every reading, regardless of which portion of the Bible that reading may have come from originally. Such a formula, Barton argues, entices both preacher and congregation to interpret parts of scripture which are not prophetic as if they were and encourages the "mistaken assumption of instant applicability."[3]

The Protestant Reformation, of course, was one of the first times such concerns about the liturgy's more negative influence were raised. Convinced that *sola scriptura* was the most effective means for knowing and understanding the Bible, reformers all across Europe sought a style of worship that would let scripture stand supreme, unmediated by what they consid-

---

[2] William Willimon, *The Bible: A Sustaining Presence in Worship* (Valley Forge: Judson Press, 1981), p. 19.

[3] John Barton, *People of the Book: The Authority of the Bible in Christianity* (London: SPCK, 1988), p. 74.

ered to be the "vain ceremonies" of the liturgy. Many, including Zwingli, downplayed the liturgy. Others, such as Calvin and Luther, tried to make worship more biblical or tried to revise the liturgy in light of scripture—all in an effort to eliminate, or at least reduce, some of the liturgy's less desirable influences on the church's experience of the Bible.

In more recent years the issue has surfaced again in light of ecumenical efforts to lift up and enhance the place of worship in the life of the church. Concerned that liturgy might overshadow scripture, a man by the name of Henry Adams, for example, began to argue almost twenty years ago that, because of the liturgy's repetitive nature, a bad liturgy was capable of undermining even the best exegetical sermon.[4] A few years later, Frederick Schroeder made the same point when he talked about "questionable liturgy" leading to "questionable" understanding of the Bible.[5] Such warnings have not disappeared, but instead have been taken up and refined in more recent years by others such as Gerard Sloyan and James Sanders.

It is at this juncture that our study of the lectionary enters into the picture. It is here that the lectionary becomes important, because, by virtue of its place as the main point where the Bible and the liturgy intersect, the lectionary by definition is an interpreter of scripture. Indeed it is one of the most powerful interpreters of scripture in the entire church.

Often this powerful interpreter is seen in the same positive light as the whole liturgy. The lectionary is frequently pictured as that same kind of benevolent, indispensable, and, above all, objective teacher that the liturgy has been thought to be. And in many respects it is true. In fact, this is one of the lectionary's main selling points: it helps guard against the subjective "hobby horses" of individual preachers.

In spite of its reputation, however, the lectionary is not completely objective. It is not theologically neutral, and if its history is any indication, it was never meant to be. Instead, the lectionary contains within it certain *a priori* assumptions and principles by which its lessons are chosen and arranged.

---

[4] Henry B. Adams, "The Liturgical Subversion of Theology," *The Pulpit* 35.6 (June 1964). Interestingly enough, years later James W. Cox, in his book, *Preaching* (San Francisco: Harper and Row, 1985), makes a similar point on p. 43 when he discusses how liturgy can hinder preaching when it is not itself biblical.

[5] Frederick Schroeder, *Worship in the Reformed Tradition* (Philadelphia: United Church Press, 1966), p. 29.

For example, the lectionary, by its very nature, serves an editorial function, creating as it were a "canon within the canon."[6] The lectionary dictates which biblical passages will or will not be read. It dictates at which point each of the biblical passages chosen will begin and end. It also dictates whether particular verses are to be included or excluded from within a given passage.

This editorial function is probably the single most important way the lectionary influences the Christian community's knowledge and understanding of the Bible. By dictating, for example, which passages will or will not be read, the lectionary determines what parts of the Bible worshipers will hear. Passages or stories that are not in the lectionary effectively become lost. The same is true for individual verses that are excluded from a lectionary passage. Because they are not read, they too are effectively lost.

The lectionary also serves an interpretive function by associating particular passages with one another or with the days and seasons of the church year. By design and by deliberate repetition, these passages become indelibly linked and are seldom ever heard in worship outside their particular association. Certain passages, then, become associated with certain other passages—the way readings from the Hebrew Bible are often linked to the Gospel reading, for instance. In the same way, other passages become associated with particular holy days or seasons—the way John the Baptist has been linked to Advent, or the way Handel's *Messiah* has linked the restoration prophecies of Isaiah to the birth, death, and resurrection of Christ.

Unfortunately, most preachers are largely unaware of these editorial and interpretive functions of the lectionary. They may know what readings are listed for a particular Sunday. They may know about the lectionary's three-year structure. They may even be aware of when the reading from the Hebrew scripture is linked to the Gospel reading and when it is not. But most preachers, even those who use the lectionary regularly, are often totally unaware of the many *a priori* assumptions and principles inherent in the lectionary and the way those assumptions and principles affect the way they, and their congregations, view the Bible.

---

[6] Gary Pense actually refers to this feature of lectionaries as censorship in his article, "The Inclusive Language Lectionary and the Church's Holy 'Censorship' of the Bible," *Currents in Theology and Mission* 13.5 (October 1986), pp. 261-265.

As both a feminist and a biblical scholar, I believe it's time to raise awareness, and I believe this for two reasons.

First, my experience has led me to believe that most mainstream American Christians are not likely to encounter the Bible in any significant way outside worship. Today, most churchgoers depend almost entirely on the Sunday services as the place where they hear the scriptures read, and the place they most often hear them interpreted. In many communions, not even church school classes or private devotions can compete with the liturgy as the place where most believers come to "acquire their basic knowledge of the nature and content of the Bible."[7]

Second, no system for choosing liturgical readings from the scriptures is completely without bias. Practical, psychological, and theological preferences (both acknowledged and unacknowledged) often govern the choices. I believe that preachers, particularly those of us who use the lectionary, need to be aware of these biases and their often subtle influences. As faithful interpreters of the Word, we need to know the assumptions and principles behind the lectionary. We need to understand how the lectionary works, in order that we might ensure that the Bible passages people hear in the liturgy, abridged as they must be for worship, reflect as accurately as is possible the whole of the biblical witness. Otherwise, the Bible we preach will be distorted, either by our own hermeneutical inclinations or, more often, by the hermeneutical inclinations of the compilers of whatever lectionary we choose to use.

In this *Guide*, I will be calling attention to several ways to go about this task. The first is: *approach the lectionary with a hermeneutic of suspicion.* Do not trust it completely. Do not accept it entirely at face value. Instead, use the lectionary critically and thoughtfully, with full awareness of the hermeneutical tendencies and guiding principles that have gone into its making.

Ask questions of the lectionary. Ask about its intended purpose and intent. Ask about its theological perspectives. Ask about its use of liturgical tradition, too.

Also, ask questions of the individual lections. Ask, for example, why the particular passage you are working on was chosen over other possible passages. Ask why that particular passage appears in the lectionary where it does. As part of your

---

[7] See Phyllis Bird, *The Bible as the Church's Book* (Philadelphia: Westminster, 1982).

exegetical study, compare the passage's biblical context with its context in the lectionary. Does its place in the church year, and its relationship to other passages also chosen for that same day, do justice to the passage's place within scripture?

Ask questions about possible editing too. Are verses cut out of the middle of a passage? How might the absence of those verses affect its meaning? Where does the lectionary passage begin and end? Is this the same place where the biblical passage itself actually begins or ends? Does that also make a difference in its meaning?

Second, *be alert to those times when the lectionary's more liturgical interests threaten to overshadow the text itself.* Watch for texts that have obviously been chosen for their relationship to the church year and make a special effort to hear the text speak on its own first. Look for passages that are clearly linked to one another and carefully do your homework on them separately. If you use both texts in your sermon, be extra diligent and careful so that in combining them neither text gets misunderstood.

Such details may seem insignificant, but they are not. As long as the lectionary is based on the church year, the ongoing tension in it between "proclamation and teaching" and "calendar and canon" will nearly always be weighted in favor of proclamation and calendar.[8] That's how deeply the year's hermeneutical tendencies and the problems that come with it are imbedded within the structure and lessons of the lectionary. Our job as preachers is to even the scales a bit.

Third, *be reasonable in what you expect of the lectionary.* Know its limitations as well as its advantages. Know what you can expect of the lectionary and, even more important, know what you cannot expect of it. The lectionary is not perfect. It is not objective. It is not all things to all people. In fact, the lectionary often cannot accomplish many things typically claimed for it.

Be cautious then. Don't expect the lectionary to give you all the Bible your congregation is ever likely to need. Don't expect

---

[8] This imbalance was particularly noticeable in the Consultation's efforts to balance their "concern for women's issues, for Jewish-Christian understanding, and for other justice issues" (all of which heavily influence the lectionary's ability to teach effectively) and their concern to not "further distance the *Common Lectionary* from the Roman, Episcopal, and Lutheran lectionaries" (all of which heavily emphasize proclamation). Minutes of the November 1988 meeting of the Consultation on Common Texts.

the lectionary to substitute for a good biblical commentary. Don't expect it to substitute for the Bible itself, either. It can't.

Instead, use the lectionary as it was intended to be used, as a tool. Think of it as a guide, one guide among many, for choosing the scriptures to be read in public worship. In some respects, the lectionary is made even more effective when combined with other guides, such as preaching through a biblical book, for example, or a sermon series taken from a particular type of biblical literature.

Fourth, *dare occasionally to make deliberate and informed changes in the assigned readings.* Try not to let the lectionary enslave you. Feel free to lay it aside on occasion. Switch readings from one Sunday to the next if your work on a particular passage warrants it. When the biblical context calls for it, make purposeful, prudent, and pastoral departures from the assigned readings.

Some of these departures might be very simple. Deliberately including individual verses that may have been edited out of a particular passage is one possibility. Choosing to preach on only one passage, even when the lectionary has linked that passage with others, is another simple way to depart from the lectionary and give the congregation another point of view.

Other more drastic departures from the lectionary might also be taken in order to supplement the official readings. One might deliberately choose, for example, occasionally to read and preach on passages that never appear in the lectionary. This would give congregations the opportunity to hear and reflect on passages they would not ordinarily hear. It would also give pastors the chance to strengthen the lectionary's coverage of those areas of the scriptural literature that are presently represented inadequately.

Some departures from the lectionary might also serve to address the liturgical dominance of the church year and of the Gospel lesson that relates to it. Passages that are seldom read because they do not fit into the liturgical year, for example, could be given a new hearing. Passages that by tradition are seldom heard outside their specific setting within the year might also be heard with new ears if they are occasionally used outside their usual liturgical context.

Other departures from the assigned lections might serve to highlight the rich diversity of scripture as well. Rather than strictly adhering to the complementarily linked passages listed in the lectionary, passages with divergent, or even contradictory, perspectives could occasionally be chosen together. Passages from widely different theological viewpoints could then be set alongside each other, letting the juxtaposition give rise to new and possibly unexpected scriptural insights.[9]

After all, the lectionary is too important and too formative for the life of the church to be used exclusively or uncritically. It is too influential to be taken simply at face value, but instead deserves our best and most rigorous thinking.

The Lectionary as an Editor

The process of creating a lectionary is never completely objective. All lectionaries, even well-constructed ones such as the *Revised Common Lectionary*, have built-in biases. They are all inevitably the product of certain decisions and each is built with certain presuppositions, assumptions, and principles, both stated and unstated. In fact, it seems virtually impossible to produce a lectionary without becoming entangled in at least some *a priori* assumptions and operating principles.

In this section, I want to look at the process by which the *Revised Common Lectionary* came into being. Specifically, I want to highlight several important questions that faced those who compiled the lectionary. I want to look at the decisions those compilers had to make, the principles and presuppositions they used to make those decisions, and the role those decisions, principles, and presuppositions still play in the lectionary's treatment of scripture.

First, however, a brief overview of some specific principles used in the creation of the *Revised Common Lectionary*.

Principles Used by the Revised Common Lectionary

Fortunately, the framers of the lectionary are quite open about most of the principles they used in their work. In fact, the initial edition of the lectionary published by the Consultation itself was fully annotated, complete with an explanatory

---

[9] Gerard Sloyan has even made some specific suggestions for improving the *Common Lectionary*. He suggests the use of two substantial readings rather than three shorter ones, the first of which would come from either the Hebrew Scriptures or a non-Gospel portion of the Christian Scriptures and the second from one of the Gospels. Sloyan also recommends a de-emphasis on Acts and John during the season of Easter and a re-emphasis on the teaching function of the lectionary as an effective means of proclamation. "Some Suggestions for a Biblical Three-Year Lectionary," *Worship* 63.6 (November 1989), pp. 533-535.

introduction and editorial notes for each set of Sunday and festival readings.[10]

The principles employed in the *Revised Common Lectionary* were borrowed in large part from its predecessor, the Roman *Lectionary for Mass*. In fact, the Roman *Lectionary* is so important to the *Revised Common Lectionary* that it is necessary to first understand the principles used in the first before one can adequately understand and critique the second. Fortunately, those who worked on the Roman *Lectionary* were also open about their operating principles.[11]

The Roman *Lectionary* itself is a revision of a traditional lectionary that had been in place for years. Thus, the Roman *Lectionary* carries within it the basic hermeneutic and structure inherited from the traditional church year. The major seasons are basically unchanged and many old readings are retained, some in their original places. In fact, most changes in structure that were made purposely served to strengthen the influence of the church year on the *Lectionary*.

Revisions were made for three reasons. The first was pastoral.[12] Thus its framers emphasized the Lord's Day, when most people were more likely to be in worship, rather than saints' days, when people were not. Lessons were also kept relatively short, particularly the first (usually Old Testament) and second (usually epistle) readings. And, most significantly, those verses that the framers found difficult were excluded. This was not done quickly or easily, but the compilers felt it was necessary in cases where including difficult verses might be more problematic than excluding them.

The second major reason for revisions was to ensure that the new *Lectionary* contained more scripture, and especially more lections from the Hebrew Scriptures. Thus a multiple (in this case, three) year structure was chosen rather than a one-year structure. The framers also chose to appoint three les-

---

[10] Consultation on Common Texts, *Common Lectionary: The Lectionary Proposed by the Consultation on Common Texts* (New York: Church Hymnal Corporation, 1983).

[11] See the Introduction to the Lectionary, *The New Liturgy: A Comprehensive Introduction to the New Liturgy as a Whole and to Its New Calendar, Order of Mass, Eucharistic Prayers, the Roman Canon, Prefaces, and the New Sunday Lectionary* (London: Darton, Longman, and Todd, 1970), and the Introduction to *Lectionary for Mass*, English translation approved by the National Conference of Catholic Bishops and confirmed by the Apostolic See (New York: Benzinger, 1970).

[12] Introduction to the *Lectionary for Mass*, p. 12.

sons for each Sunday and major festival, the first of which would be a reading from the Hebrew Bible (except during the season of Easter).[13]

Gospel lessons, which had always enjoyed a premier place, were likewise enhanced. Effort was made to include more complete passages and the repetition of Gospel stories was eliminated, except in those cases where the framers found it necessary to include the distinctive versions of more than one Gospel. Semi-continuous readings from the synoptic Gospels were also chosen to emphasize a particular synoptic Gospel in each of the yearly cycles, while John continued to be emphasized on major festivals such as Christmas and Easter.

The third reason for changes was to revise the relationships between the lessons by using a combination of independent and harmonized readings. During major festivals, all three readings were harmonized and, in some cases, were even connected to readings from previous and subsequent Sundays. In Ordinary Time the reading from the Hebrew Scriptures was always linked with the Gospel and occasionally to the epistle reading as well.

The compilers of the *Revised Common Lectionary* used those same basic principles as a starting point. They presupposed the Roman *Lectionary's* basic structure and its calendar. They also borrowed its Gospel lessons with only minor revisions, most often adding or subtracting a verse here and there or moving passages from one Sunday to another nearby Sunday.

Their first new task was to address what many were already identifying as problems in the Roman *Lectionary*. Members of the Consultation looked at such things as length of passage, confusing beginning and ending points, large gaps within lessons, and the appropriateness of certain other lessons.

Several specific principles guided this editing process. Passages were edited to make them more understandable. Passages were also edited on the basis of pastoral concerns, i.e. "unhelpful verses" were cut. Passages were also edited in or-

---

[13] According to Geoffrey Wainwright, this reintroduction of the Hebrew Scriptures did not arise out of a completely objective concern that the whole of scripture be adequately represented in the new lectionary. Rather, it came out of the direct influence of a particular theological orientation—that of the Biblical Theology movement. This movement, which emphasized both the importance of the Hebrew Scriptures and their connection to early Christian writings, possibly more than any other theological stance, shaped the Roman *Lectionary's* use of the Old Testament. Wainwright, *Doxology: The Praise of God in Worship, Doctrine, and Life* (New York: Oxford, 1980), p. 172.

der to tie them to specific themes or to relate them to other passages.

The Consultation's most important new task, however, was to improve the choice of lections from the Hebrew Bible. This was a concern for two reasons. First, the compilers of the *Revised Common Lectionary* felt that certain parts of the Hebrew Bible had not been adequately represented. They viewed the minor prophets and the wisdom literature as having been particularly slighted.[14] Thus, they revised many of the Roman *Lectionary's* Old Testament readings and added others of their own choosing.

Second, the compilers of the *Revised Common Lectionary* were concerned about the Roman *Lectionary's* heavy use of typology. This too was thought to not truly represent the Hebrew Scriptures. They were not willing to completely eliminate typology, however. So, when their work was revised and republished in 1993, the Consultation included two sets of readings from the Hebrew Bible for every Sunday during Ordinary Time—one reading linked to the Gospel lesson for the day and one that was part of a series of semi-continuous readings.

With that brief overview in mind, then, let us look in more detail at the questions involved in the making of a lectionary and the impact the answers given by the *Revised Common Lectionary's* compilers has had on the lectionary's treatment of scripture.

The Question of Purpose

The first and fundamentally most influential question faced by the compilers of the *Revised Common Lectionary* was the question of purpose. Before the first list of Sundays and festival days to be included was even considered, before the first passage was even chosen, those who put the lectionary together had to ask themselves, "What do we want this lectionary to accomplish? What purpose do we want it to serve?"

This is not as simple a question as it might seem at first. In fact, there is quite a difference of opinion on the matter, with most views generally falling into one of two major camps.

On the one hand, there are those who view the lectionary primarily through the lens of the liturgy. They argue that the primary purpose of any lectionary is to proclaim Christ. In this view, a lectionary is primarily a vehicle for proclamation. On

---

[14] *Common Lectionary*, p. 21.

the other hand, there are others who would argue that the most important purpose of a lectionary is to provide the Christian community at worship a faithful, organized, and systematic presentation of the full range of scripture. In this view the lectionary is first and foremost "the Church's catechism,"[15] and its primary purpose is to strengthen the church's understanding of the scriptures.[16]

Those who worked on the *Revised Common Lectionary* itself worked hard not to take sides between these two views of the lectionary's purpose. They have viewed the lectionary both as a teaching tool and as a vehicle for the church's proclamation of Christ in the liturgy. Both purposes are included in the guiding principles used by the Consultation. Both are reflected in the Consultation's choice of passages. Both can be found in the way the lectionary itself was finally structured.

One could conceivably argue that this taking of the middle ground is a strength of the lectionary. One could say that it makes the lectionary more flexible, more responsive to various needs, and less tied to a dogmatic view of what a lectionary should be and do.

However, one could just as easily (and I personally believe more persuasively) argue that taking the middle ground on the question of purpose has led instead to a unintended bias toward the liturgy. Given that the lectionary's structure is based on the liturgical church year and given that the lectionary's primary use is in the liturgy, this bias is not surprising. To balance it would have required an equally strong bias toward teaching on the part of the lectionary's compilers, a course they did not choose to take.

Moreover, taking the middle ground between the lectionary as liturgist and the lectionary as teacher has also led to a unintended lack of clarity. In fact, because it is often not sure of its purpose, the *Revised Common Lectionary* is at times woefully inconsistent, often choosing passages for their didactic value at one point and choosing them for their liturgical value at others.

---

[15] John Fitzsimmons, "Learning to Live with the Lectionary," *The Clergy Review* 57 (June 1972), p. 424.

[16] A sign of the strength of this position, at least among some Protestant groups, is the use of the lectionary in Christian education. An example is Joseph P. Russell, *Sharing Our Biblical Story* (Minneapolis: Winston Press, 1979). The Presbyterian Church (USA) has even based a major church school curriculum, *Celebrate*, on the structure and readings found in the *Common Lectionary*, as has the United Church of Christ (*The Word Among Us*).

Structural and Editorial Questions

Once the question of purpose had been decided, the compilers of the *Revised Common Lectionary* then faced several important structural and editorial issues. What time frame would the lectionary encompass: one year or multiple years? Would the lectionary follow biblical readings in their canonical order (*lectio continuo*) or would it instead follow specific topics or themes? Would the lessons be related to one another or would they be completely independent? What method would compilers use to choose lessons? How long would the chosen lections be? Would lessons be edited, and if so, for what reasons?

Those questions are just as crucial as the question of purpose, for the answer to each of them also has an enormous impact on the way the lectionary treats the biblical passages included in it. Decisions about time frame and lesson length, for instance, affect how much of the Bible it will be possible to include. Decisions as to how the lessons are to be ordered affect the flow of thought found in the readings. Decisions about the dependence or independence of lessons affect the context in which those passages will be heard in worship. Likewise, decisions about the editing of individual passages also affect the context in which individual lessons are heard.

STRUCTURAL ISSUES

The first structural question that can carry with it heavy implications for how a lectionary like the *Revised Common Lectionary* will treat the biblical materials is the question of time frame. Although the church year is usually the basic unit of structure, lectionaries can encompass either a one-year cycle or a cycle of several years.

Each design has its advantages and disadvantages. One-year lectionaries, for example, have historical precedence. They are compact (and thus more easily bound in a single book). They are also not complicated to use. However, they can include only a limited number of lessons. As a result, one-year lectionaries are often not comprehensive, nor are they especially effective in representing fairly the various theological viewpoints found in scripture.

Multiple-year lectionaries such as the *Revised Common Lectionary*, on the other hand, usually contain a sufficient number of lessons to be both comprehensive and inclusive. This is their major advantage. Their longer length not only permits the presentation of a much wider range of biblical material, but also allows for more prolonged explorations into particular parts of scripture as well. This is not to say, however, that multiple-year lectionaries guarantee complete comprehensiveness. They do not, as we shall soon see, but they do make comprehensiveness much more probable than single-year lectionaries.

One major disadvantage to multiple-year lectionaries is their cumbersome length; they often require more than one volume to print each lesson in full. More importantly, though, they are also more complex and hence take more effort and sophistication on the part of those who use them[17] (thus creating the need for books like this one). Still, because multiple-year lectionaries offer far more passages of scripture than do one-year lectionaries, their advantages often far outweigh whatever disadvantages might be involved in using them.

The second structural question that can carry with it heavy implications for how a lectionary like the *Revised Common Lectionary* will treat the biblical materials involves the method by which the lessons are to be chosen. Traditionally this is done in three ways: the *lectio continuo* method, the thematic method, and the "combination" method.

In the strict *lectio continuo* method the books of the Bible are read in sequence. Each reading begins where the last reading ended. Given the length of the Bible, however, this is extremely impractical. More frequently a modified version of *lectio continuo*, or semi-continuous reading, is used. This entails reading a particular biblical book sequentially, omitting certain passages between the chosen readings (1 Kings 19:1–5; 1 Kings 19:9–14; 1 Kings 19:15–21; and 1 Kings 21:1–3, 17–21, for example).

In either form, continuous readings have much to commend them as a way of presenting scripture in as comprehensive and accurate a way as possible. Continuous readings assure that a sizable portion of the biblical material will be covered. They assure that most, if not all, of the biblical narratives will be heard in their entirety. And most important, continuous readings present the scriptures in order, as they are, unmediated by ecclesiastical tradition or editing. Continuous readings are,

---

[17] A case in point is the way in which the new Roman *Lectionary*, and the *Common Lectionary* that followed it, seem to presuppose an understanding of redaction criticism. According to Reginald Fuller, this is particularly true in regard to the Gospels, since each year of the two lectionaries' three-year cycle is designed to emphasize the distinctive flavor of one of the Synoptics. Reginald Fuller, *Preaching the New Lectionary: The Word of God for the Church Today*. (Collegeville, MN: Liturgical Press, 1971), pp. xx-xxi.

in many respects, the best method available to lectionaries for handling the scriptures with accuracy and respect.

The second most common method for choosing lessons is the topical or thematic. This method takes readings from various parts of scripture according to stated themes. Most often these themes are related to the church year, but they can also be theological or doctrinal, as in the case of the readings chosen for Trinity or Reign of Christ Sunday.

The pedagogical advantages to this method are obvious, for in many respects thematic choices make a lectionary an effective teaching tool. Through it, congregations not only become more acquainted with the great themes of Christian tradition but they also have that teaching regularly reinforced through repetition.

Thematic lectionaries also give a needed structure and discipline to the reading of scripture.[18] They present the Bible in an organized and orderly fashion. They connect passages in ways that make the lessons easier to learn and remember. They also encourage the well-respected practice of allowing scripture to interpret scripture.

The thematic/topical method, however, does not always present the scriptures accurately. In fact, this is the thematic method's primary drawback. First, lessons for one Sunday are often disconnected from lessons for the next. This unfortunately encourages a piecemeal presentation of scripture. It also gives little sense of the continuity of the scriptural witness.[19]

Second, the thematic method often uses many parts of the Bible without fully allowing the distinctive aspects of any particular portion of scripture to be given adequate expression. In fact, with thematic lectionaries, congregations seldom, if ever, get the full impact of a particular Gospel's character, for example. In some cases, congregations using thematic lectionaries may never even hear an entire narrative read in full.

Third, and maybe most important, the thematic approach can often draw more attention to the theme than it does to the text. Especially when the theme for the day is given in a prominent title, it easily catches the eye, overshadows the text, and

---

[18] See John Gunstone, "Contemporary Problems of Liturgical Time: Calendar and Lectionary," *Studia Liturgica* 14.2, 3, and 4 (1982), pp. 74-88.

[19] Interestingly, Sherman Johnson argues that rather than a disadvantage, this piecemeal character is actually an advantage in that it more accurately reflects the way in which the biblical tradition itself came into being. *The Year of the Lord's Favor: Preaching the Three-Year Lectionary* (New York: Seabury, 1983), pp. 145-146.

leads many to go no further than the title to understand what the text might be saying. Thus, in a highly thematic lectionary, the theme, and not the text itself, can all too easily become the guiding principle for interpreting a given passage of scripture.[20]

Fourth, the thematic approach often assumes a structure that is not actually present in the biblical readings. Such a structure can be doctrinal, theological, ecclesiastical, liturgical, or even, as in most cases, a mixture of each. As we shall see in the next chapter, this is particularly evident in the festival seasons when the themes of the church year impose a structure on Gospel narratives, such as the one in Mark, which actually have a very different structure.

By using these structures, then, thematic lectionaries tend to homogenize the Bible. They often blend passages from different time frames, from different theological perspectives, even different literary contexts and mix them all together under a single, overarching theme, often operating on "an implicit assumption that wherever one opened the Bible, one encountered a unified doctrinal structure."[21] This is especially true for readings chosen for a Sunday such as Reign of Christ, when all the readings are linked together under the same theme, even though in their biblical context they are not related to one another at all.

The third method of choosing lessons is a combination of the first two methods. This is the method used by the *Revised Common Lectionary*, having inherited it from the Roman *Lectionary for Mass*. Thus, during major festivals and seasons, primarily Advent/Christmas and Lent/Easter, lessons in the *Revised Common Lectionary* are most often chosen themati-

---

[20] Howard Hageman, "A Brief Study of the British Lectionary." *Worship* 56 No. 4 (July 1982), p. 358. A telling example of a theme drawing attention away from the biblical texts themselves can be found in the highly thematic lectionary produced by the Joint Liturgical Group. The theme for Pentecost 6, for instance, is "The New Man." The Gospel reading for that day in Year One is Luke 15:11–32, the "parable of the prodigal son." Traditionally, interpreters have concentrated on the relationship between the prodigal and his father, seeing it as a type for the relationship between the believer and God. Scholars such as Jeremias, Crossan, and Via, however, maintain that the more original meaning of the parable more likely rests with the figure of the jealous elder son. Seen in this way, the parable both defends Jesus' ministry with sinners and challenges the religious establishment of his day. A sermon could be preached from either viewpont, but the theme, "The New Man," strongly implies the first.

[21] Clark Hyde, "The Bible in the Church: The Lectionary as Paradigm," *Worship* 61.4 (July 1987), p. 323.

cally in order that the character of the festivals might be reflected in the readings. During nonfestival seasons, semi-continuous readings are more often chosen.

This combination method takes advantages from both the thematic and the continuous methods of choosing lections. It is able to accommodate the church year while also allowing significant portions of the Bible to be explored in depth. It also avoids some disadvantages inherent in the other two methods. It is not as disjointed as the thematic method, nor is it as inflexible as the strictly continuous or even semi-continuous method.

Unfortunately, even though it is probably the best method for choosing texts, the combination method is more complicated than either of the other two methods alone. As a result it demands much more of the preacher and congregation than choosing a passage by either the strict *lectio continuo* or thematic method. Lectionaries based on the combination method assume a basic acquaintance with the principles underlying the lectionary. They also assume that those who use it will have more than a basic acquaintance with both the scriptures and the church year.

The last and possibly most influential structural issue that can impact the way a lectionary like the *Revised Common Lectionary* will treat the biblical materials involves the relationship between lessons. In other words, should the lessons chosen for any given Sunday be entirely independent of one another or should they be connected in some way? Or, more specifically, should each lesson stand on its own or should there be a "controlling lesson" around which other lessons are arranged or "harmonized?"[22]

In the *Revised Common Lectionary*, the Gospel lesson is always the controlling lesson, although it exerts that "control" in different ways depending on the time of year. During festival seasons such as Advent or Easter, both the lesson from the Hebrew Scriptures and the epistle lesson are usually chosen specifically to harmonize, or correspond in some way to the Gospel lesson for that particular Sunday or feast day. During other more ordinary times of the year, both independent and harmonized readings are offered from the Hebrew Bible, while the epistle lessons are primarily independent, semi-continuous readings.

---

[22] The framers of the 1969 Roman *Lectionary for Mass* were the first to call this the "Principle of Harmonization."

This principle of harmonization has several advantages. Like the thematic approach, to which it is closely related, harmonization of lectionary readings can be an effective teaching tool. It also gives a structure to the Sunday readings that can be useful to the preachers using it.

Harmonization, however, has many more disadvantages, particularly when it comes to the way it uses the Bible. Like the thematic approach, the principle of harmonization often imposes an extra-biblical structure onto the chosen passages. It links passages that were not originally meant to be so connected. It often disregards the uniqueness of various parts of scripture, and it encourages preachers to "fit the lessons together" even when such connections may not be constructive or even intended by the lectionary in the first place.

The most important disadvantage to harmonizing lectionary readings, however, is the way in which such harmonization often links the Hebrew Scriptures to the Gospel lesson by a prophecy/fulfillment kind of hermeneutic. Thus one often finds a passage from the prophets, for instance, read on the same Sunday as its supposed fulfillment in the Gospel reading. In the same way, a narrative from the life of King David, for instance, is often read on the same day as a similar story in the life of Christ.

This is not a totally illegitimate methodology. It was one of the first ways the early church interpreted the Bible. However, as one commentator has pointed out, it is "not the best possible handling of the Hebrew Scriptures."[23] In fact, today harmonization of this type is a very problematic handling of the Hebrew Scriptures, as we shall see later on.

EDITORIAL ISSUES

The next set of issues faced by the compilers of the *Revised Common Lectionary* were editorial ones. These issues involve choosing which passages to include or not include. They involve choosing appropriate passage lengths. They involve editing verses within passages. Each of those choices, too, has an enormous impact on how the lectionary treats the Bible.

Not surprisingly, the first and most significant editorial decision involves the initial selection of passages to be included. For example, Lewis Briner has noted that the lectionary initially proposed by the Consultation on Common Texts was rightly criticized for a lack of Old Testament readings showing

---

[23] Clark Hyde, p. 361.

the role of women in sacred history.[24] Such a selective use of scripture, he argued, limits a community's perception of the biblical material. If a particular story (for example, one about a biblical woman) never appears in the lectionary, it is virtually lost to those who hear the Bible only in worship. To them, it is as if the story never existed. Likewise, a congregation using a lectionary that includes the parable of the lost sheep (in which a male shepherd figures prominently) but not the parable of the lost coin (a similar parable with a woman as leading figure) will also have a somewhat limited view of scripture, most likely one that emphasizes the experience of men to the exclusion of women.

The selection of passages to be included in a lectionary can be made in several ways: by a didactic approach, by a doctrinal approach, or by relying on previous precedents. All three approaches can be found in the *Revised Common Lectionary*. In some instances all three approaches played a part—as when passages that originally had been read in worship for their didactic or doctrinal content later found their way into the lectionary because they had gained a measure of precedence through the years.

In the didactic approach, lessons are chosen for their teaching value. Passage selection is made on the basis of how well they build up and edify the church. It is made on the perceived pedagogical value of the lessons.

Choosing passages for their didactic qualities has some advantages. It is practical. It is pastoral. It emphasizes time-honored passages of scripture, and it encourages homiletical reflection on those passages.

However, choosing passages primarily on the basis of how well they are thought to edify the church does not encourage homiletical reflection on less familiar, and possibly more difficult, passages. This is the major disadvantage to a heavily didactic approach to passage selection. It often shies away from difficult texts and thus frequently cuts a congregation off from whatever word those more challenging passages might have to say. A heavily didactic approach also keeps congregations and their preachers from having to wrestle with those hard but important textual and interpretive questions raised by the biblical material.

---

[24] Lewis A. Briner, "A Look at New Proposals for the Lectionary," *Reformed Liturgy and Music* 17.3 (Summer 1983), p. 126.

Although the didactic approach was not the primary way lessons were chosen for the *Revised Common Lectionary*, the Consultation on Common Texts used it frequently. Sometimes their use of the approach was helpful, as when they decided to cut out the graphic description of Judas' suicide in Acts 1:18 in favor of the more simple statement of fact in 1:19. Often, though, the Consultation's use of the didactic approach was not so helpful, as when they purposefully did not include certain passages from the Davidic narrative that might have given congregations a picture of the complex political issues of the time specifically because the Consultation felt those passages were "not edifying" enough.

Another approach by which lessons are chosen is doctrinal. Under this principle, readings are chosen by how well they support the traditional teachings of the church. They are chosen for their doctrinal, catechistic, and theological value.

Again, there are some admitted advantages to choosing lessons on a doctrinal basis. Such a method is pedagogically sound, it gives a lectionary a solid theological grounding, and it ensures that the important themes of Christian tradition will find a proper place in the liturgy.

However, like the thematic method to which it is related, choosing passages for their perceived doctrinal value has one major flaw. It tends to place those passages into a doctrinal structure that is foreign to them. Doctrinally chosen lections are often taken out of their biblical context and forced instead into a doctrinal framework that was never envisioned, nor intended, by the biblical writers. Yet, it is most often in that very doctrinal context that such a passage is read and interpreted for worship.

Readings for more doctrinally oriented holy days are especially susceptible to this tendency. For example, there is debate among biblical scholars as to how much of the New Testament actually teaches the doctrine of the Trinity. Hints of it can be found, of course. That's how the doctrine was first developed. But there are, at least in the minds of many biblical scholars, very few, if any, passages from the New Testament that directly teach the Trinity. In that light, to make any New Testament passage into a reading for Trinity Sunday, is, at the very least, a questionable procedure and, at the very most, a deliberate attempt to put words into the mouths of the biblical writers that they did not intend.

Inflexibility is another disadvantage to the doctrinal method, for it can often bind a lectionary to the particular doctrinal concerns prevalent at the time a particular lectionary was compiled. Thus it is not as sensitive as it might be to the many inevitable shifts in theological issues and concerns faced by the church throughout the years.

Again, although it was not the primary approach to passage selection in the *Revised Common Lectionary*, the Consultation often chose passages on the basis of their perceived doctrinal value. As with the didactic approach, sometimes the Consultation's use of the doctrinal method was helpful, often it was not. Again readings chosen for more doctrinally oriented holy days, such as Trinity Sunday, are probably some of the worst examples.

The most common method for choosing passages for including in a lectionary is to rely on precedents, either from traditional use or from earlier lectionaries. In most lectionaries, such traditional precedents often account for the bulk of all the lessons chosen.

This time-honored method of choosing lectionary passages has much to commend it. It connects modern congregations to their roots in the faith and opens up to them the treasures of centuries of Christian devotion and experience.

However, heavily relying on tradition does not guarantee a systematic treatment of scripture, nor does it guarantee that such treatment will be accurate to the biblical witness as a whole. First, traditional precedents encourage but do not ensure a balanced biblical diet. This is particularly true if the precedents being used are heavily influenced by the more liturgical concerns of the church year.[25]

Second, traditional precedents also do not guarantee that important but more difficult passages will be included. (This is particularly true for passages that could be understood to challenge the tradition, such as the story of the Hebrew mid-wives.) In some respects, traditional precedents may even encourage a certain resistance and inflexibility toward needed change in the liturgical readings.

Most important, however, is how the principle of precedence indirectly makes use of an older theology than is used elsewhere in the church. How this happens is very simple. As we saw in the first chapter, the tradition behind some readings in the lectionary is very old. By using such ancient traditions, traditional precedents also borrow ancient theologies, some of

---

[25] James A. Pike in his foreword to *Preaching the Christian Year*, Howard Johnson, ed. (New York: Scribner, 1957), p. v.

which stretch back to medieval times and others to the second and third centuries. Sometimes such borrowing is helpful, but often it is not, especially when what is borrowed is itself less than helpful.

The choice of passages to be included is but one editorial issue that can heavily influence the way a lectionary like the *Revised Common Lectionary* interprets scripture. A second is that of passage length. This is not as simple an issue as it may appear at first, for many passages of scripture are too long for modern congregations unaccustomed to public reading. Should such long passages be read as a unit? Should they be somehow broken up into several units read over successive Sundays? Or should they be edited in some way to make a single, albeit shorter, unit? Each of those methods has been used by the lectionary and each has its own particular hermeneutical consequences.

The best example of preserving a long unit of scripture is the lectionary's use of the passion narratives. In this particular case, the entire narrative (which can encompass several chapters) is read in its entirety. Sometimes music or a period of silent prayer is inserted into blocks of reading, but essentially the complete unit is read in one sitting.

Preserving the long unit in such a way has the distinct advantage of preserving the biblical form of the passage. By keeping the unit intact, it also best preserves the theological intent of the passage. Thus, like *lectio continuo*, reading the entire unit is probably the best of the three choices for dealing with passage length.

Admittedly, preserving the entire unit sometimes makes the passage cumbersome to work with. It can also force preachers to choose between using a passage that is too long to effectively interpret within the time frame of worship or not using the passage at all. But even so, preserving the unit is still the most systematic and faithful way for a lectionary to deal with the passages within it.

Breaking long passages into sequential units read over successive Sundays (as is done in the historical narratives characteristic of the lectionary's readings during the summer months) also preserves the biblical form of the passage, but not nearly so effectively. Splitting passages also requires deciding where the unit should be split, which is not an easy task in a passage that is meant to be taken as a whole. Moreover, splitting passages also risks a misunderstanding of the passage if only part of it is heard at a time.

Shortening the passage by selective editing gives the desired length, and most of the time the flavor of the passage as well. But (as we shall see later) it often sacrifices some of the delicate nuances of the whole. Selective editing to shorten the passage also requires making decisions about what to leave out, which is again not an easy task when interpreting passages that are often a skillfully integrated unit of literature.

The Influence of the Church Year

Of all the structural decisions made by the compilers of the *Revised Common Lectionary*, the most influential of all was the decision to base it on the days, seasons, and structure of the traditional church year. That decision was by far the most far-reaching, and the most powerful in its impact on the lectionary's treatment of the Bible. In fact, the decision to use the traditional church year was so far-reaching that it often came close to threatening the middle ground the lectionary's compilers sought to steer between the lectionary as liturgist and the lectionary as teacher.

This is largely because the influence of the church year is so pervasive. The church year significantly influences the choice of passages to be read in the lectionary. It influences where the chosen passages will be placed. It also influences which passages will be read with what other passages.

Probably the best example of this is the way in which certain festivals and seasons of the year often call for specific passages of scripture to be included in the lectionary, either because the passages relate the origin of the particular festival or because the passages have been historically associated with it. Thus we find readings about John the Baptist along with prophecies from Isaiah in Advent, readings from the birth narratives of Luke at Christmas, the story of the Magi from Matthew on Epiphany, the temptation narratives in Lent, and resurrection appearances from John during Easter.

This influence of the church year is not only pervasive, however; it is also quite subjective. Some, like myself, might even call it biased, for in many respects the church year is no more value-neutral than the lectionary itself. It, too, comes out of a particular theological perspective. It, too, carries with it certain assumptions and operating principles that prefer certain themes and emphases in the Christian faith over others.

Whether such pervasive influence (and its attendant biases) is good or bad depends in large part on whether one believes the purpose of a lectionary is to teach or proclaim the tradition. Biblical scholar James Sanders, for instance, sees the enormous impact of the church year as detrimental, even dangerous, to the lectionary's ability to teach the scriptures accurately. In his words, "the calendar tyrannizes the canon in the lectionary format as traditionally conceived."[26]

Liturgist Horace Allen, on the other hand, sees the year in a much more positive light. In his view, it is only right that the year, rather than the biblical canon, should serve as the determining factor in a liturgical document such as the lectionary. In fact, he argues, in the context of worship, "domination of the calendar over the canon" is not only right; it is assumed.[27]

Either way, though, for good or for ill, the church year is as much a part of the lectionary as the lectionary passages themselves. The seasons of the year give the lectionary its structure. Its holy days and festivals give the lectionary its themes. Even the way readings in the lectionary relate to one another shift as the year shifts from one season to the next.

I will not take time here to describe the church year and its seasons. Nor will I walk through an explanation of the themes connected to those seasons. Most of that information is already common knowledge to most users of the lectionary. What I want to do here is to take a closer look at the year, but not from the liturgist's standpoint (which is the view most often taken). Rather, I want to look at the year from the standpoint of the biblical scholar.

In other words, I want to look at the way the church year interprets the Bible. I want us to look at the church year's theology. I want us to look at some of those often unstated assumptions, principles, and theological tendencies underlying the year that the year has in turn bequeathed to the lectionary.

The first, and possibly most influential, of these tendencies in the church year is its use of a hermeneutic that is more ancient than that which is prevalent today. In fact, the hermeneutic employed by the church year, and thus by the lectionary as well, is quite old, in some places dating as far back as the second century.

---

[26] James A. Sanders, "Canon and Calendar: An Alternative Lectionary Proposal," in Dieter Hessel, *Social Teaching of the Christian Year* (Philadelphia: Geneva, 1983), p. 258.

[27] Horace Allen, "Using the Consensus Lectionary: A Response," *Ibid.*, p. 265.

Thus, the hermeneutic of the church year is one that was developed by the early church. Primarily this hermeneutic arose out of two major concerns faced by that church. First was its attempt to make sense of the death and resurrection of Jesus within the context of the Hebrew faith. Being Jews, the disciples were not prepared for what happened to Jesus. The Messiah was not supposed to die. But when the one they had become convinced was the Messiah did indeed die, those faithful Jewish followers of Jesus naturally looked to the Hebrew Scriptures to help them explain the apparent contradiction.

Second was the early church's attempt to deal with the growing tension between it and the synagogue. This, too, was a crisis, and, like the death and resurrection of Jesus, necessitated a new look at the scriptures of the Hebrew faith.[28]

The hermeneutic that developed out of these concerns was twofold. It was both a hermeneutic of proclamation designed to "prove" that Jesus of Nazareth was indeed the Messiah "according to the scriptures," and it was a defensive hermeneutic designed to justify the followers of the "way" before Jewish authorities.

This hermeneutic, which the church year inherited and later passed on to the lectionary, employed several specific methodologies in its interpretation of scripture. It made heavy use of typology. It interpreted the Hebrew Scriptures from a prophecy/fulfillment mode. And it employed an eschatology that was primarily a realized eschatology.

Typology—the identifying of certain events and persons of the Hebrew Scriptures as prefiguring events and personages in the Christian Scriptures—is probably one of the oldest exegetical models known in the Judeo-Christian tradition. In fact, it was first employed in the Hebrew Scriptures themselves. Taking this same methodology, the early church, in its attempt to defend itself in the synagogues, searched the Hebrew Scriptures for types prefiguring Christ. Certain passages, such as Psalms 22 and 89, became increasingly identified with the life of Jesus. The readings for the Easter Vigil and the use of Isaiah 50 on Passion Sunday are prime examples of this typological association.

Soon these images from the Hebrew Scriptures (Moses lifting up the serpent in the desert, the paschal lamb, the "humble king" in Zechariah, the suffering servant of Isaiah, and so on)

---

[28] See Donald Juel, *Messianic Exegesis.*

became increasingly understood as referring to Jesus. Through this association, these texts, which had never been considered messianic types by Jewish interpreters, came to be understood as "messianic" by the early church.

It was these very passages, and their attendant associations with events in the life of Christ, that were then incorporated into the church year as it began to develop. As the practice of established liturgical readings grew, it inherited this typological tendency. By the patristic era, typology had become so well integrated into the liturgical life of the church that it was considered by most to be a significant characteristic of the Christian tradition.[29] It continues to be a significant factor, particularly when the scriptures are used in worship.

In fact, this inherited typological hermeneutic has become so important in some communions that even as late as 1964, it could be asserted that "unless seminary students are introduced to a serious consideration of typology as a key to the interpretation of scripture, it is hard to see how they will ever begin to appreciate the use which the liturgy makes of the Bible."[30]

A second and related characteristic of the ancient hermeneutic passed on to the lectionary by the church year is the use of prophecy/fulfillment exegesis. In this type of exegesis, events and persons in the Hebrew Scriptures are not only understood as "types" of the events and persons in the life of Jesus, but are also understood as having prophesied those events, sometimes in great detail. In fact, one commentator has taken prophecy/fulfillment so far as to say that "the Old Testament...is not an end to itself, and indeed cannot be understood save in reference to its fulfillment by Christ."[31]

Like typology, the prophecy/fulfillment type of exegesis is also very old. In fact, it is at least as old as the earliest Christian writings themselves, reflecting again the church's perceived need to defend itself before the Jewish authorities of the day. In the passion narratives, for instance, Matthew cites Zechariah 11:12–13 (attributing it to Jeremiah, however) as a

---

[29] Edmund Hill, "The Word of God in the Liturgy," *Liturgy* 33.4 (October 1964), pp. 85-86.

[30] *Ibid.*, p. 85.

[31] Paul-Marie Guillaume, "The Reason for an Old Testament Lesson," in *The New Liturgy: A Comprehensive Introduction to the New Liturgy as a Whole and to Its New Calendar, Order of Mass, Eucharistic Prayers, the Roman Canon, Prefaces and the New Roman Lectionary*, Lancelot Sheppard, ed. (London: Darton, Longman, and Todd, 1970), p. 60.

prophecy of the thirty pieces of silver paid to Judas. Mark alludes to Psalm 41:9 as a prophecy of the betrayal (14:18), and to Zechariah 13:7 as a prophecy of the abandonment by the disciples (14:27). Luke uses Isaiah 53:12 as a prediction that Jesus would be crucified between thieves (22:37). And John quotes Psalm 22:18 as a prophecy of the soldiers' casting lots for the clothing of Jesus (19:24).

As with typological exegesis, these "prophecies" and their attendant "fulfillments" were subsequently incorporated into the church's liturgy. Gospel passages, such as portions of the birth narratives from Luke and Matthew and portions of the passion narratives from all Four Gospels, were linked quite early to the passages from Hebrew Scriptures that had become associated with them. Thus, Micah 5:2–5 became traditional for Advent, Isaiah 9:2–7 became traditional for Christmas, Isaiah 53 became traditional for Lent and/or Passion Sunday, and Isaiah 25:6–9 became traditional for Easter.[32]

The third aspect of the ancient hermeneutic bequeathed to the lectionary by the church year is realized eschatology. As defined by Gerard Sloyan, "This is the triumphal understanding that all that has been realized in the Christ of glory has been realized in Christians."[33] Realized eschatology is the conviction that in Christ everything God intended for the creation was accomplished, and that the church now lives in the age of the fulfillment.

Sloyan cites the Fourteenth Sunday of Year B in the Roman *Lectionary* as an example of the lectionary's use of this eschatology. The first lesson is Ezekiel 2:2–5, which relates the "rebelliousness" of the prophet's Israelite contemporaries. The Gospel reading is Mark 6:1–6, the story of Jesus' rejection in Nazareth. The epistle is 2 Corinthians 12:7–10, in which Paul talks about God's power being manifest in weakness. This combination of readings, Sloyan argues, invites the interpreter to contrast the unbelief of the Israelites and the residents of Nazareth, with the perfected belief of the church embodied in Paul. "The intended meaning," he says, "is the preeminence of

---

[32] Goulder, in *The Evangelists' Calendar: A Lectionary Explanation of the Development of Scripture* (London: SPCK, 1978), argues that such a method of interpreting history as "fulfillments" of the Law and Prophets can even be found as early as the book of 1 Maccabees, which he says, "bridges the gulf between the Chronicler and the evangelists," p. 138.

[33] Gerard S. Sloyan, "The Lectionary as a Context for Biblical Interpretation," pp. 131-38, esp. p. 135.

Jesus. What may emerge is the superiority of those of the Christian dispensation, in their own minds, to all who have gone before."[34]

As with typology and prophecy/fulfillment exegesis, this element of realized eschatology is also of ancient origin, and again can be related to the early church's growing conflict with the synagogue. It can be related, as well, to the early church's conviction concerning an imminent Parousia of Christ. Convinced that they were living in the last days, many of the earliest Christian writers spoke as if all things had indeed been completed in Christ. Many of them wrote as if the Christ-event was indeed the ultimate and final crowning achievement of God's activity in the world, and although other later writers modified this position considerably, the earlier convictions did not fade away but were instead passed on, along with the later, more modified eschatologies.

Traces of this form of eschatology still exist in the lectionary even today, however. They are particularly evident in the readings from the book of Acts and the heavy concentration on the various apostolic speeches recorded there. It is also evident in the heavy use of the passion narrative from John and its themes concerning the "unbelief" of the "Jews." And it is evident, too, in many of the lections chosen from the Pauline corpus, particularly those chosen for the Advent and Easter seasons.

Several critical issues are raised by the use of such an ancient hermeneutic. First, its use in liturgy gives this more ancient hermeneutic a far more favored place in the life of the church than other, newer views of the Bible. Given the repetitive and often subliminal influences of the church year, its ancient hermeneutic can often overshadow newer ones. Not only does the hermeneutic of the church year enjoy the advantages of constant reinforcement through the lectionary readings, it is also at the same time reinforced with the use of symbols,

---

[34] *Ibid.*, p. 135. In this particular case, the *Common Lectionary* has made an improvement by appointing 2 Samuel 7:1–17 as the first lesson. This is in keeping with its semi-continuous reading of the David material at this point and is far less susceptible to the temptation of realized eschatology. However, the *Common Lectionary* is not completely free of cases in which the reading from the Hebrew Bible could conceivably be used as a foil for contrasting it to the "fulfilled" experience of the church.

The readings for the Third Sunday in Lent Year A, for instance, might lead to a contrast between the "rebellious" response of the Israelites to the water given them from the rock (Exodus 17:3–7) and the "faithful" response of the Woman at the Well to the "living water" Jesus promised to give her (John 4:5–42).

color, and music. All of these exert a more powerful impact than the words of the sermon alone, which is where the newer hermeneutics are most likely to be found.

Second, the ancient hermeneutic of the church year is also a simpler hermeneutic that does not require the more sophisticated biblical and theological knowledge demanded by other, later hermeneutics. It is more easily expressed, more easily understood, and as such is more easily assimilated by a larger number of people. This, too, can give the hermeneutics of the church year a greater impact on the lives of ordinary congregations than might be possible for other, more complex, hermeneutics.

The most important issue raised by the ancient hermeneutic of the church year, however, is the negative impact such a use has on the church's understanding of the Hebrew Scriptures. Generally the hermeneutic inherited by the church year views the Hebrew Scriptures as "incomplete," "imperfect," and "limited." According to this hermeneutic, the Hebrew Scriptures are of only secondary importance. Their role is primarily a supporting one, which either "prophesies" what was later "fulfilled" in Christ, or supplies the "imperfect" type that was later perfected by its counterpart in the life of Christ.

At the very least, such a hermeneutic leaves congregations with a misleading impression of the Hebrew Scriptures. One might expect, for instance, that a lectionary that was designed to give the Christian community a sense of the grand sweep of God's activity through history (which was the intention of both the Roman and *Revised Common Lectionary*) would naturally concentrate on the narrative portions of the Hebrew Scriptures. Instead, as biblical scholar Arland Hultgren has pointed out, the narrative portions make up only 32 percent of all the readings taken from the First Testament in the Roman *Lectionary*.[35] Readings from the prophets, however, comprise 48 percent of the readings over three years, which then prompts him to ask:

> Does this not mean, then, that the common assumptions of churchgoers gets reinforced, that is, that the Old Testament...when it is not prescribing laws, is predicting the coming of Christ, which usually it is not? We should be aware, then...that the lectionary may not

---

[35] Arland J. Hultgren, "Hermeneutical Tendencies in the Three Year Lectionary," in John Reumann, ed., *Studies in Lutheran Hermeneutics* (New York: Fortress, 1979), p. 164.

lead people into a better understanding of the sweep and edificatory nature of the Old Testament.[36]

At the worst, however, the ancient hermeneutic inherited by the church year not only misleads but it can also lead to a overall disregard for the Hebrew Scriptures in general. In such a hermeneutic, the Law and narrative portions of the Hebrew Bible become "preliminaries" for the prophets, and "the Old Testament religion an intermediate form of the final New Testament religion," thus reducing the "Hebrew revelation to a matter of little consequence apart from the fact of Jesus Christ."[37]

Taken to its logical conclusion, this hermeneutic can be found to have such a low regard for the Hebrew Scriptures that even a reputed scholar such as Geoffrey Wainwright is able to say that "there are perhaps positive conclusions to be drawn from the fact that churches managed for a thousand years with scarcely an Old Testament lesson at the eucharist, so that we should hesitate now to consider such a lesson 'indispensable.'"[38]

Wainwright may have meant his statement as hyperbole, but just six years later Concordia Publishing Company did indeed dispense with the Old Testament lesson. In 1968, responding to what they considered customer pressure for more open space, Concordia decided to discontinue printing the text of the first lesson on the bulletins of their Every Sunday Bulletin Service. The decision was quickly rescinded, but that it was possible to make it at all is a sign of the extent to which this line of reasoning has influenced even the nonliturgical life of the church.[39]

---

[36] *Ibid.*, pp. 164-165. Fortunately, the compilers of the *Common Lectionary*, recognizing the problem that Hultgren has identified, have redressed the imbalance by appointing semi-continuous reading of major narratives in the Hebrew Scriptures. The Patriarchal narratives are found in Year A, the David narratives in Year B, and the Elijah/Elisha narratives in Year C. Thus lections from the narrative portions of the First Testament now make up 56 percent of the total lections used, giving a much more accurate picture of their relative importance.

[37] Rudolph Boon, "Bringing the Old Testament to It's Legitimate Place and Function in the Church's Liturgical Reading of Scripture," *Studia Liturgica* 17 (1987), p. 138.

[38] Wainwright, *Doxology*, p. 173.

[39] "Marcion Strikes Again?" editorial, *Concordia Journal*, March 1986, Volume 12, Number 2, p. 42.

The most ominous aspect of this view of the Hebrew Scriptures, however, is the latent anti-Semitism contained within it. First, such a view can encourage Christian triumphalism. Limiting the witness of the Hebrew Scriptures to mere background for the Christian Scriptures and emphasizing contrasts between the people of Israel and the church entices congregations to identify too quickly with Jesus, Paul, or the apostles. It encourages them to identify too quickly with those the Bible calls the good and righteous ones and at the same time also keeps congregations from identifying with our "just counterparts, the good religious folk who rejected Christ."[40] This in turn, gives the unbiblical impression that Christendom is the culmination of God's activity in the world and therefore superior to every other religion that is or ever has been.

Second, not only does the view of the Hebrew Scriptures found in the ancient hermeneutic of the church year and lectionary lead to Christian triumphalism; it also can lead to a denigration of first- and second-century Judaism. The process is often a subtle one as typological and prophecy/fulfillment models exert their influence upon the choice of lections taken from the Hebrew Scriptures. As James Parkes has pointed out in his article, "The Bible in Public Worship: A Source of Anti-Semitism," such influence can often lead to a preponderance of readings picturing the Israelites as rebellious and unbelieving. This biased selection from the Hebrew Scriptures, he maintains, then "prepare the mind for the condemnation induced by readings from the New" and encourage the erroneous view of Judaism as mere "background" to a more faithful and more spiritual Christianity.[41]

Going another step further, one can find even still another level to this anti-Semitism inherent in the hermeneutics of the church year: the denigration not only of the Judaism of the Hebrew Scriptures but of modern Judaism as well. By selectively reading the Hebrew Scriptures, by allowing our view of them to be influenced by an ancient (and in many ways outdated) hermeneutic, and by refusing to honor the development of Judaism after the scriptures were canonized, Judaism is denied as a legitimate, viable, and contemporary faith. In fact, Gerhard Sloyan argues, "by attending to them anciently but not modernly," we, in effect "declare the Jews a non-people."[42]

---

[40] Sanders, "Canon and Calendar," p. 263.

[41] James W. Parkes, "The Bible in Public Worship: A Source of Anti-Semitism," *Face to Face* (Summer/ Fall, 1976), II, p. 4.

[42] Sloyan, "The Lectionary as a Context...," p. 138.

Of course, it could be argued, as it was in an editorial published in the *Concordia Journal*, that the lectionary was not meant to "instruct a congregation in the history of religion, not even biblical religion, but to be a vehicle for the proclamation of the Word of God, Jesus Christ."[43] It may even be argued that the traditional image of the Hebrew Scriptures discussed above is not even problematic at all, since the proclamation of Jesus Christ, and not Christianity's relationship with Judaism, is the primary intent of the lectionary. Even so, the seeds of anti-Semitism that have been inherited by the lectionary are far too dangerous to be ignored. They must be addressed if the church is ever to rid itself of the anti-Semitism that is so prevalent in its tradition.

Another and equally disturbing feature of this ancient hermeneutic is the way it tends to ignore women and their contribution to the faith. This, too, can be traced back to concerns present in the early church when this hermeneutic was first being developed.

What historical evidence we have now indicates that the very earliest Jesus movement may have been quite egalitarian. We know from the Christian Scriptures themselves that women traveled with Jesus and in some cases helped finance his ministry. The letters of Paul also hint that women held positions of importance within the first-generation church.

By the time the pastoral epistles were written, however, a number of social forces had begun to make these egalitarian practices more difficult to sustain. One of the most important of these social forces was a general increase in a sense of upheaval and stress within the society at large. Another was an increase in persecutions against Christians and the tension that created within the church.

In response to the social forces around them, leadership in the second-generation church increasingly became concerned with helping the church "fit into" its society and not call attention to itself. More radical behavior, which would have been perfectly acceptable earlier, was increasingly looked down upon. Increasingly stringent doctrinal lines were also drawn. Fidelity to the church and its leadership, as well as fidelity to certain doctrines and teachings, became more and more important.

---

[43] "Changes in the New Lectionary?" editorial, *Concordia Journal*, January 1984, Vol. 10, No. 1, p. 3.

Women in particular bore the brunt of this shift in the life of the church. Because their participation had always been a bit controversial, and because some had been attracted to less orthodox versions of Christianity, women soon became suspect. Eventually they became expendable, particularly women who were leaders.

Much of the liturgical tradition that developed at that time reflected this tension about the role of women in the church. Leadership in worship increasingly became the sole purview of men. Biblical readings that included the stories of women were increasingly downplayed and in some cases even ignored. Only Mary, the mother of Jesus, retained a place of importance.

This feature of the early church's ancient hermeneutic was also passed on through the lectionary. We can see it in the number of biblical women who are missing in the lectionary. We can see it in the remarkably small number of stories of women included in the lectionary. We can also see it in the way the lectionary has treated some of the stories of women that do appear.

In addition to its use of an ancient hermeneutic borrowed from the early church, a second problem the lectionary has inherited from the church year is its strong christological character. Von Allmen particularly emphasizes this in his classic, *Worship: Its Theology and Practice*, when he asserts that the very legitimacy of the church year is "subject to one absolute condition: the cycle of the year should be a celebration of Christ."[44] For many, the whole purpose of the church year and of lectionaries based upon it is to bring congregations face-to-face with Christ. In fact, for some, this christological emphasis is even more important than a systematic presentation of Jesus' teaching.[45]

The church year, then, is unapologetically a yearly rehearsal of the life of Christ. It is a cyclical rehearsal of the birth, life, death, resurrection, and ascension of Christ. Of course, this is no doubt more true for the festivals than it would be for Ordinary Time, yet even Sundays of the church year often carry with them a strong christological bent, largely due to the great emphasis that is always placed on the Gospel reading.

There are some distinct advantages to the church year's christological emphasis. Such a strong christological tone, for

---

[44] J. J. von Allmen, *Worship: Its Theology and Practice* (New York: Oxford University, 1965), p. 232.

[45] Johnson, *Year of the Lord's Favor*, p. 147.

instance, guards against a cluttering of the church calendar. It also keeps the church's attention focused on Christ, rather than on whatever special interests, or even secular interests, might arise to claim the congregation's time and resources.[46]

There are, however, some important consequences to such an emphasis that should not be ignored. One is the unique perceptual framework it gives to the community's understanding of the faith, for the way we arrange time, particularly liturgical time, shapes a community's way of thinking. The ordering of time affects a community's very perception of its God and of its social environment. A comparison of two very different liturgical years, that of the English and early American Puritans and that of sixteenth- and seventeenth-century Anglicanism, might illustrate.

Unlike the church year reflected in the *Revised Common Lectionary*, the Puritan calendar was dominated by the Sabbath Day. Aside from Election Day, there were no other regularly set liturgical days, although days of fasting and humiliation or days of thanksgiving might be irregularly called when the occasion seemed to warrant it. The Sabbath was the "queen" of days to the Puritans, who saw in it a foretaste of the eternal realm of God and the heavenly rest promised to all the faithful.

Such a calendar encouraged the Puritan faith to be a forward-looking one. By emphasizing the eschatological Sabbath, it urged the Puritans to concentrate on the future and on the blessings that awaited them there. Thus, instead of concerning themselves with such things as a historical tradition, both the English and American Puritans focused primarily on the world to come, preferring to view tradition, history, and the things of this world as largely a preparation for the next.

In contrast, in the Anglican communions of that same time period, where the yearly cycle of the church year festivals dominated, God's great acts in history became the focus. This historical emphasis encouraged a past-centered faith that did not so much stress the coming realm of God but rather stressed the liturgical meeting of the present with the past—specifically the past found in the life, death, and resurrection of Christ. Thus, Anglicanism, rather than concerning itself with eschatological concerns, primarily focused instead on helping the faithful live the Christian life in this world.[47]

---

[46] Donald Macleod, *Presbyterian Worship: Its Meaning and Method* (Atlanta: John Knox, 1980), p. 114.

[47] I am indebted to Dr. Horton Davies for bringing these differences in the Puritan and Anglican calendars to my attention.

The difference may often be more subtle than the above description indicates, but even so, the probable influence of each communion's liturgical calendar is clear. Seeing through different liturgical lenses, each developed a different perspective on the Christian faith. Using a different "church year," each came to a different view of what was most important regarding the things of God.

Similar dynamics are also operating today. Employing a church year similar to that of the sixteenth- and seventeenth-century Anglicans, communions that use the *Revised Common Lectionary* tend to be more historical in focus. In fact, this is so true that even when more eschatological themes are sounded, as in Advent, they are most often sounded within a historical framework—i.e., the preaching of John the Baptist, the Magnificat of Mary, and so on. Likewise, far less historical focus is found in those communions which de-emphasize the traditional church year. One finds there an emphasis on more eschatological concerns—i.e., heaven, hell, personal salvation, and so on.

This then leads into a second hermeneutical issue in a christocentric church year: an overly christocentric reading of the Bible. Again this raises the same sorts of consequences that were earlier raised by the church year's treatment of the Hebrew Scriptures. For instance, by placing it in a theological framework that is foreign to it, a christocentric church year encourages a depreciation of the First Testament. It entices congregations to not take the Hebrew Scriptures on their own terms, but instead to read into them a christology that is simply not there.

Likewise, by emphasizing the life of Christ while at the same time not recognizing the importance of the Jewish religion of which he was a part, a christocentric church year also encourages a depreciation of Judaism. Such a strong christocentric focus not only entices congregations into a simplistic image of ancient Judaism, it also lures them into ignoring developments in Judaism since the second century.

And by emphasizing the life of Christ above other aspects of the Christian tradition, such as his teachings, a christocentric church year encourages as well a depreciation not only of Jews but of any others who may share similar religious concerns, but do not share a veneration of Christ. A christocentric church year encourages a Christian egoism, and does little to address Christendom's lingering anti-Semitism, or its tendency to look down on other faiths as somehow "inferior."

Another consequence of the heavy christological emphases in the church year is the liturgical exaltation of the Gospel reading. This may be expected of a church year that quite early in its development became shaped around the events in Christ's life that are recorded in the Gospels. In such a context, it is not surprising to find the Gospel reading given special deference.

Thus in most lectionary systems, including the *Revised Common Lectionary*, the Gospel is the lesson that "controls" the other readings and determines the liturgical tone of the day. If, for instance, all three lessons are not read, the Gospel reading is usually one that is. When other lessons are read, the Gospel is usually read last, the liturgical position of honor. In some communions it is often reverenced by the congregation being asked to stand, or by a liturgical kiss, genuflection, or censing. And in some cases, its reading is reserved only to specially trained liturgical leaders, i.e., deacons, priests, or other ordained ministers.[48]

This concentration on the Gospel accounts of Christ's life also raises some important issues regarding the lectionary's use of scripture. Howard Hageman cites this concentration as a particular problem, noting that "when the controlling lesson is always the Gospel lesson, other parts of the scripture are given no opportunity to speak for themselves."[49] This is especially true in respect to the place of the Hebrew Scriptures within the church year, particularly whenever the readings from the Hebrew Scriptures are specifically harmonized with Gospel readings.

However, not only does the church year's christological emphasis on the Gospel deliberately allow the Gospel reading to overshadow the readings from the Hebrew Scriptures, it even allows the Gospel reading to overshadow other lections from the Christian Scriptures as well, notably the epistle lesson. Because the epistles are often used even in congregations that do not always read the first lesson, and because they are often not harmonized with other lessons, the epistle readings are frequently given better expression than readings from the Hebrew Scriptures. But even so, the dominance of the Gospel lesson can be considerable. In fact, for some, "the Gospels are so

---

[48] In his article "The Word in Christian Liturgy," *Liturgy* 2.3 (Summer 1982), p. 15, Jerome Kodell writes that this reverence for the Gospel was in many respects virtually identical to that given to the consecrated host.

[49] Hageman, "A Brief Study...," p. 364.

important that the epistle lessons may be considered only sub-
sidiary and even neglected in liturgical preaching."[50]

A fourth hermeneutical tendency of the church year is its
heavy dependence on the calendar and structure of the Gospel
of Luke. This Lukan dependence may not be as immediately
obvious as some other tendencies, but it becomes more evident
when one considers that Luke is the only Gospel that contains
the record of all the events now celebrated as festivals of the
church year. Luke is also the only Gospel whose sequence of
events exactly matches the sequence of the church year.

For instance, Luke is the only Gospel that begins with Ad-
vent/Christmas. It is the only Gospel that records the census,
the trip to Bethlehem, the search for lodging, the angels' an-
nouncement to the shepherds, and the birth of Jesus. The Gospel of Matthew also contains a birth narrative, but it is remarkably short compared to the one found in Luke and is more
concerned with events related to the festival of Epiphany. Neither Mark nor John mentions the birth or any events leading
up to it. Their Gospels begin some years later, with the ministry of John the Baptist.

Luke is also the only Gospel to record the events now com-
memorated at Pentecost. Matthew stops his record at a very
brief mention of the ascension. Mark ends his at the women
fleeing the empty tomb on Easter morning. And John stops at
the commissioning of Peter and the other disciples, an event
that precedes even the ascension.

Many of the major emphases and themes of the church year
are also Lukan. For instance, the church year reflects Luke's
interest in historical narrative, which is in sharp contrast with
the emphasis on the actions of Jesus in Mark and the theologi-
cal/spiritual interests of John. The church year has also borrowed Luke's stress on social justice and ethics, which contrasts with Matthew's more ecclesiastical concerns.

The most important consequence of such a strong dependence on Luke is what some have called "synoptic fundamen-
talism." In other words, because the church year is so heavily
Lukan in character, and Luke is a synoptic Gospel, the view of
Jesus presented in the lectionary is primarily the synoptic one.
It tends to view Jesus historically and chronologically. It also
emphasizes him as teacher, preacher, and healer. (In contrast,
the Johannine tradition is less concerned with history and tends
to emphasize Jesus as a revealer of the Divine.)

---

[50] Johnson, *The Year of the Lord's Favor*, p. 205.

For years the synoptic tradition was assumed to be the best source for proclaiming the deeds and teachings of Jesus. It was often the place scholars began whenever they sought "the historical Jesus." In recent years, however, biblical scholars have begun to question this assumption. They have found, for instance, that the history and chronology of the synoptic Gospels may in fact be no more reliable than that given in John. Scholars have also found that in some instances, John may even be more historically accurate.

Yet, because of the church year, the synoptic version, particularly that of Luke, still dominates the lectionary. The synoptic/Lukan image of Jesus is still used as if that image is the only image of Jesus found in the Gospels. Thus, in spite of the fact that more of John is read than any other Gospel, the unique character of John is almost lost because when it is read, it is usually read in the context of a Lukan church year.

Similarly, according to Robert Smith, even other synoptic Gospels are often "forced into a Lukan mold" by the lectionary. This, he says, is especially hard on Mark, but Matthew "suffers" from it as well.[51] To illustrate his point, Smith imagines what the church year would be like had it been based on Mark. A Markan year, he says, would have no Christmas, no Epiphany, no Ascension Day, and no Pentecost. Instead, he imagines, it would be a year in which we would find ways to commemorate the mighty struggle the Markan Jesus has with the powers of evil in the world. Rather than observing the historical events of our present Luke-influenced year, a Markan church year would concentrate on the twelve disciples, on the way of the cross, and most of all, on the church's present need "to write in our lives an ending to the Gospel more satisfactory than the one provided by the nervous second-century author of Mark 16:9–20."[52]

Smith's illustration is telling, for it reveals vividly just how much the unique viewpoint of even another synoptic Gospel like Mark has been muted by the Lukan character of the liturgical year. In fact, even in Year B, when Mark is the lectionary's featured Gospel, it is still forced into a liturgical and theological structure that is foreign to it, as the additions of Lukan readings during Christmas, Ascension Day, and Pentecost testify.

---

[51] Robert H. Smith, *Augsburg Commentary on the New Testament: Matthew* (Minneapolis: Augsburg Fortress, 1989), p. 341.

[52] *Ibid.*, p. 347.

ADVENT

*T*here are several important features about the lectionary readings for this year that preachers will want to note as they prepare sermons for Advent. First, with the exception of a short reading from James, all the readings for Advent this year are from either Isaiah, Romans, or Matthew. In fact, we will be spending much time with all three of these books during the course of the entire year, particularly Romans and Matthew. Each book has its own unique background, style, and theology. For this reason alone it might be a good idea to read at least one good introductory volume on each.

Second, nearly all the readings for Advent Year A are of a long-standing tradition. Most have been read during Advent for centuries. Some, such as Matthew 24 and the prophecies of Isaiah, have been associated with this season for as far back as the second century. Because these passages have become so layered with tradition and association, preachers will want to be particularly careful to listen to each passage separately. Each one should be interpreted on its own terms first before being listened to in the context of Advent.

Third, it should be noted that none of the lectionary readings follows the canonical order of the books from which it was taken. In most cases, readings skip around from one chapter of the book to another. In every case, readings for the Fourth Sunday in Advent revert back to an earlier chapter in order to reflect the approaching season of Christmas. Those of us pre-

41

paring Advent sermons this year will want to take this shift into account, particularly as we prepare sermons for the Final Sunday in Advent.

Fourth, it should also be noted that stories of women often associated with Advent (primarily Elizabeth and Mary) are missing this year. Instead, because the lectionary's principal Gospel for Year A is Matthew and Matthew highlights Joseph, the lectionary also highlights Joseph. Mary shows up only briefly, once on the Fourth Sunday in Advent, (Matthew 1:18–25), where she appears largely in absentia, and then once more on the Third Sunday in Advent, where her Magnificat appears as an alternative psalm reading.

Finally, having looked at some of the general issues raised by the lectionary readings for Advent this year, let's take a closer look at some issues that are specific to the readings from the Hebrew Bible, the epistle lessons, and the Gospel lessons.

Lessons from the Hebrew Bible

The "prophet" for Advent Year A is Isaiah, or more accurately, what biblical scholars call First Isaiah (Isaiah 1—39). All the readings taken from First Isaiah during this Advent season, though, are either "messianic prophecies" or prophecies regarding the restoration of Israel following the exile in Babylon. Given the way the church year has influenced the lectionary, this kind of heavy concentration on "messianic" and restoration prophecies is to be expected. Restoration prophecies have been a part of the Advent liturgical tradition for centuries.

However, such prophecies are not the primary emphasis of First Isaiah. Instead, Isaiah 1—39 emphasizes denunciations of idolatry and oppression. It is filled with repeated calls for repentance. It also includes a historical appendix that recounts Sennacherib's siege of Jerusalem in 701 B.C.E. None of these more characteristic passages, however, appear in the lectionary this year during Advent, even though a number of them could be quite appropriate for Advent preaching.

This heavy emphasis on restoration prophecies slights what is the primary focus of First Isaiah. It also invites a misunderstanding of the restoration prophecies themselves. Isaiah's denunciations of idolatry and his repeated calls for repentance are the context out of which the promise of restoration arose. For Isaiah, repentance and promise should not, indeed cannot, be separated. If we try, we risk offering people either a paralyzing sense of guilt or cheap sense of grace. Unfortunately, by focusing almost exclusively on the restoration prophecies, the lectionary automatically predisposes the preacher toward the latter.

In an effort to address this situation, a preacher might consider lengthening the lectionary's present readings to include some of First Isaiah's oracles of judgment. Even if these oracles are not read in the liturgy, they should at least be read in the study as background material for the restoration prophecies that do appear in the lectionary. One might also want to consider preaching on one of First Isaiah's judgment oracles all by itself. Such a text could easily lend itself to a number of traditional Advent themes, particularly justice, peace, or self-examination. A good choice for such a sermon might be either Isaiah 2:6–22 or Isaiah 5:1–7 (which will be read later on in this year for Proper 22).

Epistle Lessons

The Advent "epistle" for this year is Paul's letter to the Romans. Like the readings from Isaiah, these Advent epistle lessons are also very traditional. They have all been associated with Advent for centuries. Since Romans is a Christian writing and always has been, this long association with the church year is less of a problem for Romans than it is for an originally Jewish writing like Isaiah. Still, those of us preaching on these passages will want to remain on guard here, for even in Romans the temptation to hear these passages primarily in light of the church year is considerable.

To guard against this temptation, preachers would do well to remember that Paul seemed to have very little interest in the earthly life of Jesus except in his death and resurrection. In fact, it could be argued that Paul was distinctly uninterested in the historical Jesus. This means that we should not expect to find anything in the epistle to the Romans about Jesus' birth, even though the placement of these lessons might tempt us to do so. Such an expectation, however, reads into the texts something that was not originally there.

Preachers would also do well to remember that the lectionary has purposely chosen these particular epistle lessons from Romans for use in Advent because they either discuss the second coming of Christ or refer to it in some way. Indeed, this reference to one of Advent's most cherished themes is one reason these passages have become so associated with it.

However, while the return of Christ is of primary interest in Advent, it is but a secondary concern in the book of Romans as a whole. There Paul is more interested in issues of grace, salvation, and, most importantly, the place of the Jewish people in the Christian understanding of sacred history. For this reason, those wishing to emphasize the Second Coming might want to consider preaching from one of the Advent Gospel lessons for this year instead, particularly Matthew 24:36–44. Those wishing to use the words of Paul on this subject might want to consider choosing passages where Paul addresses the Second Coming more directly, passages from 1 Thessalonians, for example.

(Comments on James 5:7–10 can be found in the comments on Advent 3A on pages 50-51.)

Gospel lessons

Since Year A is the year the lectionary has chosen to emphasize Matthew, all four Gospel readings for Advent this year are from Matthew. Again, the influence of the church year on our understanding of these readings is considerable.

Those preaching on the Gospel lessons this year should be aware, for example, that Matthew's story line has been completely twisted in order to fit into the demands of the church year. Thus, on the First Sunday in Advent we find that a reading from near the end of Matthew has been chosen because it fits the traditional theme for this day, the second coming of Christ. On the Second and Third Sundays in Advent, when the tradition has often emphasized John the Baptist, the readings chosen send us back to near the beginning of Matthew, to chapters 3 and 11, where John the Baptist appears. On the Fourth Sunday of Advent, again in response to demands from the church year, we are sent even further back toward the beginning of Matthew, to chapter 1, where Matthew records the birth of Jesus.

Those preaching on the Gospel lessons for this year should also be aware that because the church year is so heavily based on Luke, the lectionary will tempt them to unconsciously interpret these passages in light of their Lukan counterparts. This is even true for Matthew's version of the birth of Jesus in 1:18–25 (Advent 4A). This passage has no direct counterpart in Luke, but when read, as it is in Year A, on the Sunday before Christmas, it can become almost a de facto prelude to the events recorded in the Christmas Gospel from Luke.

Careful attention should be paid, then, to the unique characteristics of the Gospel of Matthew. Background reading about this particular Gospel, background reading in the structure of the lectionary, and work in a Gospel parallel comparing Matthew and Luke's respective versions of the chosen lectionary readings would all be helpful strategies. It might also help the preacher to begin by taking a few moments to deliberately listen to these Matthew passages as if Luke's Gospel never existed.

First Sunday in Advent

This Sunday has traditionally been a day for emphasizing the Second Advent, or the promised return of Christ to the earth in glory. Traditional scriptures chosen for this Sunday often sound a clarion call to the people of faith to awake and prepare for the coming Day of God. For this reason, passages for the First Sunday in Advent are often filled with eschatological and apocalyptic language and thought.

Year A is no exception to this tradition. The Romans 13 passage and the Matthew 24 passage both announce the nearness of God's coming Day with images typical of Jewish and Christian writings on the end of the world. In a similar way, the passage from Isaiah 2, while not strictly eschatology or apocalyptic, has often been reinterpreted by Christian tradition to be so as well.

To prepare to interpret such texts, preachers would do well to refresh their knowledge of both Jewish and Christian thought concerning the end times. Special attention should be paid to the difference between apocalyptic and prophecy, to the variety of opinions ancient Jewish groups held about the coming of the Messiah, and to the way early Christian groups took those opinions and shaped them to fit their own needs and expectations.

Isaiah 2:1–5

This is a clear example of the lectionary's linking a restoration prophecy to the coming of Jesus, in this case, the second coming of Jesus. Fortunately, this passage is being heard more and more outside the context of Advent (particularly the verse about beating swords into plowshares). However, because the association this passage has with Advent is still so strong, those of us who choose to preach on it should make every effort to be aware of its original historical and literary context. We should also make our congregation aware of this context by giving a brief historical note before the reading, or lengthening the reading to include some of the verses that precede it.

Preachers should likewise be very careful about how we use this passage in connection with the other readings for the day. Special care should be taken to avoid a simplistic use of prophecy and fulfillment. At the very least, the vast differences between each of the lessons for today should be noted. In most cases, it is probably best not to try to make connections among these lessons at all, even though the lectionary encourages us to do so.

Romans 13:11–14

This traditional passage appears in the lectionary on this particular Sunday primarily because its theme (proper Christian conduct in light of the imminent second coming of Christ) matches so well with the traditional theme for this Sunday. In this case, the link is an entirely appropriate one. In fact, if used well, this passage can even serve as a kind of corrective to the triumphalism that is often misread into the Isaiah passage when it is used alone.

Even so, we would do well to keep two important caveats in mind with respect to this lesson: (1) it is not exactly representative of the book of Romans as a whole, and (2) Paul's emphasis here is on the behavior he expected of the Roman Christians, not on the Second Coming itself.

Matthew 24:34–44

This lesson, too, is a traditional one that has long been associated with Advent. Again, this association is entirely appropriate. The lesson is taken from a part of Matthew's Gospel where the author is consciously talking about the Second Coming. This makes Matthew 24 the least problematic of the lectionary readings available to the preacher this week.

Those who choose to preach on this passage, though, will want to note the parallels to it that are also in the lectionary. For instance, Mark's version of verses 34–36 (Mark 13:30–32) appear as part of the Gospel lesson on the First Sunday of Advent Year B. Luke's version of the same verses (Luke 21:32–33) appear on the First Sunday of Advent Year C. Verses 42–44 appear in their Lukan version (Luke 12:39–40) as part of Proper 14C. Only verses 37–41 appear in the lectionary solely in their Matthean form. Because so many verses in this lesson appear in more than one form it is often tempting to read into them things that are actually in one of the parallels from either Mark or Luke. Care should be taken with the Lukan parallels in particular since the church year often predisposes us to think in terms of Luke, especially during Advent and Christmas.

Second Sunday in Advent

On the First Sunday in Advent this year, the lectionary focused almost exclusively on anticipating the second coming of Christ. This Sunday, largely because John the Baptist now enters the Advent picture, the focus of the lectionary broadens to include anticipation of the birth and ministry of Jesus as well. In some cases, passages that mention Jesus' birth and passages that refer to his coming again have been placed right next to each other. Sometimes anticipation of both events is alluded to within the very same passage. For the preacher, this complicates the picture in several ways.

First, the lectionary's dual focus for this week deliberately blurs important distinctions between anticipating the birth of Jesus and anticipating the Second Coming. The lectionary has woven both these anticipations together so tightly that it is often hard to tell one from the other. In fact, by choosing these particular lessons for the same Sunday, the lectionary has created in some cases a deliberate ambiguity as to that coming of Jesus is being referred to, an ambiguity that only heightens a similar ambiguity within the texts themselves.

However, while this ambiguity has long been traditional for Advent, it is not very helpful to the preacher. It invites confusion. It invites a misunderstanding of the relationship between Jesus' coming and his coming again. It also invites a superficial use of prophecy.

Second, the dual focus of the lectionary this week deliberately connects the readings for today in a number of different ways. All three readings, for instance, are linked together by common themes related to Advent. The lesson from Isaiah and the lesson from Romans both refer to the coming "branch [or root] of Jesse." They both also describe this "branch" as one who will gather the Gentile nations together under God. The lesson from Isaiah and the lesson from Matthew are also clearly related. The first describes the "branch of Jesse" as a judge, the second contains John the Baptist's very similar description of Jesus as judge.

Again, while these connections have long been traditional for Advent, they are not especially helpful to the preacher. They encourage us to rely heavily on a prophecy/fulfillment model of biblical interpretation. They also encourage us to read into a passage themes that are actually more related to the church year or to other passages chosen for this Sunday.

Obviously, very careful biblical and theological work is called for here as a way of sorting though the many layers of expectation and connectedness found in these passages. Those of us who preach on them should be careful to not intermingle the various layers we find here too early in the sermon-writing process. We should also be careful to not make assumptions about what these passages have to say based on their placement in the lectionary.

Isaiah 11:1–10

This passage is a very familiar one even though it appears in the lectionary only once every three years. Such familiarity not only testifies to the lectionary's power of association, it can also entice us into thinking that we know this passage better than we do.

For instance, those who choose to preach on this reading should be aware that the lectionary is using it as a messianic prophecy. This is a very traditional way of interpreting this passage, but as we found with Isaiah 9 last Sunday, it is not the only way.

Preachers should also be aware that the lectionary has again edited out the historical context behind this passage. We should not feel confined to the official reading, however. In fact, some of the historical references in chapter 10 might even help give the lofty promises found in the lectionary reading itself a more realistic focus.

Preachers should also be aware that the lectionary has once again neglected to include Isaiah's words of judgment that preceded the promises contained in this passage. As before, including historical references and background verses to the appointed reading could help here. At the very least, such verses would discourage us from identifying too easily with the returning exiles.

Romans 15:4–13

Standing on its own, independent of the lectionary, this passage from Romans contains very little that is characteristic of Advent. There is no sense of anticipation or expectation. There is no reference to Christ's birth or his appearing again in glory. Only a short, one-word reference in the last line to hope would make one think of Advent. Yet, we are enticed by the lectionary into thinking Advent as we read these words because of their place in the lectionary.

Here Paul is actually talking about the full inclusion of Gentiles into the people of God and the role of the "branch of Jesse" in bringing that full inclusion into being. Again, as was the case last Sunday, those of us who preach on this passage should study Paul's complex argument here in full. As much as possible, we should try to listen to this text outside the context of Advent. We should make every effort to hear it independent of its associations with the church year, at least until these words have had a chance to speak for themselves first. Otherwise we run the risk of interpreting them in a much too superficial way.

Matthew 3:1–12

Unlike the passage from Romans, this passage is full of Advent images, references, and themes. In fact, John the Baptist's appearance on the Second Sunday of Advent is so traditional that it is difficult to imagine Advent without him, or to imagine the Baptist in any other place in the church year other than Advent. The two fit together very nicely.

Even so, there are a few factors preachers should keep in mind as we prepare for this Sunday. First, in placing John the Baptist before the *birth* of Jesus, the lectionary has played a little with biblical history. John did not announce the birth of Jesus. He announced the public ministry of Jesus, particularly that part of Jesus' public ministry that is traditionally associated with the Second Coming (clearing with the winnowing fork, gathering the wheat, burning the chaff, etc.).

Second, all three of the synoptic Gospels present a slightly different picture of John. Matthew's version is heavily dependent on Mark, except for verses 7–10, which Matthew shares with Luke. Preachers will want to make sure that Matthew's own unique voice has a chance to be heard this year.

Third Sunday in Advent

Many of the complexities and issues we encountered last Sunday we meet again on this Third Sunday in Advent—passages with long associations to Advent, a blurring of distinctions between the birth of Jesus and his Second Coming, and an intricate pattern of connection between passages, either with the church year or with one another.

This week there are also several additional elements of which to take note. First, the epistle lesson is from James rather than Romans. This puts us into a very different historical, literary, and theological context. Since the lectionary sends us back to Romans again for the Final Sunday in Advent, care should be taken to see that the reading from James this week is not inadvertently read with Pauline lenses.

Second, Mary's Magnificat from the Gospel of Luke is listed this Sunday as a possible alternate to the psalm reading. This, too, puts us into a very different context from the Gospel readings we have been following in Matthew. For this reason, it is probably best not to preach on the Magnificat this year, but instead save it for Year C, the year of Luke. However, preachers would still do well to use the Magnificat in the worship service itself. It gives us one of the few opportunities we will have in Advent to hear from a biblical woman, and it is an especially appropriate reading for the season.

Isaiah 35:1–10

Again the lectionary has linked still another prophecy about the restoration of the Hebrew people's fortunes following their exile in Babylon to the birth and second coming of Jesus. This time however, the oracle from which this passage is taken is so long that it will be difficult to find nearby verses to provide historical background. A short introduction before the reading or purposeful historical references within the sermon itself might be better options in this case.

Interestingly, this passage also appears (in a shorter form) during Ordinary Time Year B (Proper 18). Preachers might want to consider preaching on it then, in the more expanded form we have here in Advent. There are two advantages to doing this. One, the preacher will not have to deal with this passage and the influence of Advent at the same time, and two, the congregation will have an opportunity to hear verses long associated with Advent at a very different time of year.

James 5:7–10

This is another well-established reading in the Advent lectionary. As was the case for the passages from Romans chosen for the First Two Sundays in Advent, this passage, too, was chosen for its reference to the second coming of Jesus. Again, however, the Second Coming is not the main point here. James mentions it largely as a means for heightening his exhortations to ethical living.

One of the most important things to remember in working on this passage is that James is *not* Paul. James has a very different theology and a very different agenda here than Paul has in Romans. For this reason, preachers who wish to preach on this passage might do well to read the whole book of James at one sitting in order to get a better idea of his particular style and viewpoint. Reading a short introduction to James would also be a good idea, if only to refresh the memory. Such preparation will be especially important for those who have already preached on one of the Romans passages this Advent, or who are planning to do so next Sunday.

Matthew 11:2–11

Again we have a very old, established reading for Advent and again we have John the Baptist as a principal player. Literarily, though, this passage is part of a longer speech given by Jesus. The lectionary did not include the whole speech for at least two reasons. One, it was too long, and two, it contained several difficult verses (notably 11:12) that could conceivably detract from the main point of the passage if read without comment. Those who choose to preach on this reading, however, would do well to keep the whole speech (11:2–30) in mind, even if only part of it is read in worship.

Obviously, this passage was placed in the lectionary on this particular Sunday because of the way it points to the advent of the realm of God in Jesus and the way it defines the role of John as forerunner to the Christ. In fact, for the lectionary's purposes, this is the perfect Advent passage. It has everything: anticipation, expectation, prophecy, and an almost point-by-point correspondence to the words of the reading from Isaiah.

John's question, however, is an important one that offers a needed counterpoint to the lectionary's enthusiasm for prophecy/fulfillment. His question not only reminds us that even John himself was uncertain that Jesus was the fulfillment of prophecy; it also reminds us that the relationship between prophecy and fulfillment is often not as clear-cut as we might imagine. Both reminders are important caveats as we prepare sermons for Advent and Christmas.

Fourth Sunday in Advent

Following long-standing liturgical tradition, the lectionary on this Fourth Sunday in Advent focuses entirely on anticipating the birth of Jesus. This completes the gradual shift in focus begun on the First Sunday in Advent when the lectionary was almost entirely focused on the second coming of Christ. Now we are pointed directly toward Bethlehem in preparation for Christmas.

In some respects, this narrowing of focus makes the preacher's job easier than it has been for the last two Sundays. We are not expected to switch back and forth between references to Jesus' birth and to his coming again, nor are we expected to sort through ambiguous references that could refer to either of those comings, or in some cases to both at the same time.

With this more pointed focus also comes heavier use of a strict prophecy/fulfillment model of interpretation. Today there is no ambiguity about the lectionary's intentions—it is the birth of Christ that we are to understand is the fulfillment. This is especially true for Isaiah 7, which is linked to the birth of Christ not only by the lectionary but by the text of the Gospel lesson itself. Because of this, preachers should be particularly careful this week about their use of prophecy/ fulfillment theology.

Isaiah 7:10–16

This familiar Advent reading has been interpreted by Christian tradition for centuries as having "predicted" the birth of Jesus. Isaiah 7:10–16 has long been considered a messianic prophecy and was used as such by the author of Matthew in the Gospel lesson for today. In fact, this particular passage from Isaiah was specifically chosen for this day because of the way it was used in Matthew's birth narratives.

Again, however, according to Jewish tradition these verses are no more messianic than any other verses from the Hebrew Bible we have studied so far. Because of this, preachers should take special care to respect the Jewish roots of this passage and not treat it as merely a signpost pointing the way to Christ. We should also be careful about simplistic uses of prophecy/ fulfillment. It is one thing to say that Isaiah 7 prefigures or foreshadows the birth of Jesus. It is quite another to say these words were meant to predict his birth.

To get a better sense of a more appropriate understanding of this reading from Isaiah, preachers would do well to read verses 1–9 as well as 10–16. Those are important verses because they give the historical reason Ahaz needed a sign in the first place. Verses 1–9 also tell us what the sign of Emmanuel was originally all about—standing up to the military might of Ephraim and Syria.

Romans 1:1-7

This passage is what biblical scholars call a salutation. In it, Paul briefly outlines some of the key issues he will be dealing with in his letter. These particular verses, though, were chosen for this Sunday in large part for two reasons, Paul's reference to the prophets and his reference to Jesus as Son of David and Son of God. We must be careful, though, to not let the season of Advent overly influence what we see here. We must be cautious, for instance, about zeroing in on the first part of this passage (where Paul talks about Jesus) without also taking into account the other part of the passage where Paul talks about his ministry to the Gentiles. For Paul, the work of Jesus and his own work are inseparable.

We must also be cautious about reading Paul as if he were Matthew or Luke. Paul's view about the nature of Jesus is very different from both Gospel writers and it can easily get lost in this season when both Matthew and Luke are so much in our minds.

Matthew 1:18-25

This passage comes from the "birth narratives" of Matthew, which is the largest block of material in the Gospel not shared by either Mark or Luke. However, since Christmas plays and stories often mix this narrative with Luke's, it will be especially important today to let Matthew speak for himself. In this respect, it might even be a good idea to save this passage for Christmas and this week preach on one of the other readings instead.

This is also one of those places where we see how much the structure of the lectionary is influenced by the Gospel of Luke. Since Matthew does not have nearly as much "Advent" material as Luke, and since Luke is the traditional Gospel for Christmas Day, the lectionary has been forced by its own structure to place Matthew's version of the Christmas story on this last Sunday in Advent. This is another reason to consider saving this lesson for Christmas.

Whether we preach on this passage now or later, we ought to do so with full knowledge that Matthew has not told Mary's part of the story. For Matthew, Mary is a secondary character. In this Gospel her story is hidden, although it is not completely wiped out. It is well worth the time it takes reading between the lines to find it.

CHRISTMAS

With the shift in season we see a dramatic shift in the biblical books from which the lectionary readings are taken. Except for two readings, lessons from the Hebrew Bible continue to come from Isaiah, but all are now from chapters 40—66, or Second and Third Isaiah. The Gospel lessons now come from Luke, then shift to John. The epistle lessons, which have steadily come from a single book during Advent, now jump from Titus first, to Hebrews, then to Ephesians.

Christmas also brings with it a dramatic shift in the arrangement of lessons. For example, unlike readings for Advent, which are read every three years, most of the lessons for Christmas are meant to be read every year (although circumstances may not always make that possible).

Moreover, many of these readings come from some of the lectionary's most favored portions of scripture, Isaiah 40—66 and John 1. In fact, more verses are read (and reread) from Isaiah chapters 40—66 than any other portion of scripture except the Psalms.[1] This means that some of the readings we will see this season are among the most often repeated parts of scripture for those churches that use the lectionary.

---

[1] Not only is this portion of Isaiah frequently included in the lectionary, it is also highly associated with the festival seasons. Of the 36 readings taken from Isaiah chapters 40—66, 19 are festival readings and 5 are read both during a festival season and during Ordinary Time. Of the 20 readings taken specifically from chapters 55—66, 9 are festival readings and 3 are read both for a festival and Ordinary Time.

Special care must be taken so that neither we nor our listeners are lulled by this familiarity. Perhaps in the process of preparing the sermon we might try looking at these passages from a number of various translations. Perhaps we might read a new book or commentary as part of our preparation.[2] We also might make a special effort to pay attention to what is going on in the society around us in order to interpret these well-known passages of scripture anew in light of current events.

Christmas also brings with it more sets of lessons than there are opportunities to read them. There are, for instance, three sets of readings for Christmas itself. There are also two sets of readings for Sundays after Christmas, even though there is often only one Sunday between Christmas Day and Epiphany.

We would do well to make the most of such an opportunity. Less frequently read passages might be purposely preached on in lieu of more familiar passages. For example, readings listed for the Second Sunday in Christmas could occasionally be read instead of readings for the First Sunday in those years when the Christmas season is only one Sunday long. In those years when Christmas has two Sundays, readings for Christmas Proper 2 might be substituted at some point in the cycle for readings that are heard more often.

Readings from the Hebrew Bible

For the Christmas season, the lectionary continues to emphasize the restoration prophecies of Isaiah, but with some important new twists brought on by the shift to Isaiah 40—66. First, except for the reading from Isaiah 9, all the prophecies this Christmas (including that from Jeremiah 31) were written *after* the exile prophesied in Isaiah chapters 1—39. This means that we are looking at a sharply different historical, literary, and theological context from that of the prophecies that were read during Advent. In the case of Isaiah 40—66, we may even be looking at the work of an entirely different author from the one we encountered in Advent.

In the logic of the lectionary, such post-exile readings make perfect sense. Liturgically, Christmas fulfills the hope expressed in Advent. In a similar manner, these readings are understood by the lectionary to do the same for the pre-exile readings of Advent. They are then presented to us by the lectionary as

---

[2] I personally recommend, *The Illegitimacy of Jesus* by Jane Schaberg (New York: Crossroad, 1990) and *The Woman's Bible Commentary* edited by Carol A. Newsom and Sharon H. Ringe (Louisville: Westminster Press, 1992).

elaborations and expansions of earlier promises now fulfilled in the birth of Jesus.

This is, of course, one possible way to interpret these lessons from Isaiah (and Jeremiah as well), but as we have discovered before, it is not the only way. In this case, it might be particularly helpful to read commentary Jewish scholars have made on these passages.

Second, the Christmas readings from Isaiah 40—66 have fewer readily available historical references than did the Advent readings from chapters 1—39. There is less concern for time and season here. There are fewer place names, and fewer datable events or people are mentioned. In many respects, these passages have a timeless quality about them, a timelessness heightened even more by the place given them in the lectionary.

Without adequate historical and theological grounding, such timelessness can invite inappropriate Christian triumphalism. Care must be taken to understand these passages in context. Unfortunately, simply adding verses to the beginning or ending of a reading or even taking verses from a previous chapter will not suffice in this case. Instead, those of us who preach on these lessons have to be creative, possibly employing some of the same techniques we may have used to historically ground the passage from Isaiah we read on the Third Sunday in Advent.

Epistle Lessons

Because the lectionary jumps from one biblical epistle to another this Christmas, the most immediate temptation facing us is the temptation to unconsciously meld these readings together as if from a single author. They are not, of course. In fact, the epistles chosen for this season are not even from the same time period, nor do they share the same congregational concerns. This is an important point to keep in mind as we navigate from one very different reading to another.

One thing these readings have in common, though, is that none of them are about the birth of Jesus specifically. This is also an important point to remember, particularly in regard to the readings for Christmas itself when the church year is at its most influential point this season.

Gospel lessons

Now that Christmas has arrived, the lectionary's unequal treatment of the Four Gospels comes to the fore. Rather than readings from Matthew, which we would expect in Year A, we have readings from Luke and John instead: Luke, because the season of Christmas is derived primarily from Luke's account, and John because John is often used by the lectionary to "fill in" for Gospels like Matthew that are thought to not have enough material for a full series of Christmas readings.

One possible option for tempering the lectionary's dependence on Luke and John here was suggested last Sunday—reading Matthew 1:18–25 (Fourth Sunday in Advent) for Christmas. Another possibility is to take an opportunity during Christmas to reflect on the genealogy in Matthew 1, or some other passage from Matthew that might be relevant for the congregation's particular situation in this season.

Christmas Proper 1
(Years A, B, and C)

Whether they are read as part of a Christmas Eve service or for Christmas morning worship, this first set of readings for Christmas has been traditional for this season for centuries. This is particularly true for the passages from Isaiah 9 and Luke 2, which became associated with Christmas around the fourth century when the season was first established in Rome.

As was the case in Advent, such long-established associations should put us on guard. With these readings we should be especially watchful for ancient methods of biblical interpretation that have influenced the lectionary and layers of tradition that through the years have come to almost obscure the intent of the biblical author. Those who take the time to sort through it all first (before writing the sermon) will undoubtedly find that the extra effort was worth it.

Of all the readings in this season, the readings for Christmas Proper 1 are also no doubt the most familiar of all the readings in the lectionary. Again, this is especially true for Isaiah 9:2–7 and Luke 2:1–20, which appear not only in worship, but also on Christmas cards and in Christmas plays and music. Such familiarity, too, should put us on guard, lest we become overly confident about our understanding of these passages.

Isaiah 9:2–7
Once again we have a restoration prophecy from First Isaiah indelibly linked to the birth of Jesus, a continuation of the pattern well established in Advent. In this case, though, the lectionary has made the link even stronger.

The lectionary has not only linked this passage generally to the birth of Jesus, it has also linked it specifically to the Christmas Gospel from Luke. Every year the two are read together. Every year they are heard one right after the other, as if that is the way they were meant to be,

Moreover, the lectionary has also clearly edited this passage with the specific purposes of the church year in mind. Verse 9:1, for example, is missing in the lectionary's Christmas version of this passage, no doubt because it detracted from the association to Christmas the lectionary intended to convey here. (The effect of this editing is made even more striking when we see what happens to this same passage during Epiphany, when associations to Jesus' birth are less important to the lectionary. In the version for the Third Sunday After Epiphany Year A, verse 1 is restored and those verses most associated with Christmas [5–7] are omitted.) Even if it means reading some verses twice in less than a month, it is still better use of this passage to read it all, including verse 1.

Titus 2:11–14

This passage echoes in tone many of the Advent epistles that exhorted believers to live godly lives while awaiting the coming of Jesus in glory. This particular passage was chosen for Christmas, though, primarily on the basis of its first verse, which speaks of the grace of God as having already appeared. In this respect, this reading from Titus is a fairly appropriate epistle for the Christmas season.

However, this passage and the epistle lesson for Christmas Proper 2 are the only passages from Titus to appear anywhere in the lectionary. This has two important consequences. One, it means that these Titus readings will receive more emphasis than other equally compelling parts of scripture because they are read almost every year and not just once every three years. Two, because both readings are also read only at Christmas, most people in our congregations will not hear them interpreted outside the season of Christmas. For this reason, preachers might want to consider preaching on these lessons, or on other passages from Titus not listed in the lectionary, at another point in the year.

Luke 2:1–14 (15–20)

This is no doubt the best-known passage from the Gospel of Luke, if not one of the best-known passages in all of scripture. It has been an obvious choice for this point in the Christmas season for centuries. In fact, were it not for the Christmas Gospel from Luke there might not be a Christmas season at all. The lectionary and the church year are that dependent on Luke's chronology of the life of Jesus.

Actually, this passage has become so traditional that people expect to hear it. They look forward to it. In some cases, they even demand it. It is now so much a part of Christmas that most of us never even consider reading something else, even though in this year of Matthew, the Gospel lesson we read last Sunday might be just as appropriate, if not more so.

If we do preach from this passage, there are several considerations to keep in mind. First of all, now that the lectionary has shifted us from Matthew to Luke, it will be especially important to keep a distinction between the two Gospels clearly in our minds. The temptation to mix these Gospel accounts will be strong especially on Christmas Eve and Christmas Day itself since many Christmas activities and events intermingle elements of the birth narratives from both Matthew and Luke. It might be helpful to begin sermon preparation by refreshing ourselves a bit on the style and theology of Luke.

Second, even though the lectionary lists verses 15–20 as an alternate ending, it is a more accurate reflection of Luke's intention to include them. The visit of the shepherds recorded in 15-20 is important to Luke's intention in this passage. It allows him to show the way Jesus was welcomed most by the lowly people of the world.

Christmas Proper 2
(Years A, B, and C)

Some of the same issues raised by the readings for Christmas Proper 1 appear again in the readings for Proper 2. The lectionary continues to associate restoration prophecies from Isaiah with the birth of Jesus. We have a second reading from Titus linked to the Christmas season. Again, the Christmas Gospel from Luke dominates the scene.

This second set of readings, however, seems to have fewer problems than the first. For instance, we do not have to deal with major shifts in the books from which the readings are taken. Except for Luke, these readings are not as encrusted with tradition, either. Because they are designed as extra readings for Christmas, these readings are not read nearly as often, nor are they as familiar as the readings for Proper 1.

Isaiah 62:6–12

In this passage, the lectionary now begins using restoration prophecies from the second half of Isaiah. This particular reading is one of the lesser known passages from this often used portion of scripture. In this respect it carries less "baggage" than the other passages of Isaiah we will meet during this season.

Also, this passage is less heavily associated with Christmas. There are a few obvious Christmas images (the highway in the desert, and the cry, "Behold, your salvation comes") but they do not predominate here in the way such images do in Isaiah 9:2–7, for example.

The editing done on this reading reflects its historical context better than many other readings taken from Isaiah for Advent and Christmas this year. This alone might make it the best of the Christmas readings from the Hebrew Scriptures from which to preach this year.

Titus 3:4–7

This passage presents us with the same issues as did the first passage from Titus, with one additional consideration—the way in which this particular passage was edited by the lectionary. In most translations, this reading begins in the middle of a sentence with the conjunction "but." This is a clear sign that the lectionary has left something out. If we read the entire sentence, the "appeared" referred to in the passage (which sounds like a clear reference to the birth of Jesus) becomes much more ambiguous than the editing of the lectionary would lead us to believe. Whether we read these earlier verses or not, however, the context they give us should be taken into account in our preaching.

Luke 2:8–20

Here we have again the Christmas Gospel from Luke, this time with the birth itself edited out. Such editing, of course, assumes that the longer version listed for Proper 1 has already been read. It also assumes, following the church year, that the birth is already an accomplished fact and need not be read about a second time. This, then, could be a good opportunity to read Matthew's narrative in 1:18–25, or to read Luke 2:1–20 in its entirety if Matthew 1 was read earlier.

Christmas Proper 3
(Years A, B, and C)

In this third set of readings for Christmas, we find a pattern very similar to the one found in the readings for Christmas Proper 1. Once more we are presented with passages that have long been associated with Christmas. In many respects, their association with this season is the primary reason all three of these readings appear in the lectionary where they do.

Like the readings for Christmas Proper 1, these readings are also passages that have been highly emphasized by the lectionary. For instance, the Isaiah 52 reading again comes from one of the lectionary's favorite portions of scripture. Part of the reading from Hebrews 1 appears again during Ordinary Time Year B, when it introduces a long string of semi-continuous readings from Hebrews. Parts of the reading from John 1 also appear in the readings for the Second Sunday in Christmas Years ABC and on the Third Sunday in Advent Year B.

These particular lessons are not only highly emphasized by the lectionary, they have also been singled out for special prominence. For while some readings in the Christmas season are read only once every three years and others may or may not be read depending on the length of the season, the lectionary suggests that these particular readings always be read at least once in the Christmas cycle. This is true no matter how long the season might be, which means that in some years these readings could actually replace other equally valuable Christmas readings.

Isaiah 52:7–10

The lectionary continues its pattern of choosing for Christmas restoration prophecies from the last half of the book of Isaiah. This passage, though, is particularly full of images which Christian tradition has appropriated from the Hebrew Scriptures especially for this season—"good news," "announces peace," "Your God reigns," "sing for joy," "comforted [the] people," "redeemed Jerusalem." Those who preach on this passage should be sensitive to the original meaning of these images and recognize that our use of them at Christmas is indeed a secondhand appropriation.

Hebrews 1:1–4 (5–12)

This passage, too, has many images we might easily associate with Christmas—"spoke...in many and various ways by the prophets," "heir of all things," "angels." If the alternate verses are also read, even more Christmas-like images can be found—"You are my Son," "the firstborn," "Let all God's angels worship him," "Your throne, O God, is forever and ever," "the righteous scepter." This association is exactly what both tradition and the lectionary intend. A close reading of the passage, however, reveals that the ascension of Jesus, rather than Christmas, is more likely the focus here. In fact, according to the author of Hebrews, it is really not until after the crucifixion and resurrection that Jesus becomes the "heir of all things." This does not mean we should shy away from using this passage now. On the contrary, a sermon that deliberately explores Hebrew's unique understanding of Jesus might yield a very fruitful Christmas message.

John 1:1–14

This is the first of many times during the liturgical year when the lectionary will use John as its "festival Gospel." In this particular case, this means that the prologue of John (John 1:1–18) will now begin to dominate most of the subsequent lectionary readings for Christmas. In fact, this Gospel lesson is the very reason this particular set of readings has been given such a preeminent place in the lectionary.

Yet, even this passage does not escape being edited according to the church year. In this set of readings for Christmas itself, for example, the most Christmas-like verses (1–14) are read. On the Second Sunday of Christmas, however, verses 1–9 are merely alternate verses while 10–18, which are not as Christmas-like, are read instead.

Because this passage so dominates the Christmas scene, it is probably best to preach from it sparingly. If we do preach from this passage, it might be helpful to consciously hold a dialogue between these words in John and the epistle lesson from Hebrews. Each has very different views on the nature of Jesus. It also might be helpful to read all 18 verses of the prologue regardless of when it is read, either as part of this set of readings or the readings listed for the Second Sunday in Christmas.

First Sunday in Christmas

This set of readings mitigates many patterns we have seen so far in the lessons chosen for Christmas. First, it is the only set of three-year readings. Second, none of the readings is as familiar, nor as encrusted with tradition, as many of the other sets of Christmas readings. Third, none is particularly associated with the church year. And fourth, all three readings have a surprising hint of the Passion in them.

There are two warnings that preachers should heed in regard to these lessons. One is to be especially watchful about the way the lectionary has edited the passages from which these readings come. The other is to not try to force the readings here into a Christmas mold.

Isaiah 63:2–9

The lectionary compilers have rightly taken this passage to be a literary unit. Taken as it appears in the lectionary, though, these words could easily be understood as simply another restoration prophecy associated with the birth of Jesus. Read in its literary context, however, this verse actually describes God's grace given to the people of Israel in the Exodus. In that context, it serves as the beginning of a long recitation of sacred history in which the prophet explains why the people were exiled into Babylon.

Compared to other Christmas readings in the lectionary, this reading is not very Christmas-like. In fact, in places it has a distinctly Passion-like tone. For that reason alone, this passage could be well worth the effort it would take to preach on it.

Hebrews 2:10–18

This reading, too, is not especially Christmas-like. It not only hints about the Passion, it is a full-fledged reflection on the Passion in which the Incarnation is seen as a first and necessary step in the process leading to Calvary. Whether or not we personally accept this view (and some biblical writers do not), this is a powerful theological move on the part of the author of Hebrews and a powerful move on the part of the lectionary tradition to include it in Christmas. At the very least, we should not let the sentimentality of Christmas cause us to overlook this passage or gloss over it too quickly before we have had a chance to struggle with its meaning.

Matthew 2:13–23

With this reading the lectionary returns to the Gospel of Matthew, its primary Gospel for this year. The shepherds, the angels, and humble stable of Luke and the lofty, almost dreamy words of John are all gone now and in their place is the angry King Herod of Matthew.

If we are going to preach on this passage there are several things we should note about it. First, depending on the number of Christmas services held in our particular congregation, this is probably the third time in less than a week that the lectionary has us reading from a different Gospel. Diligent biblical work will be required to make sure that each Gospel's unique perspective is given its due.

Second, the lectionary has once again bent Matthew's chronology in order to fit it into a Luke-inspired church year. According to Matthew, both the killing of the innocents and the flight into Egypt occurred *after* the visit by the magi. It is through them that Herod learned of Jesus' birth, and it is through them that he learned approximately where and when that birth took place. In the chronology of the lectionary, though, the magi (whose visit actually set the events of today's reading in motion) do not appear until Epiphany.

Third, except for Mary, this is the first time this year that women appear in the lectionary readings. This is not entirely the fault of the lectionary, however, for Matthew's own text does not include women in the Christmas story in quite the same way Luke's did. Their presence here is secondary to the action of the men in the story. In fact, as mothers of murdered children, the women in this reading are in a real sense victims of male violence. This text is a "text of terror" for women and ought to be read as such. Perhaps the best way to do this would be to consciously imagine this story from the viewpoint of the mothers in it (including Mary) and to reflect on the untold story that is between the lines we read there.

Second Sunday in Christmas

In these readings the lectionary returns to the pattern it used for the readings assigned to Christmas itself. There is a restoration prophecy traditionally associated with the birth of Christ (or at least a prophecy containing Christmas-like images), an epistle lesson with Christmas-sounding phrases, and a Gospel lesson either from Luke or John. Preachers should note, however, that while the pattern of readings may be similar, two of the three readings are from biblical books we have not seen previously—Jeremiah and Ephesians. Special care should be taken to familiarize ourselves with these books. This is especially true for Jeremiah because readings from the Hebrew Bible have been so consistently from Isaiah up to this point.

In the lessons for today the lectionary also returns to its pattern of yearly readings for Christmas. In this case, though, such a pattern does not necessarily give these readings special emphasis. For while today's readings may be listed for every year, they are often not read that often in practice, largely because the Christmas season is seldom two Sundays long.

Jeremiah 31:7–14

Because we have just spent almost six weeks reading from Isaiah, the words of this lesson can sound deceptively like the ones we've already heard. They are similar, but Jeremiah has his own unique voice that is well worth the effort to try to hear. Reviewing some background material on Jeremiah or looking over an introductory commentary could be very useful in helping us sort out what Jeremiah in particular has to say to us.

This reading is also taken from one of the lectionary's favorite sections of Jeremiah. Parts of chapter 31 appear in several places—Easter Year A, and in Lent and Ordinary Time Year C. From this particular reading, verses 7–9 appear again in Proper 25 Year B. Because the church year is less likely to influence our understanding of this passage during Ordinary Time, it might be advisable to preach on it then rather than here during Christmas.

Ephesians 1:3–14

This is another example of how important it is to read the verses that precede or follow a reading from the lectionary. In this case, verses 1–2 have been left out, no doubt in an effort to make this passage more universally applicable. Verses 1–2, however, are important because they give the literary context for the rest of the passage. Reading them makes it clear that we are not in just any part of Ephesians; we are in the salutation that opens the book. This is vital information because the primary purpose of a salutation is to introduce the major themes that will later be taken up by the author. Customarily a salutation is not a place for theological discussion, although the editing of the lectionary makes it appear so here.

John 1: (1–9) 10–18

For the second time in this short season the lectionary again gives us the prologue in John. As was noted the first time this passage appeared (Christmas Proper 3, Years ABC), even this well-favored passage has not escaped being edited by the lectionary to conform to demands of the church year. In this case, now that the Christmas season is about to close, the most familiar Christmas-like verses (1–9) have been taken out and verses 15–18, which expand on John's witness to Jesus, have been added. Again, to really do this passage justice, it is probably best to read all eighteen verses.

EPIPHANY

*A*s it stands in the *Revised Common Lectionary* today, Epiphany is a curious and often confusing mix of liturgical traditions. Even the parenthetical title given to it betrays the sometimes uneasy marriage that has come to characterize the period of the church year between the day of Epiphany and the beginning of Lent.

This confusion should not surprise us, given the wide variety of traditions that have historically been associated with this part of the liturgical year. Epiphany was first celebrated in the Eastern churches on January 6 as far back as the third century. This one-day festival celebrated both the birth of Jesus (including the visit by the magi) and his baptism. In the early part of the fourth century, Western churches, too, began celebrating Jesus' birth, but they celebrated it on December 25 with neither magi nor the baptism as part of the celebration.

Eventually both traditions began to influence each other. By the latter part of the fourth century, many Eastern churches added a December 25 celebration of the birth of Jesus to their observance of Epiphany and many Western churches added a January 6 celebration of the visit by the magi to their observance of Christmas. Western churches, however, did not celebrate the Baptism of Jesus until much later, when Gospel readings about Jesus' baptism were added to the traditional series of readings for Epiphany that celebrated God's unfolding reve-lation in Christ.

Traces of all these traditions can be seen in the lectionary today. Following Western tradition, lectionary readings for the day of Epiphany now focus on the visit by the magi and on the Sunday following on the Baptism of Jesus. Even vestiges of the traditional Western readings for Epiphany can also be found today in the readings from the Gospel of John on the Second Sunday After Epiphany and in the optional readings listed for Transfiguration when celebrated on the Last Sunday of Epiphany.

Following Eastern tradition, however, Epiphany in the *Revised Common Lectionary* is not a season at all but is more properly thought of as part of the Christmas cycle. Today, Epiphany, the Baptism of the Lord,[1] and, in some respects, the Second Sunday After Epiphany all function in many ways as a continuation of the Christmas part of the lectionary. The Sundays after that are Ordinary Time (with the exception of Transfiguration Sunday for those churches that celebrate the Transfiguration on the Last Sunday After Epiphany).

This curious mix of traditions presents us with a challenging situation very different from the one we encountered in Advent and Christmas. First, unlike the seasons before it, Epiphany presents us with a complex pattern of readings, some of which are meant to be linked to one another and others which are not. The readings for Epiphany Day, the Baptism of the Lord, and the Second Sunday After Epiphany, for example, are all clearly linked by the lectionary according to the theme of their respective Sundays. On subsequent Sundays, however, readings from the Hebrew Bible are often linked to the Gospel lesson, but both the epistle and the Gospel lessons are semi-continuous readings and are in no way meant to be linked together. If the Last Sunday After Epiphany is celebrated as Transfiguration Sunday, all three readings will again be deliberately linked.

Second, and also unlike the seasons before it, Epiphany lacks a consistent theme or liturgical tone to carry us through from one Sunday to the next. It begins with a lingering Christmas-like atmosphere on Epiphany Day, shifts to a baptismal theme on the First Sunday After Epiphany, returns to themes more characteristic of Epiphany Day on the Second, and then shifts again to Ordinary Time from the Third Sunday After Epiphany on. In many churches still another shift comes on the Last Sunday

---

[1] Note later on, calling this Sunday, Baptism of Jesus Sunday, avoids the sexism and patriarchialism implied in the title, Lord.

After Epiphany when Ordinary Time gives way to a celebration of the Transfiguration as the dominant theme.

Such lack of consistency is a mixed blessing for the preacher. On the one hand, more is demanded of us during Epiphany than was the case during Advent or Christmas because now each Sunday's readings present us with a different situation than the one before it. To keep track of it all will require deliberate awareness, constant vigilance, and a consistent willingness to plan in advance. It will also require that we take time to understand what the lectionary intends on any given Sunday, whether we choose to follow that intention or not.

On the other hand, the lack of a consistent theme or pattern in Epiphany gives us some marvelous flexibility. We can, for example, move sets of lessons around much more easily in Epiphany than was the case during either Advent or Christmas because no one theme indelibly ties these lessons together. We even have flexibility regarding the special days that occur during Epiphany. Epiphany itself, for instance, may either be celebrated on January 6 or the First Sunday in January. Likewise, the Sunday of the Transfiguration may either be celebrated as the Last Sunday After Epiphany or it may be celebrated during Lent. Such choices offer all kinds of possibilities that are not usually available in the lectionary unless we depart from it entirely.

Moreover, the lack of a consistent theme during Epiphany also means the Hebrew Bible will not be as dominated by the Gospel lesson as it was during Advent and Christmas. In most cases, the readings will still be linked, but the linking in Epiphany is far less long-standing and far less indelible. We are now freer to let the Hebrew Bible stand on its own.

Finally, the lectionary readings for Epiphany are complicated by one additional factor. Like Christmas, Epiphany is variable in length. It can last from as few as six Sundays to as many as nine. Again, advance planning will be important in order to make the best use of the number of Sundays available. This will be particularly true for years when Epiphany is short and more decisions are required about which lessons will or will not be read.

There are several possible approaches we might take to such a challenging pattern of readings. One approach might be a sermon series based on the semi-continuous readings from either Corinthians or Matthew. Matthew is especially attractive in this case because readings for both Epiphany and the Baptism of the Lord could also be included in the series. Another approach is to deliberately ignore the lectionary's intended linkings and preach a series of sermons on the Epiphany readings from the Hebrew Bible. These readings are a wonderful collection of God's self-revelations that can easily stand independent of the Gospel lessons they have been associated with in the lectionary. (This option might be especially good for years when Epiphany is short and fewer semi-continuous readings are available for use.)

A third approach is to dispense with the lectionary's suggested readings from the Hebrew Bible and do a sermon series on the Servant Songs of Isaiah. Even the Isaiah passages for the day of Epiphany and for the Baptism of the Lord, which are already taken from these Songs, could be incorporated into such a series. This option will take more work than the others, but it could prove quite fruitful, particularly if one studies what Jewish scholars have to say about the Servant.

Readings from the Hebrew Bible

All the readings from the Hebrew Bible for Epiphany have been chosen primarily for the way they illuminate or relate to their corresponding Gospel lesson. In Year A, these readings come primarily from the book of Isaiah, as was the case for Advent and Christmas this year as well. Again, most of these readings come from Isaiah 40—66 (Second and Third Isaiah), and again, many are taken from Isaiah's prophecies of restoration. In addition to these lessons from Isaiah are a lesson from Micah and a couple of lessons from Deuteronomy.

The Isaiah passages are of particular interest for several reasons. The first has to do with the reading from Isaiah, chapter 9. This well-known passage is usually associated with Christmas, and indeed was read on Christmas just this year. Now it appears again here in Epiphany, although in slightly different form. Also of interest is the continued use of the last half of Isaiah. During Advent and Christmas this part of Isaiah was primarily associated with the birth of Jesus.

In Epiphany it is linked to a more general revelation of God. We also see in Epiphany examples of the many times when the Servant Songs of Isaiah will be linked to Jesus.

Epistle Readings

With the exception of Epiphany, the Baptism of the Lord, and the Ninth Sunday After Epiphany (and Transfiguration Sunday if it is celebrated in Epiphany), epistle readings for Epiphany this year are taken from the first four chapters of

1 Corinthians. These are deliberately semi-continuous readings. Unfortunately, these semi-continuous readings are given short shrift by the lectionary. Some will not even be read if Epiphany is short or if Transfiguration Sunday is celebrated as part of Epiphany. But even if Epiphany is long, however, and all these readings are used, the cycle of semi-continuous readings will still only cover the very beginning of 1 Corinthians.

To help rectify this situation, preachers might consider celebrating the Transfiguration during Lent. This would give an additional Sunday for these semi-continuous readings.

Gospel Readings

Except for the reading from John on the Second Sunday After Epiphany, all the Gospel readings for Epiphany this year come from Matthew, the lectionary's Gospel for Year A. The lesson from John seems a bit out of place among all those passages from Matthew, and in respect to the semi-continuous readings from Matthew, it is. This reading appears where it does primarily because of the church year. Readings from John's Gospel are "ancient Epiphany Gospels" and they appear on this Sunday every year. This year's reading contains John the Baptist's testimony concerning Jesus.[2]

The lessons from Matthew, like those from 1 Corinthians, are deliberate semi-continuous readings. In this case, however, they will pick up again after Pentecost. Because the readings for Epiphany Day and for the Baptism of the Lord Sunday are also from Matthew, this means a quite respectable series of semi-continuous readings from the Gospel of Matthew. If the Transfiguration is celebrated during Epiphany, still another reading will come from Matthew, although it is not strictly semi-continuous.

Even this series of readings, unfortunately, is slighted by the lectionary. Not only are they interrupted twice (once by the Gospel of John, and then once more by Lent, Easter, and Pentecost), but some of these lessons will not be read at all due to the variable length of Epiphany. Again, one recourse is to celebrate Transfiguration in Lent. Another recourse is to leave out the set of readings listed in the lectionary for the Second Sunday After Epiphany and begin this cycle of semi-continuous readings a Sunday early. Still another is to save the readings from the Sermon on the Mount and do some shifting of

---

[2] *The Common Lectionary*, p. 58.

lessons to include them in Ordinary Time when semi-continuous readings from Matthew, resume again after Pentecost.

Before making any such shifts, however, care should be taken to first understand the relationships between the lessons as the lectionary has conceived them. Some of these relationships are positive ones and ought to be considered whenever we shift lessons around. This is particularly true whenever a set of lessons is broken up or the shift of one set of lessons is made, for example, on account of the Gospel lesson, and it ends up unintentionally affecting the pattern established in the epistle lesson.

Epiphany of the Lord

The first issue to face us in this set of lessons is the official title given to this day by the lectionary. Historically, the day of Epiphany has always been known as simply that, Epiphany (Epiphany Day). That is the way most people still refer to it. The lectionary, however, insists on Epiphany of the Lord. There is no need to be so specific, especially when doing so leads us into the use of patriarchal language.

The readings for Epiphany Day, been associated with this day in the church year for centuries, much like the readings for Advent and Christmas. In fact, the readings for Epiphany have always been associated with this time of year from the very beginnings of the lectionary. This actually makes the tradition behind the Epiphany readings even older than the tradition behind the readings for either Advent or Christmas, because the celebration of Epiphany itself is at least half a century older than both its predecessors in the church year.

Such ancient associations should immediately put us on our guard once again. As during Advent and Christmas, we should again be alert to ancient methods of interpretation like typology (which may or may not agree with what we know about the Bible today). We should be alert to ancient ways of thinking, too, which also may or may not be of help to us today.

The readings for the day of Epiphany also receive heavy emphasis from the lectionary, again like many of the readings we saw during Advent and Christmas. Not only are these lessons read every year, they also come from parts of the Bible that are highly favored by the lectionary. This favoritism should again put us on guard.

Interestingly, the readings for today do differ from the readings for Advent and Christmas in one respect. They are meant to be read on the actual day of Epiphany (as one might expect), but they can also be read on the Sunday before. This provision is somewhat unusual for the lectionary and was done specifically to ensure that the Baptism of the Lord Sunday would be observed on the Sunday following the celebration of Epiphany, even in those churches that do not hold midweek Epiphany services.

At first glance, celebrating the Epiphany on the Sunday before January 6 is a tempting option. It means that both the Eastern and Western traditions for Epiphany will each get their due. But there are hidden costs involved, too, for the "First Sunday in January" option also means that the already short Christmas season will be shortened even more.

In the logic of the lectionary, an abbreviated Christmas season is no great loss because Epiphany itself is already a continuation of Christmas. The preacher, however, would lose the flexibility the lectionary has so carefully built into the Sundays after Christmas, and congregations would lose the opportunity to hear some of the better chosen readings for Christmas.

Isaiah 60:1–6

The lectionary's treatment of this passage presents us with many of the same issues we saw regarding similar passages for Advent and Christmas. For example, the lectionary has once again followed a centuries-old tradition and deliberately linked a restoration prophecy in Isaiah to an event in the life of Jesus. In this case, the lectionary's habit of making the Gospel lesson the controlling lesson is particularly ironic. It would have been historically more accurate to have made this lesson from Isaiah the controlling lesson. The truth is, Matthew 2:1–12 actually depends on Isaiah 60. The Epiphany-like references to visiting kings and precious gifts that we find here in Isaiah are not just types prefiguring the magi, they were the inspiration for them. In fact, if it weren't for Isaiah, the magi might not have appeared in Matthew's Gospel at all, or might have appeared in a very different form.

Unless one is prepared to spend a good part of the sermon explaining the literary parentage of Matthew's account of the magi, it is probably best not to preach on both the Isaiah and Matthew readings at the same time. By the same token, unless one is prepared to discuss the dynamics of Hebrew prophecy and the way such prophecy differs from simply telling the future, it is also probably best not to preach on this passage at all during Epiphany. It could be a very interesting and challenging passage during Ordinary Time, however, particularly if more of chapter 60 is included in the reading.

Likewise, the lectionary has once again deliberately played down the historical context of a reading from the Hebrew Scriptures. There is no mention as to why those returning had been exiled in the first place. (They had fallen into worshiping other things than God, had mistreated the poor, and refused hospitality to strangers.) There is no mention as to why they are being allowed to return, either. (It was so that they and everyone else would know that God was indeed God.) Instead there is only a triumphal procession into Zion, without any acknowledgment at all of the pain and effort it took to get there or the purpose God had in mind in bringing it all about.

Moreover, the lectionary has also played down a very important political dynamic inherent in this passage—the tendency of oppressed people, once they have gained victory, to become oppressors themselves. In Isaiah we see this dynamic played out in the people of Israel. Nations that once oppressed Israel are now described as subservient to it. "The nations" *and their wealth* stream into Zion. But, unlike the rest of Isaiah 60, the verses chosen by the lectionary only hint at such dynamics. As a result, we (and our congregations) are not given a chance to adequately wrestle with what is a major issue in the prophetic literature.

Care should be taken to honor and address this historical and political context. The first is fairly simple. We would do well, for example, to read and study chapter 59 of Isaiah as background for sermon preparation. We would also do well to let the congregation in on this background as well by giving them a brief overview of chapter 59 before reading the actual lesson for today.

The political context is a bit more difficult to address, particularly on a festival day when the liturgy tends to be pretty clearly focused. In this case, perhaps it is best to read this lesson from Isaiah as it is for today and leave the political implications in it for another time, perhaps during Ordinary Time. Not only would we not be competing with the festival of Epiphany then, we would also have more time to adequately reflect on the "politics of revenge" so blatantly played out in the rest of chapter 60.

Last, the lectionary has again chosen a reading from the Hebrew Bible primarily on the basis of how well it fits into the liturgical themes of the church year. In this respect, this passage from Isaiah has everything one would want for Epiphany:

light, rising, brightness, and kings bearing gifts from afar. Again the imagery is so familiar we hardly notice it.

But we should notice, especially the images of light and brightness, for what we have here is the very same issue we encountered in Advent—darkness being equated with bad and evil while light and brightness are equated with all that is good. That is popular biblical imagery, and it is legitimate imagery, but it must be used sensitively and with respect to people of color for whom darkness is a source of pride.

Ephesians 3:1–12

The conjunction that begins this passage is an immediate clue for us to look back at the verses that precede it. In this case we find the author discussing the enmity that has often characterized the relationship between Jew and Gentile and the way in which Jesus had broken down that ancient "wall of hostility." This is the mystery of which the author speaks in the reading for today—Jew and Gentile have both been brought together in the body of Christ, the church.

No doubt it is this note of revelation that first led to this passage being read for Epiphany. However, it is the content of that revelation that makes the choice of this lesson one of the lectionary's better moments. This passage from Ephesians not only mitigates some of the triumphalism in the Isaiah passage, it also helps us rightly interpret the Gospel lesson for today. In the light of Ephesians, we see that the visit of the magi was more than just a simple story of people from far off lands being led to the Christ Child. They are revealed for who they really were, Gentile outsiders being welcomed by Christ.

Because today is a festival, and the lectionary is so focused on the Gospel lesson, it might be tempting to pass over this passage in light of the more "Epiphany-like" images of the other two lessons. It would be wise to resist the temptation and let this passage do its important interpretive work. Even if we do not preach on it directly, its message should inform what we say about either Isaiah or Matthew. At the very least, it should be regularly read each year along with the other lessons, possibly even accompanied by a brief introductory statement about its significance.

Matthew 2:1–12

As is often the case, this Gospel lesson is the reason for today's festival. Since Matthew is the only Gospel to record the visit of the magi, his account is read every year, even in

Years B and C, when Matthew is not the principal Gospel. This is more emphasis than most other Gospel lessons receive, with the exception of Luke's Christmas narrative and the prologue and Passion narrative from John.

One very important thing to remember about this passage is this—it is emphatically not a continuation of Luke's version of the Christmas story. These magi have not followed shepherds, they have not heard angels singing in the sky, nor are they visiting Jesus in the manger. These distinctions may be small, but important, for while Luke is trying to portray Jesus as humble and one with the common people, Matthew is more concerned here with the revelation of Jesus to the world and the impact his coming had on those with power in the world.

Second (as we saw earlier), even though the lectionary and Matthew himself link this passage with the reading from Isaiah, the preacher should approach such linking with caution. A better choice would be to go with the link to Ephesians. There are fewer interpretive issues there.

Baptism of the Lord

For the Second Sunday in a row the lectionary has given us a problematic title. Again the word *Lord* here is an unnecessary use of sexist and patriarchal language. A more inclusive title is Baptism of Jesus Sunday, a title that is already being used in many parts of the church.

Today's is a fairly new festival. This is particularly true in Western tradition, which I noted earlier has only recently added Gospel readings about the Baptism of Jesus to this period of Epiphany. Even in the East, however, where the Baptism of Jesus has long been a feature of Epiphany, it was not a festival on its own. Technically, it is still not a festival, but continues as the focal point of Epiphany itself.

There are some distinct advantages to the Baptism of Jesus being such a recent festival. For one thing, it means that there are fewer traditions associated with this day. We are freer to be creative and innovative. The newness of this festival also means that even though the Gospel lesson for today has been associated with Epiphany for centuries, the other two lessons do not have such long-standing associations either with each other or with the church year. They are, however, still officially linked to the Gospel lesson, even if the links are not particularly strong ones.

Isaiah 42:1–9

Even though the passages for today are new to the liturgical year, they still follow some very old patterns. For instance, in this passage from Isaiah the lectionary has linked a Servant Song with an event in the life of Jesus. This is a common association in both Christian tradition and in the lectionary. We saw it in Advent this year and we will see it again in Lent, Easter, and on this very Sunday in both Years B and C.

Of course, to identify Jesus as the Servant is a legitimate and time-honored way to interpret this passage, but as is often the case, it is not the only interpretation possible. Hebrew prophecy is wonderfully multifaceted and often employ multiple layers of meaning. Jewish scholars have, for instance, identified the Servant as the people of Israel, the king, the Messiah, the prophet himself, and so on. Awareness of these other possible interpretations adds depth to our understanding of this passage, depth that could be particularly useful on a day when baptism is a central focus.

As usual, the lectionary has again deliberately edited out the historical context of this passage. In fact, the editing here might make this reading appear to be a self-contained song. It is not. It is the continuation of a song begun in chapter 41 when God laments the lack of a person who could give counsel to the people of Israel. Awareness of this background also helps widen the possibilities available to us in interpreting the meaning of the Servant.

Acts 10:34–43

This is a unique reading in several ways. First, it is not from an epistle, as one might expect at this time of year. Instead it comes from one of the speeches in the book of Acts. Like the use of the Servant Songs of Isaiah, this too is a pattern we will see repeated on this Sunday in Years B and C.

Second, this reading is one of the most often repeated passages read during Epiphany. It is read four times in the lectionary, twice during this year alone.

Third, it is also a very popular reading for festivals, even though it does not record an event from the life of Jesus. Acts:10:34–43 is probably best recognized as an alternative reading for Easter Day, and in that setting the pronouncement of the risen Christ contained in this passage is the primary theme. Here in Epiphany, there are several themes one might emphasize—the revelation of Jesus following his resurrection, the appointment of Jesus as the "judge of both the living and the dead," and (as the lectionary compilers themselves suggest) the baptismal theme of forgiveness found in verse 43.

If we take the historical context of this passage into account, another even more appropriate theme emerges. This is no generic sermon Peter is preaching here, although the lectionary does not tell us this. It is a baptismal sermon, and not just any baptismal sermon, either. It is the baptismal sermon for Cornelius and his family, the first recorded Gentile converts into the Christian church. Seen in this light, this passage continues the inclusive Epiphany message we saw on Epiphany in Matthew and Ephesians. This time baptism is singled out as the sign of God's all inclusive love.

Matthew 3:13–17

Once again the lectionary has altered the chronology of Matthew's Gospel in order to accommodate the church year. In this reading, we have skipped several years ahead in the life of Jesus from where we were on Epiphany. We have also skipped several verses ahead in the Gospel of Matthew, passing over verses that have already been read during Advent and Christmas. Preachers who choose to preach on this text, then, might want to read through the first three chapters of Matthew as part of their sermon preparation. This will help to keep Matthew's chronology firmly in mind and enable us to not be unduly influenced by the very un-Matthew-like chronology of the lectionary.

As is often the case when we are dealing with a familiar account recorded by all three synoptic Gospels, preachers should take care not to unintentionally combine elements from the other Gospels into Matthew's account here. Checking out the differences in each account through Gospel parallels and identifying those elements that are unique to Matthew will be time well spent and may even lead to several sermon ideas.

Second Sunday After Epiphany

Of all the readings appointed for Epiphany, the readings for this Sunday best reflect the confusion so characteristic of the lectionary this time of year. Like Epiphany itself, these readings are a curious mix. There are, for example, festival elements in both the reading from Hebrew Scriptures and the Gospel, as well as elements more associated with Ordinary Time in the epistle. There is also the remnant of a very old tradition in the Gospel lesson while at the same time there is the beginning of a newer practice (at least in Epiphany) of semi-continuous readings in the epistle lesson. And then, adding even more confusion, there is a sudden shift to the Gospel of John in the Gospel lesson, but the reading from Isaiah that is linked to it is another Servant Song similar to the one Last Sunday.

Isaiah 49:1–7

In this reading we find a pattern similar to the one we saw on Epiphany in that it was chosen primarily for the Epiphany imagery found in verses 6 and 7. The Servant is called to become a "light to the nations." Kings will see the Servant and "stand up" at attention. Even princes and rulers will bow down and worship the Servant as God's chosen one.

We also find a pattern similar to the one we saw last Sunday in the way the lectionary has again associated the Servant of Isaiah with Jesus. In this case, however, the linking made is of a more general nature and is not related to any specific event in the life of Jesus.

Neither of these patterns truly reflects the original intent of Isaiah, which was to proclaim the coming restoration of Zion and the Servant's role in that restoration. For this reason it will again be important to keep in mind the historical and political context of this passage. Again, it will be important to keep in mind what Jewish scholars have said and are saying about the Servant.

1 Corinthians 1:1–9

This passage begins the series of semi-continuous readings from 1 Corinthians that will take us through Epiphany and then begin again following Pentecost. There has been no effort by the lectionary to link this passage either with the church year or with any of the other readings for today. It is completely independent and should be treated as such in a sermon.

This passage is also the beginning of 1 Corinthians itself. It contains the salutations and thanksgivings traditional for letters of that time. It also contains a brief overview of some of the issues Paul will be addressing in the rest of the letter, a practice that was also traditional for his time.

Because it is such an independent reading and because it is part of a series of semi-continuous readings, this passage is probably the best choice of the three for a sermon. Preachers would do well, however, to study 1 Corinthians first in order to follow Paul's intricate line of thinking. This will be especially true for those who are planning to make this passage the beginning of a sermon series.

John 1:29–42

This passage from John interrupts the long string of readings from Matthew characteristic of this year in Epiphany. It was chosen for this Sunday in the lectionary primarily because it is an ancient Epiphany Gospel. Like other traditional Epiphany readings, it centers on a revelation of God in Christ, in this case the revelation that comes from the lips of John the Baptist. Also recorded in the passages is the calling of Jesus' first disciples—Andrew, Simon Peter, and another unnamed disciple.

Moreover, this passage again comes from one of the lectionary's favorite parts of the New Testament—the first chapter of John. As we have already seen, it is a particularly popular choice for the Christmas cycle. Not only do we find it this year, we will also see readings from this part of John on this same Sunday in both Years B and C.

For those who want to continue preaching on Epiphany themes, this passage could be a good choice. It has fewer lectionary and church-year-related issues involved in its choice than the reading from Isaiah. Those who preach on this passage, however, would do well to remember that John has a very different view of Jesus and his mission in the world than does Matthew. Because we have been reading from Matthew for some time now and will continue in Matthew again next Sunday, it will be important to keep that distinction in mind.

Third Sunday After Epiphany

By this Sunday, the lectionary's characteristic pattern for Ordinary Time finally emerges in full. We are now back in Matthew, so both the Gospel and the epistle readings are now completely independent semi-continuous (in the case of 1 Corinthians, almost continuous) readings. The reading from Isaiah, though, is still linked to both the church year and the Gospel. This same pattern will continue for all of the Sundays left in Epiphany except for the last.

Even though we are now in Ordinary Time, a few hints of Epiphany still remain. The Isaiah reading, for instance, talks about the dawning of a great light. The Gospel lesson not only quotes Isaiah, it also pictures the initial ministry of Jesus as the embodiment of that light. These hints, however, are not meant to indicate the continuation of an Epiphany season. They are, instead, more a reflection of the lectionary's having linked the Isaiah reading to the Gospel lesson from Matthew.

Isaiah 9:1–4

This reading is probably one of the best known and most often read passages for Epiphany. In fact, we have already seen it once this year, on Christmas Day (where part of this reading is read every year). Many comments made then also apply here.

There are, however, a few things we should note about the way the lectionary has used this passage here in Epiphany. First, it has been edited specifically to reflect the church year. The first verse has been added in order to strengthen the intended connection with the Gospel lesson. At the same time, verses 5 through 7 (which announce the birth of Emmanuel) have been omitted to soften the connection of this passage with Christmas.

Second, because this passage is from Isaiah 1—39 and all the other Isaiah passages for Epiphany are from Isaiah 40—66, it has a very different historical and literary context from the others. Not only was it written years before the Exile, it is not technically a restoration prophecy, although it does contain one of the few glimmers of the restoration to be found in First Isaiah.

Since tradition and the lectionary have imposed so many associations on this passage, it is best to handle it carefully. Those who choose to preach on it this Sunday ought to do so with eyes open. They should be fully aware that both Matthew and the lectionary have used this passage in very different ways than were originally intended and that most of us have been conditioned to follow their lead.

1 Corinthians 1:10–18

Last week we read the salutation and thanksgiving that began this letter. Today we come to the body of the letter where Paul begins his argument in earnest. His thought here is not easy to break into sections suitable for public reading, however, so even though the lectionary has ended this reading at verse 18, the line of thinking Paul is developing here is not ended. In fact, he is just beginning to lay the groundwork for what is to come later.

Therefore, no matter how we use it, this passage should not be treated as an isolated unit. We need to keep in mind what has come before, and particularly to keep in mind what is to come. For this reason, the most effective use of this passage would be as part of a sermon series based on the Epiphany readings from 1 Corinthians. A brief introduction connecting this reading to the one last Sunday is another possible approach. At the very least, it should be read in its place with the other readings from 1 Corinthians, even if we do not preach from it.

Matthew 4:12–23

With this reading the semi-continuous readings in Matthew begin in earnest. Even so, as we noted earlier, they are not completely free from being affected by the church year. Unlike the reading from 1 Corinthians for today, which takes up immediately where the last reading left off, in this reading we have again skipped over several verses from last week's reading in Matthew. Between these two readings is the account of Jesus being tempted in the wilderness (an account that will be picked up later in Lent). So, even though the lectionary does not say it, the background Matthew intended for this reading today is that forty-day fast. Those who preach on this passage should bear this in mind even if they do not directly address it in the sermon.

The lectionary has also done some extraneous editing on this passage, which once again has nothing to do with the church year. It has concluded this reading at verse 23, but the natural literary end to this unit is actually verse 25. Those two neglected verses are not essential to the passage, but there is also no reason to exclude them either. They should be read, if only to give this reading more of a sense of completion.

The second most important issue in this passage is the use Matthew makes of Isaiah 9. He has deliberately used it as a proof text for the preaching of Jesus. This, as we have noted before, is not an illegitimate use of Isaiah, but it is one that can invite misunderstanding if not used carefully. Again, it would be a good idea to refresh our memories about what Jewish scholars have said about this passage. It would also be a good idea to play down the link that has been made here and purposefully not preach on both Matthew and Isaiah together.

Fourth Sunday After Epiphany

This Sunday the semi-continuous readings from both 1 Corinthians and Matthew continue. Instead of the expected reading from Isaiah, however, the lectionary has shifted to

Micah for the reading from the Hebrew Bible. As was the case last Sunday, the lectionary intends this reading to be linked to the Gospel lesson for today, but this link is not as strong as others we have seen so far this year. For this reason, it is probably best not to force even these two readings into one sermon, unless in the course of preparing the sermon it becomes logical to use one to illuminate the other.

Micah 6:1–8

There are several things preachers will want to keep in mind when working with this passage. First, Micah is not Isaiah, even though he may sound like him at times. Micah has his own particular view of what is happening in eighth-century B.C.E. Israel, and we would do well not to make assumptions about this passage based on more familiar passages from Isaiah.

Second, this passage is one of the few passages from Micah included in the lectionary. It is also one of the few Micah readings (and one of the few Hebrew Bible Epiphany readings) that are not especially linked to the Gospel lesson for the day. This reason alone might commend this passage to us as a possible basis for a sermon.

Third, taken out of context (as is nearly always the case in a lectionary), this passage can appear to be a diatribe against the ancient Jewish sacrificial system. This is not exactly the case, as the verses in chapter 5 that precede this reading make clear. Micah is not accusing the Israelites of hollow worship; his real target is the ease by which the Israelites of his day accommodated to the worship of things other than God. Care should be taken that we not misrepresent either ancient or modern Judaism. Care should also be taken that we not imagine ourselves to be exempt from Micah's challenging words simply because we are Christians.

1 Corinthians 1:18–31

This well-known passage begins immediately where last week's lesson left off. In fact, because there are no good natural breaks in this part of 1 Corinthians, the lectionary has purposely repeated the last verse of last week's reading (verse 18) again this Sunday. This repetition not only gives us a running start, it also helps underscore the continuous nature of these readings.

Even though the lectionary (by its very nature) has to treat this passage as an isolated unit, it is not. It is part of the progression of Paul's thought here. The topic has now shifted from a discussion of divisions in the Corinthian community to a proclamation of God's wisdom, but for Paul they are very much related. In fact, his description of God's "foolish" wisdom was purposely designed to contrast with the ego-based divisions that had come up among the Corinthians.

This progression of thought is especially important to keep in mind when we get to verse 22 where Paul begins talking about "Jews and Greeks." If we see this passage as an isolated unit it is easy to begin to imagine that we are neither. Technically that may be true, but if we take this passage in the context of Paul's thought, "Jews and Greeks" include everyone and the wisdom of both camps is foolish when compared to the wisdom of God. In this case, using in our sermon the phrase "those who are not Jews" might get Paul's point across a bit better than the word *Greeks*. The readers of this passage would then be more clearly included, which is what Paul had in mind all the time.

Preachers will also want to be aware that this is not the only time these verses appear in the lectionary. Verses 18–25 are read again on the Third Sunday of Lent Year B. Since more of Paul's thought is reflected in the longer text here, this is the better of the two choices from which to preach. It also gets us involved with fewer issues related to the church year.

Matthew 5:1–12

Having skipped only verses 23–25 of chapter 4, the reading for today picks up virtually where last Sunday's reading ended. With these verses, though, we come to the Beatitudes and the beginning of a long string of almost continuous readings from the Sermon on the Mount. As with the Corinthian lessons, such a string of continuous and semi-continuous readings is an open invitation to do a sermon series. That is an especially attractive option this Sunday since this particular reading is often divorced from its literary context.

Also like the Corinthian lesson for today, this is not the only time this lesson appears in the lectionary. It will also be read for All Saints' Day this year. (Interestingly a similar pattern will be seen again in Year C, when Luke's version of the Beatitudes is likewise read both on All Saints' Day and on the Fourth Sunday After Epiphany. There, too, it forms the beginning of a series of semi-continuous readings from a sermon by Jesus, this time the Sermon on the Plain.)

Fifth Sunday After Epiphany

Today's readings continue the pattern characteristic of the lectionary in Ordinary Time. Both the Gospel lesson and the epistle lesson are semi-continuous, in this case both picking up immediately from where their respective readings ended last Sunday. The reading from the Hebrew Scriptures is once again from Isaiah 40—66 and is again deliberately linked to the Gospel lesson.

Isaiah 58:1–9a (9b–12)

This passage is a little different from most of the Hebrew Bible readings we have seen so far in Epiphany. First, it is a very popular passage with the lectionary, more popular in fact than Isaiah 9, judging by the number of times it occurs in the chosen readings. These verses from Isaiah 58 not only appear in today's reading, they also appear every year on Ash Wednesday (Isaiah 58:1–9a) and in the readings for Proper 16 in Year C (Isaiah 9b–14). Given that the lectionary can include only a finite number of passages of scripture, this number of repetitions is remarkable, particularly for a passage from the Hebrew Bible and one that is used primarily during Ordinary Time at that.

Second, this passage is not the deliberately isolated restoration prophecy we have come to expect from the lectionary in this cycle. It is, instead, a remarkably representative piece of Second Isaiah's thinking. It hints at the restoration to come (particularly in the alternate verses), but concentrates instead on the changes in behavior Isaiah believed were necessary for restoration to even be possible.

Third, this passage is one of the few times in this cycle when the reading from the Hebrew Scriptures has been definitely linked to the Gospel lesson for today but has not been linked to the life of Jesus in the process. Instead, the link here is theological and points up the similarity between the teachings of the prophet here and the teachings of Jesus.

Because it is so unusual, this could be a good time to preach on this passage. Those who do so, however, should again take care to not misrepresent Judaism but rather let these words speak to their modern congregations instead.

1 Corinthians 2:1–12 (13–16)

In this passage we continue reading Paul's thoughts concerning the controversies at Corinth. Here he relates his own teaching to the "foolish wisdom" of God we read about last week.

The first question to be faced in regard to this reading is whether to include the alternate verses. They are more difficult to understand than the other verses, which is no doubt why the lectionary made them optional. But at the same time, they are part of Paul's argument here. Since there is no compelling reason for omitting them, the best solution is to go ahead and read them, but not necessarily preach on them.

Again it will be important this week to connect this reading to the earlier readings from 1 Corinthians. If this passage is simply read and not preached on, such connection may not be as important, but it would still be helpful as a way of helping members of the congregation understand the background Paul's readers would have taken for granted.

For those who are planning to preach on this passage, it also might be a good idea to "read up" on Paul's concept and use of authority and his thinking on the "principalities and powers." Both are key concepts in this passage and also in subsequent readings from 1 Corinthians.

Matthew 5:13–20

This passage picks up immediately from the Beatitudes we read last week. Unlike last week's reading, however, this is the only time this passage appears in the lectionary.

In most cases where the lectionary has linked a reading from the Hebrew Scriptures with a reading from the Gospels, the intention is for us to understand the Hebrew Scriptures in light of the Gospel. In this reading, however, it might be more constructive if we shine the light in the other direction and let the reading from the Hebrew Scriptures illuminate this Gospel lesson. In doing so, however, we should remember that Matthew is using polemic here. His picture of the Pharisees is not without bias and we should be careful in using it today.

Sixth Sunday After Epiphany
(Proper 1)

This Sunday begins that part of Epiphany when readings may or may not be read on any given year, depending on the number of Sundays available between now and Ash Wednesday. The virtually continuous readings of both 1 Corinthians and Matthew continue. The reading from the Hebrew Scriptures, however, has shifted out of the prophetic literature into a reading from Deuteronomy. While there may be a weak link with the church year, this time there is no clear link with the Gospel lesson.

Deuteronomy 30:15–20

This passage is an excellent representative of the book of Deuteronomy as a whole, but unfortunately it is a bit isolated here in Epiphany. It is also read during the longer period of Ordinary Time following Pentecost in Year C, but even there it is still somewhat isolated from other readings from Deuteronomy.

One consequence of this isolation is that it does not give the preacher the opportunity to adequately address the historical, ethical, and theological issues contained in this passage, particularly those surrounding the conquest of Canaan. What does it mean to say that God commanded the forced displacement of people from their land? Does obeying God always bring blessing and does disobedience bring a curse? What about people like Jesus who have suffered and even now suffer on account of their obedience to God? These are important questions that should be raised at least in the preacher's mind whenever we deal with a passage like this one.

One possible option is to hold off preaching on this passage until summer Ordinary Time (perhaps in Year C) when there is room to take more than one Sunday to reflect on readings from Deuteronomy. If we plan in advance, another option is to dispense with the official Epiphany readings from the Hebrew Bible and make the same kind of room during Epiphany itself.

1 Corinthians 3:1–9

This passage continues Paul's discussion on the conflicts in the Corinthian church. If the alternate verses from last Sunday's reading were used, the lesson today will have followed immediately from where we left off last Sunday. This is important to remember because Paul's thought here assumes that we know what has been said up to this point.

Because it is part of a series of almost continuous readings, this passage is more affected by the variable length of Epiphany than is the reading from Deuteronomy. Most of the time, of course, this passage will simply appear in the middle of this series of readings from 1 Corinthians, but in some years when Easter is particularly early it will not be read at all. In this case the preacher might want to consider moving it (along with the 1 Corinthians lessons for the Seventh and Eighth Sundays After Epiphany) to the first few Sundays After Pentecost. The semi-continuous readings from 1 Corinthians appointed for those Sundays could then be shifted to form an even longer string of readings. In other years this reading will be the final semi-continuous reading from 1 Corinthians until after Pentecost, in which case the preacher might want to consider the same kind of shift.

Matthew 5:21–37

This reading, too, begins immediately where the reading from Matthew ended last week. It is the first part of a series of "you have heard that it was said" teachings in which Jesus describes the righteousness he talked about in last week's reading. The rest of the series will appear next week. Since there is no natural division in these teachings, preachers should feel free to divide them differently than the lectionary has done. As with the reading from 1 Corinthians, the variable length of Epiphany will also affect the way this reading might be used. Again, preachers should feel free to shift lessons around to make the most of this excellent chance to highlight the Sermon on the Mount.

Seventh Sunday After Epiphany
(Proper 2)

Today we find a pattern of readings similar to the one we saw last week. Both the Gospel and the epistle lessons continue to be virtually continuous readings from Matthew and 1 Corinthians, and the reading from the Hebrew Scriptures, which is only loosely linked to the church year and Gospel, is again from the Pentateuch. These lessons are also likely not to be read in any given year depending on the length of Epiphany.

Leviticus 19:1–2, 9–18

This is the only passage from Leviticus to appear in the lectionary at all and it appears twice, in slightly different forms. This is the first appearance. The other is as one reading from the Hebrew Scriptures appointed for Proper 25 Year A. It is a good example of the thinking found in Leviticus even if it does not give us the kind of detail that characterizes the rest of Leviticus.

The first thing we notice about this passage is that verses have been cut out of the middle of it. These verses contain instructions for performing an animal sacrifice and as such were probably considered less important than the more ethical regulations in the rest of the passage. In some respects, this is a logical assumption, even though it is not an assumption shared by Leviticus itself. Why the lectionary compilers chose to also omit verses 3 and 4 is not clear. Those verses speak about respect for parents, the Sabbath, and the avoidance of idolatry. Those are more universal concerns and probably should be included when this passage is read or preached.

It may be tempting to ignore this passage in favor of the others appointed for today. We should resist the temptation, for even if we do not preach on this reading specifically, it ought to be read if only for the way it reflects the heart of the Law, which is justice and ethical consideration for others, especially the disadvantaged. As we shall see, this will be especially important if we are preaching from the text from Matthew.

1 Corinthians 3:10–11, 16–23

This passage is a continuation of the thought we have seen in the earlier readings from 1 Corinthians, and it is best understood in that context. It continues the discussion about divisions in the church, this time employing the image of the builder. It concludes by returning us again to a consideration of the "foolish" wisdom of God that Paul talked about earlier.

Once again we find that the lectionary has chosen to edit some verses from the middle of this reading. The reason for this omission is not as clear as the reason for the omission in Leviticus, but it lies in the history of the lectionary. Historically this reading did not even include verses 10 and 11. The lectionary compilers added them to give the reading an "ecclesiastical context."[3] They did not, however, add verses 12–15, no doubt because they are somewhat more difficult than other verses included in the passage. There is no compelling reason, though, to omit them from the reading, even if they are not exactly the best material for a sermon.

Matthew 5:38–48

This lesson continues and completes the "you have heard that it was said" series of teachings we began last week. In Matthew's eyes, these teachings form a unit, and even though the lectionary, of necessity, has had to break the unit in two, it should be treated as one. Unfortunately, this lesson is even more likely to fall victim to a short Epiphany than the reading

---

[3] *Common Lectionary*, p. 59-60.

last week. In such a year, preachers might want to consider reading the entire unit in one Sunday. While it is a bit longer than most lessons, it is not unreasonable, particularly if only one other reading is used with it.

A good choice for that other lesson would be the reading from Leviticus for today. In the Fifth Sunday After Epiphany we saw an example of where the reading from the Hebrew Scriptures helped shed light on the Gospel lesson for the day. This is another such example. The high-minded ethics of the Leviticus reading help us see that the Jewish Law is not (and was not) all letter and no spirit, a conclusion one might be tempted to reach if this lesson from Matthew were the only guide. Using the Leviticus passage to illuminate this Gospel lesson also helps us see the way Jesus' teaching echoed the best of his Jewish tradition.

Eighth Sunday After Epiphany (Proper 3)

Today's readings present us with some interesting shifts. We continue with virtually continuous readings in 1 Corinthians. We have skipped over several verses in Matthew from the end of the lesson last week, but the reading is still semi-continuous. And we are back once again in Second Isaiah for the reading from the Hebrew Scriptures.

Isaiah 49:8–16a

In this reading we have still another restoration prophecy from Isaiah. Interestingly enough, it follows immediately the prophecy we saw on the Second Sunday After Epiphany. In this case, however, there are few if any attempts to link this passage to either the Gospel lesson or the church year.

This passage contains some excellent feminine imagery for God (and God's Servant). That reason alone ought to commend it to our attention. Unfortunately, it is quite likely that Epiphany will not be long enough for this lesson to come up in the lectionary. Preachers who do not want to miss the opportunity to preach on it might try reading it on the Third Sunday After Epiphany. At the very least such a move would restore the biblical order of both this reading and the reading from Isaiah appointed for the Second Sunday After Epiphany.

1 Corinthians 4:1–5

As has been the case for several Sundays now, this reading picks up where the last reading in 1 Corinthians ended. It is in many respects a fitting ending to this series of readings, for in it Paul comes to his main point: no one, including the Corinthians, ought to boast except in Christ.

Preachers who use this passage will probably want to make some adjustments in the editing done by the lectionary. First, since this passage begins with the phrase, "So then," it seems to come out of nowhere. A short introduction connecting this passage to the one last week would help place it in the proper context.

Second, it also might be helpful to lengthen this reading to also include verses 6 and 7. These verses help bring out the point Paul has been trying to make all along.

Matthew 6:24–34

To get to this reading, the lectionary has again passed over several verses in Matthew from where we left off last Sunday. Those verses, which deal with giving alms, praying, fasting, and collecting treasure in heaven, have been taken out of this cycle of semi-continuous readings and are read instead on Ash Wednesday. Today's lesson picks up with Jesus teachings' on anxiety.

Once more, the variable length of Epiphany will affect the way we might choose to use this reading. If this reading is the last reading in Epiphany before either Transfiguration Sunday or Ash Wednesday, one need only acknowledge the parts of Matthew that have been skipped over here. A short introduction to the passage before it is read is one way to do this, particularly if we are not going to preach on this lesson specifically. If we do choose to preach on this passage, a brief introduction might still be sufficient if we have done our homework on the passage and let that homework be reflected in the sermon.

Should Epiphany be short, however, the lectionary will not include this passage at all. In that case, preachers again might choose to shift this passage to the period of Ordinary Time following Pentecost so that none of the Sermon on the Mount is missed, even if consideration of it is interrupted by the Lent and Easter cycle.

Verses 25–33 of this lesson are also read on Thanksgiving Day in Year B. If one is going to preach on this lesson, though, it is probably best to do it here in Epiphany or in Ordinary Time after Pentecost, when this lesson could join the renewed semi-continuous readings from Matthew. The proper context of this passage will be clearer now and after Pentecost when there are fewer church year distractions than will be the case on Thanksgiving.

Ninth Sunday After Epiphany
(Proper 4)

This final set of Epiphany lessons is very different from most of the Epiphany lessons we have seen so far. The Gospel lesson is still a semi-continuous reading from Matthew, but the epistle lesson is from Romans rather than 1 Corinthians. The reading from the Hebrew Bible is again from Deuteronomy, but this time it is clearly linked to the Gospel lesson.

The most important difference between these readings and those we have seen earlier is that these readings will be read no matter how short or how long Epiphany might be in a given year. In fact, these lessons have been included here in Epiphany only for those churches who do not celebrate Transfiguration during Epiphany. For those who do, these exact same readings are also listed for the Sunday between May 29 and June 4 this year. This is a pattern we will also find in Years B and C as well.

Deuteronomy 11:18–21, 26–28

The most important feature about this reading is that once again the lectionary has cut verses right out of the middle of it. Since these missing verses show God as blessing the forcible displacement of the Canaanites and seem to view conquest as a reward for faithfulness, they were probably left out in an effort to make this passage sound more "politically correct."

The trouble is, this passage is not politically correct according to today's standards. To try to make it appear otherwise may not be the best way to deal with it. In fact, removing these verses may actually contribute to the problem the lectionary compilers were attempting to address by denying us and the people in our congregations the opportunity to reflect on this less than seemly side of our history.

Romans 1:16–17; 3:22b–28 (29–31)

At first this lesson from Romans seems out of place among all the lessons from 1 Corinthians we have seen up to this point. This reading seems less out of place, though, when we consider that this set of lessons is more likely to appear in Ordinary Time after Pentecost than it is here in Epiphany. When read after Pentecost, this reading from Romans becomes the first in a series of semi-continuous readings. That is a more appropriate setting for this lesson and, even if it is possible to read it now, preachers might want to consider holding off preaching from it until a year when it falls after Pentecost.

Even more significant for the understanding of this text, however, is the remarkable number of verses missing from it in the lectionary. In going from Romans 1:17 to 3:22b, the lectionary has passed over nearly two chapters of text. It is not difficult to see why the lectionary has excluded these verses. The argument here is not easy to follow, many of the verses are obscure, and most of them center around the topic of God's wrath. All of these are common reasons for the lectionary to edit verses.

This is a major omission, however, that bypasses a large part of Paul's thought. Some of this omission is understandable. It avoids troubling verses about God's condemnation of various people's behavior, verses which could easily be misunderstood out of context. At first glance, these verses appear to single out certain people for special condemnation. When one reads past the condemnatory verses, however, Paul's real point becomes clearer — no one is in a position to condemn anyone because *all* have sinned. The reading then resumes with Paul expanding on his point.

In the alternate verses, verses 3:29–31, Paul connects this point specifically to his controversial ministry to the Gentiles. Everyone, he says, both Jew and Gentile, is saved by faith, not by the Law. These verses, no doubt, were made alternates because they were historically so specific. It is also easy to infer from these verses that Paul believed that Jews have to believe in Jesus to be saved. What Paul really thought about this matter is still hotly debated among scholars. Thus, unless one is willing to address both the history and the ambiguity inherent in these verses, they are probably best left as merely alternates.

All the excluded verses should be acknowledged in some way, whether or not we preach on this lesson. It would not be feasible, however, to simply add the verses back in. That would make the reading too long and not give us adequate time to address the complex process of thought these verses represent. Instead, preachers might choose to study these missing verses along with the others as part of their sermon preparation. When this passage is read, they might also explain to the congregation that verses have been edited and give a short, one-sentence synopsis of what is missing.

Probably the most productive use of this passage would be to let it dialogue with the reading from Deuteronomy. Christians are used to thinking about the Jewish law as strict and spiritless. They are also used to thinking of Christianity as superior to the Law. When we look at both these readings together, though, we see that the distinctions are not that clear. The writer of Deuteronomy and Paul are both after the same things, life and blessing.

Matthew 7:21–29

This reading concludes the semi-continuous readings from the Sermon on the Mount. It does not, however, conclude the semi-continuous readings in Matthew, which will resume again after Pentecost.

The structure of the lectionary itself is even more of a problem for this lesson that it was for either of the other two lessons for today. First, to get to this lesson at all, the lectionary has skipped the first 20 verses of chapter 7. This does not mean that these verses are completely lost, only Matthew's version of them. Luke's version of most of these verses will appear in the lectionary two years from now, in Epiphany Year C. Only verse 6, on throwing pearls before swine, and verses 13–14, on the narrow gate (the only teachings in these missing verses that are unique to Matthew), never appear at all.

Second, if these verses are read as part of Epiphany, they serve as a natural break in those semi-continuous readings, which will resume after Pentecost. This is probably the best situation for understanding this reading, particularly if it is also the conclusion of a sermon series.

If, however, Epiphany is short, or if Transfiguration is celebrated on the Last Sunday After Epiphany, this reading will probably not be read at all, or will be read on the First Sunday after Trinity. In either case, the continuity of these semi-continuous readings is compromised and should be addressed if we are going to do justice to Matthew and his Sermon.

What the preacher will do about this situation depends in large part on what decisions have been made earlier in Epiphany. If the preacher has been working on a sermon series from either 1 Corinthians or the Hebrew Bible, the loss of continuity here in Matthew is not so critical. This is also true if the preacher has been simply preaching from one Sunday to the next without regard for the semi-continuous nature of either the Gospel or epistle lesson. In either case, this lesson will probably appear after Pentecost and the preacher can give whatever brief introduction might be appropriate to help set the literary context then, before the passage is read.

If, on the other hand, the preacher has been working on a series of sermons from Matthew, it is probably best to assure that this passage is read and preached on here in Epiphany. Dispensing with the John reading on the Second Sunday After Epiphany or moving Transfiguration Sunday to Lent are two ways to do this that have already been mentioned. Both have advantages and disadvantages.

A more difficult but possibly more satisfying solution is to divide the verses of the Sermon on the Mount for oneself according to the number of Sundays available in Epiphany. In that case, even verses that the lectionary has left out might then be included. The most serious disadvantage to this plan is that whatever positive linkages there are between lessons as they stand now would be lost.

Last Sunday After Epiphany (Transfiguration Sunday)

This is the first of two sets of lessons provided by the lectionary for Transfiguration Sunday. The second appears on the Second Sunday in Lent. Of the two sets of lessons, this set is the most clearly influenced by the Transfiguration theme found in the Gospel. Not only has the reading from the Hebrew Bible been chosen for the way it relates to the Transfiguration Gospel, but so has the epistle lesson. This is not the case during Lent, when the Transfiguration Gospel appears as an alternate reading that is not linked specifically to either of the other two readings.

Preachers who wish to emphasize the Transfiguration theme would do better to choose this set of lessons here in Epiphany. It offers more possibilities for exploration of the theme from various viewpoints, more opportunity for reflection, and it does not involve juggling competing themes related to Lent.

Exodus 24:12–18

This lesson was obviously chosen because the experience of Moses in this passage seems to prefigure that of Jesus in the Gospel lesson today. This is a clear example of early Christian typology and should be understood as such. The temptation, naturally, is to understand this passage in light of the

Gospel. As we have seen, however, when understood correctly, typology actually works the other direction. This passage should be thought of as shedding light on today's Gospel lesson. In fact, this reading may have been one of the passages Matthew himself used to shape his account of the Transfiguration.

Those who use this passage for preaching, should use it with full awareness that it has been taken out of context here and isolated from its moorings in the book of Exodus. This is not so important if one is merely reading this passage, but if one is preaching from it, care should be taken to familiarize oneself with that context in preparation for the sermon.

As before, it might also help to read what Jewish scholars have said and are saying about this passage. That would help us keep this passage in proper perspective. It might also generate some sermon ideas that otherwise might be missed on such a heavily Christian day as Transfiguration Sunday.

2 Peter 1:16–21

This passage was obviously chosen for today because of its reference to the "holy mountain" and of being "eyewitnesses of his majesty." At first glance, it appears to be another example of appropriate linking when a passage from Christian Scripture is used to illuminate another passage of Christian Scripture. This is not the case here, however, because this passage is not actually about the Transfiguration at all. Rather, it is about the authenticity of the author's teaching as opposed to the teachings of others. The reference to the Transfiguration is more a means of establishing the author's credentials than it is a comment on the meaning of the event itself.

Preachers who try to preach a Transfiguration sermon from this passage will probably end up either frustrated or inappropriately stretching the meaning of the text. There is no reason not to read this lesson, but today is probably not the best day for preaching on it.

Matthew 17:1–9

The lectionary has made quite a leap from the Sermon on the Mount, where we have been now for several Sundays, to this account of the Transfiguration. Not only have we skipped over nearly half the Gospel of Matthew, we have also moved into a more narrative section of it. Preachers must be aware of this shift and consciously take it into account as they use this lesson.

Most scholars today agree that Matthew used Mark's account of the Transfiguration (Mark 9:2–8) to write his own. Matthew made some stylistic changes of his own, however, that not only differ from Mark but from Luke as well. These stylistic changes are important for understanding Matthew's particular view of this pivotal event in the life of Jesus. For this reason, a Gospel parallel and a commentary that discusses the literary composition of Matthew would be especially helpful if not indispensable tools for preparing a sermon on this passage.

L<u>EN</u>T

With Lent, we enter into one of the oldest seasons of the church year. Only the celebration of Easter is older. In fact, Lent originated out of a desire on the part of the church to help its members become better prepared for the Easter celebration. This was especially true for catechumens, who received instruction in the faith throughout the season of Lent in preparation for their baptism on Easter morning.

There are several important features about Lent as it appears in the *Revised Common Lectionary* that preachers will want to note as they prepare for these next six weeks. First, Lent is really two "seasons"—Lent itself and Monday through Saturday of Holy Week. Both seasons resemble each other but have their own unique flavor. This is important to remember, for Lent is commonly observed as an extended meditation on the events of Holy Week. That is certainly a time-honored way of observing Lent, but it is not the intent of the lectionary.

For the lectionary, the focus of Lent is on the believer's baptismal journey of faith. This is the historic emphasis of Lent and for this reason Lenten readings either emphasize great stories of faith, such as Abraham and Sarah's journey and the temptations of Jesus, or they offer reflections on baptism. It is really only Holy Week alone that focuses on the last days in the earthly life of Jesus.

Thus, preachers who wish to emphasize the Passion throughout the entire six weeks of Lent will need to improvise and substitute more Passion-oriented passages for the ones listed in the lectionary. Some preachers may also want to create their own Lenten "lectionary" that would more clearly reflect an emphasis on the Passion.

Second, there are several times during Lent when the lectionary, often with mixed results, attempts to combine very different liturgical traditions. The first of these occasions comes on the Second Sunday in Lent. On that Sunday, an account of the Transfiguration of Jesus always appears as an alternate Gospel lesson in order to accommodate those churches who have traditionally celebrated the Transfiguration in Lent. In doing this, however, the lectionary reveals a subtle bias toward an Epiphany Transfiguration. In Epiphany, the Transfiguration Gospel was the controlling Gospel and as such was supported by the other lessons for the day. Not so here in Lent. Not only is the Transfiguration Gospel not supported by the other lessons, it is itself treated as a mere alternate lesson.

Preachers who wish to emphasize the Transfiguration for Lent may want to consider using the set of lessons that were listed for Transfiguration during Epiphany. They are not particularly Lenten readings, but they are more appropriate for a celebration of the Transfiguration than are the readings here, which are intended primarily for the Second Sunday in Lent.

A second attempt to combine different liturgical traditions occurs on the Sixth Sunday in Lent, which the lectionary not only celebrates as the Sixth Sunday in Lent, but as Palm Sunday and Passion Sunday as well. This particular melding of traditions is a fairly new feature in the lectionary. It is also somewhat of a mixed blessing, as we shall see later on when we get to the readings for that day.

The third attempt to combine traditions can be found in the readings for Holy Thursday. Here the lectionary tries to combine both a supper and a footwashing tradition. This, too, is somewhat of a mixed blessing, but not nearly as difficult to sort out as the Palm/Passion traditions on the Sixth Sunday of Lent.

Readings from the Hebrew Bible

All readings from the Hebrew Bible for Lent are of long-standing liturgical tradition. They recount important narratives of faith that were expressly chosen for the way they illuminate their respective Gospel lessons. This year these narratives are drawn from Genesis, Exodus, 1 Samuel, Ezekiel, and in Holy Week, Isaiah. These narratives appear in historical order, but they are not meant to be connected to one another, nor do they follow a particular theological line of thinking the way the readings for the Easter Vigil will do.

The most important and most troublesome feature of these lessons, however, is the almost exclusive use of very old forms of typology and prophecy/fulfillment to link these lessons to the Gospel. This is particularly true in the readings for Palm/Passion Sunday and Holy Week, but ancient examples of typology and prophecy/fulfillment can also be seen in a couple of sets of readings during Lent itself.

As was noted in the Introduction, some Lenten readings from the Hebrew Bible have been linked to the death and resurrection of Jesus from as early as the second and third centuries. The connections between them came out of an attempt by the early church to defend itself and its messianic claims for Jesus in the face of a rapidly deteriorating relationship with the synagogue of the time. Today, that concern is still reflected in the manner these lessons are used, even though the present relationship between church and synagogue is now quite different.

The most effective way for us to deal with the influence of this ancient "baggage" is first to be aware of its presence. Second, as has been suggested before, find out what Jewish tradition has said about these passages. All the readings from the Hebrew Bible chosen for Lent have meaning on their own apart from their use by Christian tradition. This meaning should not be overlooked or dismissed, because it is often an excellent starting point for sermons.

A second and equally troubling feature of these lessons is the absence of women as examples of faith. Since these lessons are from long-standing tradition, such absence is not surprising, but it is also not very helpful to us today. We would do well here to purposefully supplement the lectionary's list of great believers with stories from the lives of exemplary biblical women. Esther would be an excellent choice for Lent, as would Hagar. Neither is given adequate attention anywhere else in the lectionary.

Epistle Lessons

The epistle lessons for Lent this year come from 2 Corinthians, Romans ((four readings), Ephesians, and Philippians. Traditionally, epistle lessons during Lent highlight baptismal texts, and for the most part this is true for Year A, but baptism is not as evident a theme this year as it will be in Years B and C. In fact, these readings for Year A are fairly independent readings, independent of each other and their respective Gospel lessons. Occasionally they will offer the theological rationale that connects the reading from the Hebrew Scriptures to the Gospel lesson for the day, but most often, the primary association these passages share is with the season of Lent itself.

Gospel lessons

It is in the Gospel lessons that we see the church year most at work. First, in order to accommodate the church year, these readings interrupt the semi-continuous readings in Matthew that were begun in Epiphany. Second, even though Matthew is the primary Gospel for this year, half or more of the Lenten Gospel lessons come from John. This is also an accommodation to the church year, for these texts from John are all traditional Lenten readings and all are associated with baptism. Third, there is a definite church-year-influenced pattern to these lessons. On Ash Wednesday the theme is always prayer and fasting. On the First Sunday of Lent the theme is always related to the Gospel account of the temptations of Jesus. There are readings from John that highlight baptism for a couple of Sundays. Then, on the Final Sunday of Lent readings begin with the story of the triumphal entry and close with a reading of the Passion Narrative. We will see this pattern again in both Years B and C when Mark and Luke are the principal Gospels.

Ash Wednesday
(Years A, B, and C)

There are four lessons appointed for today, Isaiah 58:1–12 being an alternate reading from the Hebrew Scriptures. As usual, the Gospel lesson is the controlling lesson and all the others are linked to it by sharing the same general theme of prayer and fasting. All are very old traditional readings for Ash Wednesday. All are highly emphasized readings that not only appear every year on Ash Wednesday but often appear on other Sundays during the lectionary's three-year cycle as well.

Joel 2:1–2, 12–17

The first thing we might notice about this passage is the way it has been edited by the lectionary. Verses 3–11, which clearly tie this reading to the Exile, have been omitted for several reasons: to downplay the political implications of the passage, to give the passage a more general application for Ash

Wednesday, and to make it short enough for public hearing.

This editing, while helpful for liturgical purposes, is not as helpful when it comes to an accurate proclamation of Joel's message. Contrary to the way it appears in the lectionary, this passage is not a general call to confession. It is historically very specific. The people of Israel are being called together in the midst of great political turmoil in hopes of averting a national calamity. They know the Exile is imminent and they are turning to God in a last-ditch effort to change the course of events. Such a historical context is full of sermon possibilities, even more than the general call to confession the lectionary would have us use. With verses 3–11 restored to the reading, we could reflect on the way people wait for a calamity before calling on God. We could reflect on whether God brings trouble upon people to make them repent. And we could reflect on what it says about a God who would bring calamity in the first place.

The decision to include or not include the omitted verses, then, depends on the way one intends to use this reading. If it is used as a call to worship, for example, or even as one reading among others, the omitted verses are not necessary and may even distract. If, on the other hand, one intends to preach on this passage, verses 3–11 should be restored, if only to give the congregation the proper historical context for the reading.

A second, less obvious feature of this passage is the way the lectionary has subtly linked the "day of God" with Lent and therefore, albeit indirectly, with the Passion of Jesus. This link is so ingrained in Christian tradition it would be virtually impossible to avoid it completely. If we allow ourselves to step back from this link, however, we might again find some unexpected homiletical treasures. Seen through this wider lens, the "Day of God" could become any day when people are confronted with a truth or reality they would prefer to ignore.

Isaiah 58:1–12

If Epiphany was long enough, this passage may have already been read this year, for it also appeared in part on the Fifth Sunday After Epiphany. This time, however, it appears with other, very different passages. Moreover, verses 9b–12 are now part of the reading, not alternates, and the fasting theme is no longer so unusual now that we are in Lent.

One of the most important differences from the way this reading was used in Epiphany is that the link with the Gospel lesson is even stronger here in Lent. This is a mixed blessing. The stronger link highlights the fasting theme, but it also invites us to look unfavorably upon Jewish piety as more shallow than its Christian counterpart. The truth is that Isaiah and the Jesus of our Gospel lesson today are *both* looking for a piety based on justice and right relations with others, especially the poor. If we keep that in mind, this passage could be the basis of a very fruitful sermon.

(See also the notes on this passage under the Fifth Sunday After Epiphany, Year A.)

2 Corinthians 5:20—6:10

Unlike other passages from 2 Corinthians chosen by the lectionary, this particular passage receives a surprising amount of emphasis. Besides appearing on Ash Wednesday every three years, verses 5:20–21 also appear as part of a longer reading in Lent Year C and verses 6:1–10 appear on Proper 7 Year B. In each case, the intended emphasis is slightly different. Here the stress is on Paul's ministry of reconciliation, a theme that will again be echoed in slightly different form in Year C when verses 5:20–21 are again read during Lent.

The reading for today is another example of how the lectionary subtly influences the way we look at a particular passage of scripture. Judging from the editing done on this reading and its position here in Lent, we see the lectionary clearly intends for us to identify with the apostle Paul. This is not entirely inappropriate, for Paul himself was hoping that his readers might follow his example. However, it might be even more profitable if instead we were to identify with our real counterparts, the Corinthians. Here were people who felt pretty confident about their faith. Some even considered themselves blessed as a result of their faith, not only spiritually but also economically. Seen in that light, Paul's words here become even more challenging and thought-provoking than they are when Paul himself is the primary focus.

Matthew 6:1–6, 16–21

This reading is the controlling lesson for today, and as we saw earlier, the Isaiah lesson has been linked to it. The comment about today's Isaiah reading also applies here. We should resist the temptation to infer from the connection the lectionary has made between these two lessons that Christian piety is inherently superior to Jewish piety.

With this lesson we find another example of a controlling lesson itself controlled by the church year. First, these verses should have appeared in the semi-continuous readings from

Matthew's Sermon on the Mount listed for Epiphany. Instead, they fit so well into Lent that they were saved until now. In fact, they were the only verses omitted from that section of Matthew.

Second, the Lord's Prayer has been edited from this passage to strengthen even more the ties it has with Lent. Normally, the Lord's Prayer is the centerpiece of these verses and the comments on almsgiving, prayer, and fasting all revolve around it. By removing the Lord's Prayer, however, the lectionary was able to enhance those more Lenten themes and make the passage itself more "appropriate" for Ash Wednesday.

First Sunday in Lent

All three readings for this day are connected by the general theme, "temptation." This is the traditional theme for the First Sunday in Lent and it comes from the long association Lent has had with the account of Jesus being tempted in the wilderness. The temptation account for this year comes from the principal Gospel for Year A, Matthew. That lesson is also today's controlling lesson and both the reading from the Hebrew Scriptures and the epistle lesson have been linked with it.

The way these lessons have been linked is somewhat different from the kinds of linking we have seen so far. In this case it is not the tradition or the church year but the epistle lesson that provides the glue to hold these lessons together. Indeed, if it were not for Paul's words here in Romans, today's reading from the Hebrew Scripture (the temptation of Adam and Eve) may never have been associated with the temptation of Jesus.

Genesis 2:15–17; 3:1–7

This is the first of a long string of traditional Lenten faith stories from the Hebrew Scriptures. It has been connected to Lent and to this particular Sunday in Lent for centuries, primarily on the basis of Paul's exegesis in Romans. In fact, the influence of Paul is so important to our understanding of this passage that one could even argue theologically that Romans 5:12–19, and not the Gospel lesson, is the true controlling lesson for today.

This heavy Pauline influence affects our understanding of this passage in at least two important ways. First, it predisposes us to interpret the story here primarily in terms of concepts such as fall and redemption. This not only narrows our perspective unnecessarily, it also restricts us to almost exclusively Christian concepts that are not original to the text.

Second, because Paul's interpretation of this passage focuses on Adam, the lectionary's Pauline bias here can also predispose us to ignore a primary figure in this passage, Eve. This puts preachers sensitive to women's issues in a double bind. On the one hand, since Eve has gotten such bad press it might be refreshing to takes Paul's lead and focus on Adam for once. On the other hand, if we take our lead from the writer of Genesis and shine the focus on Eve, we might find ourselves unwittingly perpetrating the already well-entrenched sexist interpretations of this text.

In such a case, it is probably best to acknowledge the powerful influence Pauline thought has had on our understanding of this passage and address that influence directly. The best forum for this, of course, would be in a sermon based on this passage from Genesis. That would give the preacher ample time to look at this passage from various points of view.

Romans 5:12–19

Even though it appears in the lectionary only once, this passage is one of the best known passages from Romans. It has long been associated with Lent, not only through its use in the lectionary but also through its use in sacred music, most notably in *Messiah* by G. F. Handel.

As we have seen, this reading can influence our understanding and interpretation of the other passages for today. However, this reading itself does not escape completely unscathed. Verses 20–21, which form a natural break for this passage, have been edited. This significant omission alters the meaning of the text. Without these verses, the focus appears to be on fall and redemption. With these verses, however, the full context of these words emerges—Paul is talking not just about fall and redemption, but about fall and redemption in the context of the Law and its role in God's plan of salvation. Verses 20–21 complete Paul's thought and should be included in any reading of this lesson, whether we are preaching on it or not.

Matthew 4:1–11

Although this reading is meant by the lectionary to be the controlling lesson for today, several factors are likely to interfere with our hearing it the way Matthew intended. The first of these factors is the heavy influence from the epistle lesson discussed above. To counter this influence, preachers may want to pay special attention to Matthew's own unique theology and literary style.

A second factor likely to interfere with our understanding of this passage is the way it has been divorced from its proper context within the Gospel of Matthew. According to Matthew, this account of the Temptations immediately follows Jesus' baptism. In fact, for Matthew and the other synoptic Gospels, the Spirit that came to Jesus at his baptism sent him into the wilderness in the first place. However, because the baptism of Jesus has already been celebrated earlier in the church year, no mention of it is made in the reading today. We would do well to acknowledge the baptismal connections in this reading, either in the sermon or in a brief introductory remark before the reading, particularly since baptism is such important imagery for Lent.

Second Sunday in Lent

The lectionary lists four lessons for today, a set of three Lenten readings and an alternate Gospel lesson. The alternate Gospel is Matthew's account of the Transfiguration and was included for those churches wishing to celebrate the Transfiguration on this Second Sunday in Lent. The reading is completely independent and has not been linked to any of the other readings.

The three primary readings, however, have been linked together in a pattern very similar to that evident last week. The reading from the Hebrew Bible is a traditional great story of faith (Abraham's call). The Gospel lesson has deliberate baptismal overtones (the visit by Nicodemus). Both are linked by a theme provided by the epistle lesson, justification by faith. The exception to the pattern is the principal Gospel lesson, which now comes from John rather than Matthew.

All three lessons appear more than once in the lectionary. The reading from Genesis and part of the reading from Romans appear together again shortly after Pentecost this year, on Proper 5A when they are both semi-continuous readings. Verses 14–17 of the Gospel lesson appear again on this very same Sunday next year and verses 1–13 will also appear next year on Trinity Sunday.

Genesis 12:1–4a

The lectionary's treatment of this passage raises at least two issues preachers will want to note, particularly if they choose to preach on this passage. The first concerns placement, for the lectionary seems to pull us in two directions at once. On the one hand, by always placing these words from Genesis next to the lesson from Romans, the lectionary obviously intends us to understand them from a Pauline perspective. Such a perspective would have us focus primarily on Abraham's obedience. On the other hand, by placing these words in Lent, the lectionary also focuses our attention on Abraham's journey to the "land that I will show you." Neither Abraham's obedience nor his journey is the primary concern of these verses as they appear in the lectionary. The true focus of this particular reading is God's promise. Preachers who wish to emphasize the obedience theme might do better to preach on the reading from Romans. Those who wish to concentrate on the journey theme would do well to lengthen the reading a bit to include more of the journey itself in the reading.

The other issue facing us here is editing. The lectionary has edited this passage in such a way that there is no hint that the land God is promising to Abraham is already occupied by the Canaanites. This is a major piece of information that should not be so easily ignored or glossed over. Otherwise we might miss the political overtones in the promise recorded in these verses, overtones that reverberate in the Middle East even today.

In the same way, the lectionary's editing of this passage gives no hint that Sarah and other members of Abraham's household were also included in the promise. This piece of information should not be ignored or glossed over, either.

The answer in both cases is to lengthen the reading through verse 9, as will be done later on for Proper 5A. This longer reading not only gives Sarah and the Canaanites their rightful place in the story, it also takes us to a more natural literary break in the narrative.

Since this same passage will appear again in a few months, one might want to consider reserving it until then. The lesson from Romans will still exert its powerful influence on this passage, but there will be fewer issues of placement or editing to concern us.

Romans 4:1–5, 13–17

The most obvious feature about this lesson is the omission of seven verses from the middle of it. Often such omissions mean that the lectionary has edited historical references or troublesome verses in order to make the passage easier to use in public worship. The missing verses in the particular reading are a perfect example. They were clearly edited to make the passage easier for modern North American Christians to understand. The edited verses should be restored, particularly since they form the heart of Paul's argument here.

A second obvious feature of this reading is the way it breaks with canonical order and takes us to an earlier section of Romans than was the case last week. Such skipping around is common among readings from the Hebrew Scriptures and even Gospel lessons when the church year seems to demand it. This skipping is often more annoying than it is crucial to the understanding of a particular passage. In the case of epistle lessons, however, skipping back and forth between chapters can seriously interfere with our understanding of the author's line of thought. Those who wish to preach on this passage should take special effort to keep the order of Paul's thought in mind, even if the lectionary does not. They might also consider preaching on this reading when it appears again this year for Proper 6A. Then it is a part of a series of semi-continuous readings.

In a similar way, we should also remain aware of the way this passage fits into Paul's long and very complex thinking about the place of the Jewish law and its tradition within the Christian faith. These verses represent only a small part of that line of thought and for that reason might be easily misunderstood. Care should be taken that we not fall into simplistic views of Paul or the Law based only on what we find here in these few verses.

A less obvious feature of this passage is the absence of references to Sarah and the rest of Abraham's household. They have again been omitted by the lectionary. Since Sarah is briefly mentioned in verse 19, preachers might want to consider lengthening this reading, especially if verses 13–25 are not read for Proper 5A later this year. One possibility is to read the entire literary unit, verses 1–25. Those who do not wish to handle such a lengthy reading might consider simply adding verses 18–25 to the present reading.

John 3:1–17

This is the first of the two Gospel lessons listed for today. Except in those churches that are observing this Second Sunday in Lent as Transfiguration, this reading rather than the Matthew reading is the intended Gospel lesson. It is also the controlling lesson for both the reading from Genesis and the reading from Romans.

With this lesson, the lectionary has once again pushed the Gospel of Matthew aside in order to highlight festival readings from John. Since nearly all subsequent Gospel readings during Lent will be from John, it might be wise at this point to refresh our memories concerning this fourth Gospel. This will be particularly important during Lent, when passages from John are more often chosen for their relationship to the church year than for their overall reflection of the thinking in the Gospel itself.

The reading for today is a perfect example. It was chosen by the lectionary primarily for the baptismal images contained in it. The baptismal theme is further highlighted by both the lesson from Romans (which is about justification by faith) and the lesson from Genesis (which is about divine election). Even the way the lectionary has edited this passage shifts the emphasis in this particular reading to those verses most commonly associated with conversion and baptism.

John's primary concern in these verses, however, is not baptism but eternal life, particularly the work of the Spirit in bringing eternal life to believers. To be true to this text, we need to keep this in mind, even though the lectionary tempts us to do otherwise.

Matthew 17:1–19

Because this lesson has been included here principally as an option for those churches observing Transfiguration this Sunday, it is completely independent of the other readings listed for today. Often such independence is a blessing. In this case, however, the blessing is mixed. We do not have the heavy-handed linking characteristic of the Epiphany Transfiguration readings, but now the Transfiguration theme is competing with the more Lenten themes characteristic of the other readings for today. With both themes coming at once, neither is likely to receive the attention deserved. Preachers who wish to celebrate the Transfiguration now might consider dispensing with all the readings for today except this one and choosing lessons of their own to accompany it, perhaps Ezekiel 1:25–28 or Hebrews 3:1–6.

Third Sunday in Lent

Today the lectionary continues its typical pattern for lessons in Lent, except that the epistle reading no longer exerts such a powerful influence over the other two lessons. Once again we have a great story of faith (this time from the life of Moses). Once again the story is linked to a traditional Lenten Gospel lesson from John. And once again the epistle lesson is from an early chapter in the book of Romans. All three lessons have long associations with Lent and clear associations with baptism.

Exodus 17:1–7

This reading is another example of the lectionary's making good use of typology. In this case the story of Moses getting water out of a rock serves as a type for at least two Christian counterparts, baptism and the living water Jesus gives the woman at the well. Neither association is so strong or so direct as to detract from the original meaning of the Exodus text. On the contrary, the typology here appropriately invites us to explore many levels of meaning, not only in this text, but in the text from John as well.

Before deciding to preach on this passage, though, preachers might want to note that it will also appear again this year during Ordinary Time (Proper 21A). It is then a part of a series of semi-continuous readings from the life of Moses. Those who wish to emphasize the baptismal associations in this reading will do better to preach on it now, when those associations are specifically highlighted. Those who prefer to treat this passage in its proper historical and literary context would do well to wait and preach on it this summer.

Romans 5:1–11

Unlike its counterparts from the last two weeks, this epistle lesson does not exert any theological influence over the other two lessons chosen for today. In fact, this reading is more related to church year than it is to either the Gospel lesson or the reading from the Hebrew Scriptures for this week.

The epistle lesson today shares several other characteristics with its predecessors. Like them, this lesson has also been chosen without regard to its original canonical order. So, even though this lesson appropriately follows last week's reading in both the lectionary and the book of Romans, last week's reading and the reading for today come from earlier parts of the book of Romans than the reading for the First Sunday in Lent. Again, preachers should keep the proper order of Paul's thought in mind here, even if the lectionary does not.

Also like its previous counterpart, this lesson appears in the lectionary several times. For instance, verses 1–5 of this reading appear again on Trinity Sunday Year C. Most importantly, this entire reading appears again shortly after Pentecost (Proper 6A) as part of a series of semi-continuous readings from Romans. Those who wish to emphasize this passage's reconciliation theme from a baptismal perspective might want to preach on it now when the season of Lent lends a baptismal cast to the verses here. Those who wish to treat this passage in its more native context might wait until the semi-continuous readings from Romans begin later this year.

John 4:5–42

This lesson is an especially long one, but well worth the time it takes to read it. For one thing, it is one of the few traditional Lenten readings that has not been heavily influenced by the church year. It is also the only Lenten reading this year to feature a woman in an unequivocably starring role. These two facts alone make this lesson an excellent choice for the sermon today. The baptismal imagery in it makes it even more attractive.

Even though the lectionary has linked this passage with the passage from Exodus, preachers should be careful about bringing the Exodus passage into a sermon from John. It is not necessary to link these two readings, particularly since doing so may even invite negative comparisons between the miraculous water of Moses and the "living water" of Jesus. For this reason, it might be better to let both readings stand on their own as independent examples of God providing the faithful with life-giving water.

Fourth Sunday in Lent

In today's readings, the lectionary continues to give us a great story of faith from the Hebrew Scriptures (the anointing of David) and a reading with baptismal overtones from the Gospel of John (the healing of the man born blind). The epistle lesson, however, is now from Ephesians, a book with even stronger baptismal imagery than that found in Romans. As usual, the Gospel continues to be the controlling lesson, but in this case it exercises little control. All three readings can easily stand independently of one another, and probably should.

1 Samuel 16:1–13

Unlike most of the other lessons in this season, this reading has not had a long association with Lent. In fact, it still does not appear during Lent in the Roman *Lectionary for Mass*. This relative independence from the church year makes this lesson one of the best readings from the Hebrew Scriptures available this Lent for preaching.

Even so, the church year still exerts its influence on this passage in at least one way. Reading it during Lent makes it easier for us to miss the political intrigue beneath the story here. One could even argue that the way the lectionary has used this passage actually encourages us to see it as a timeless example of a humble person of faith being called by God. However, even more promising possibilities for Lenten sermons can emerge if we resist that temptation and remember the rest of the story, especially those long hard years a very human David spent realizing the promise in Samuel's act.

Preachers particularly interested in the life of David should note that this is not the only opportunity they will have to consider this passage. It also appears next year as part of a longer reading for Ordinary Time. There it serves as the first in a long series of semi-continuous readings from the life of David.

Ephesians 5:8–14

This reading is part of what many scholars believe is an early baptismal exhortation. Indeed, its association with baptism is the primary reason for the inclusion of this reading in the lectionary and for its inclusion during Lent. Preachers who use this passage, however, need to find specific ways to acknowledge this association because the reading itself does not directly mention baptism at all.

The most striking feature about this lesson is the way it has been edited by the lectionary. If we look at only the verses included in the lectionary, this reading appears incomplete, and it is. It not only begins with a conjunction, "For...," it also ends with a quote that begs for elaboration. This situation no doubt arose because verses 15–20, which would help clarify the reading, appear in the lectionary as a separate reading on Proper 15B. Even so, there is no reason they cannot also appear here. In fact, they should probably be added whether we preach on this text or simply read it in worship.

This is also another reading in which we find the images of light and dark being used as symbols for good and evil. Again, preachers should watch how they use this imagery. The reading should be used carefully and with sensitivity to the way it sounds to people of color.

John 9:1–41

Like the lesson from John last week, this lesson is also long but well worth the time it takes to read it. There are two issues, however, that preachers will want to note as they use this lesson. Both issues we have encountered before. The first is John's use of polemic against those who oppose the ministry of Jesus. Here John not only uses the misnomer "the Jews"; he also paints a historically inaccurate picture of the Pharisees. As far as we know, the Pharisees never had the kind of council described in these verses and, until at least a generation after his death and resurrection (probably when John himself was writing), no one was ever threatened with expulsion from the synagogue for believing in Jesus.

Second is John's use of blindness as an image for spiritual obtuseness. This, too, is polemic, and must be treated carefully and sensitively, even if no one in the particular congregation is blind.

Fifth Sunday in Lent

In today's readings we find some of the most traditional, most highly emphasized, and most powerfully linked readings that we have seen so far this Lent. Not only that, all three readings are strong readings and full of preaching potential. To do them justice, we will need to spend plenty of time studying both the passages themselves and the intricate relationships they have with each other and the church year.

Another very striking feature about these passages is the way they each foreshadow the approaching Easter celebration. The reading from the Hebrew Bible speaks of dry bones being resurrected. The epistle lesson from Romans speaks of the "Spirit...who raised Jesus from the dead." The Gospel lesson recounts the raising of Lazarus. Such Easter imagery in the midst of Lent also calls for careful attention and thoughtful reflection as to the best way to use it.

Ezekiel 37:1–14

This famous passage about the valley of dry bones is very important to the lectionary's Lent/Easter cycle. It not only appears today, it also appears every year in the readings for the

Easter Vigil and on Pentecost Day in Year B. Except for a few passages from Isaiah, few other passages from the Hebrew Bible have received such emphasis.

This passage is popular with the lectionary largely because it fits so well into a typological link with the death and resurrection of Jesus (and here the death and resurrection of Lazarus as well). Such powerful associations should not be treated lightly. They should also not be used until one is thoroughly familiar with the message of Ezekiel first.

Of the two opportunities given to us this year for preaching on this lesson, today is clearly the best. In fact, the only drawback to preaching on this passage today is its appearance again at the Easter Vigil, only a few shorts weeks away. If we wait for the Easter Vigil, however, this reading will not only have to compete with the Easter proclamation, it will also have to compete with several other readings from the Hebrew Bible.

Romans 8:6–11

With this reading, the lectionary briefly returns to the book of Romans. This particular reading appears today primarily because of its several references to resurrection. Those references not only provide the means by which this passage is linked to the Gospel lesson for today; they also help link this passage to the reading from Ezekiel.

Resurrection themes, however, are only part of this reading and only part of Paul's thought here in chapter 8. In fact, although the lectionary may imply otherwise, resurrection is really only a tangential concern for Paul at this point. His primary concern is the work of the relationship between Law and Spirit.

For this reason alone, it is probably best to save preaching on this text until later this year when it appears again in a longer form on Proper 10A. This is not to say this lesson should never be preached in Lent. It can be, although to do so will require more of the preacher. If we wait, however, this lesson will then be free of possibly misleading links to the Gospel lesson. It will be read in context with other semi-continuous readings from Romans. And, with the addition of verses 1–5, it will also be a more complete reading.

John 11:1–45

Like the reading from Ezekiel for today, this lesson has long been traditional for Lent, though at first glance it sounds more appropriate for Easter. It is also the controlling lesson for today, and as such passes its Easter-like tone on to the other two readings.

To its credit, the lectionary has included this entire passage despite its length. This is especially noteworthy when one considers how easy it could have been to omit several of the verses here, particularly those recording Jesus' conversation with the sisters of Lazarus. In fact, the lectionary has not only retained the verses about Mary and Martha in this lesson, it also highlights them again next year for All Saints' Day. In Martha's case this is particularly helpful, for it provides a balance to the usual picture we have of Martha as a workaholic homemaker envious of her more studious sister. Here she is shown giving the very same confession of faith Peter is said to have given in the other three Gospels.

What the lectionary has excluded from this lesson is the rest of the story. John's account of the raising of Lazarus did not end with verse 45. He goes on to say that not everyone there believed. Some even went to the Pharisees and on the basis of their report the plot to kill Jesus was begun. In fact, the events recorded in this passage set John's Passion story into motion. This is important information, which not only helps us balance the "Easter" tone of this reading, but also provides us an appropriate connection to Lent.

Sixth Sunday in Lent
(Passion *or* Palm Sunday)

As we noted in the introduction to Lent this year, the readings for today reflect an effort to combine two very distinct liturgical traditions—a Palm tradition and a Passion tradition. In fact, in the edition of the lectionary published by the compilers of the lectionary themselves, there are even two sets of readings listed, one for a liturgy of the Palms and one for a liturgy of the Passion. The first consists of the traditional Palm Sunday story from Matthew plus a reading from Psalm 118. The second not only includes the expected reading from the Hebrew Bible and epistle lesson, it also includes both a long and short version of Matthew's Passion narrative.

These readings can be combined in several ways. The expectation of the lectionary is that the readings for the Palms will be used at the beginning of the service and the readings for the Passion will be used later on in the positions usually reserved for the respective readings for the day. Churches wishing to observe the Passion alone, however, might choose to ignore the Palm Sunday readings. Churches wishing to observe a Palm tradition, on the other hand, might choose to substitute the Gospel and psalm from the liturgy of the Palms for those listed in the liturgy of the Passion and read them in the main portion of the service. Such churches might also choose to use an entirely new reading from the Hebrew Scriptures and an entirely new epistle lesson to accompany the Palm Sunday psalm and Gospel lesson.

Which option we choose will probably depend in large part on the kinds of services planned for Holy Week. If the congregation has both a Holy (or Maundy) Thursday and Good Friday service, particularly if it has a well-attended Good Friday service, an emphasis on the liturgy of the Palms could be sufficient in most cases. If, on the other hand, the congregation does not have midweek services for Holy Week, or those services are sparsely attended, an emphasis on the Passion might be more appropriate here.

Another feature of the readings for today is the unique pattern of emphasis these readings receive in the lectionary. Every one of these readings is read at least once a year, except for each of the readings from Matthew.

Matthew 21:1–11

Technically, this well-known story of the entry into Jerusalem is not really a part of the Passion narrative at all. Matthew did not connect this story to the Passion, and neither did Matthew's source for this story, the Gospel of Mark. The entry into Jerusalem has been linked to the Passion, however, by a long-standing theological and liturgical tradition. To this very day, the lectionary continues to pass down that tradition to us and its influence, for good and for ill, should be dealt with whenever we use this passage.

One clear example of that influence is evident in the way this passage is treated by the lectionary. Even though the passage is a Lenten Gospel lesson, it is not intended by the lectionary to be a controlling lesson. In fact, judging from the way this passage is used, the lectionary does not even intend for us to preach on it at all. This does not mean, however, that we should never preach on this lesson. Occasionally we should. But when we do, we should do so fully aware that the lectionary has stacked the liturgical deck in favor the Passion.

Thus, whether or not we preach on this lesson, care should be taken that it not be swallowed up by either the lectionary's controlling Passion theme, or by the sheer length and power of Matthew's Passion narrative. This lesson has its own integrity apart from the Passion and taking the time to let it speak for itself could yield some powerful results.

Isaiah 50:4–9a

This famous reading has been associated with the Passion of Jesus since the second and third centuries. This association is very apparent in the *Revised Common Lectionary*. Isaiah 50:4–9a appears four times in the lectionary's three-year cycle— three times on Passion Sunday alone. Only once does it appear outside a Passion context (Proper 19B).

The lectionary's use of this reading is another example of the way associations made by the early church continue to appear in the lectionary even today. In this case, the early church associated this picture of the Suffering Servant with Jesus in order to counter the Jewish argument that God would never let the Messiah die the way Jesus did.

In the same way, this passage is also another example of legitimate typology that almost becomes a questionable prophecy/fulfillment model of interpretation. This, too, reflects concerns from members of the early church, who used such a model of interpretation in an effort to "prove" to their Jewish contemporaries that the Passion of Jesus had been foretold by the prophets.

Once again, neither of these ancient ways of looking at this reading is particularly helpful to us today. At best, they distract us from seeing what this passage has to say on its own. At worst, they contribute to a continued anti-Semitism in the Christian interpretation of the Hebrew Scriptures.

Several options are available to us for countering the way this passage has been used by the lectionary. The most important is to be aware that the lectionary is predisposing us to a particular interpretation. Using that awareness we can deliberately search for other possible interpretations, particularly among Jewish scholars. What if we were to view the Suffering Servant as the whole people of Israel, for instance? Or what if we took the Servant to represent the faithful person in general?

The second, probably more challenging option is to postpone preaching on this passage until it appears next year in Ordinary Time. The reading will then be unencumbered by the strong Passion associations we find today. The challenge, however, will be in not adding those associations unconsciously.

Philippians 2:5–11

This early Christian hymn has also been long associated with the Passion. Like the reading from Isaiah, it also appears every year on this Sunday and then once more on a Sunday in Ordinary Time, in this case, Proper 21A.

The lectionary selectively edited this passage in a clear effort to emphasize the Passion theme. In doing so, the lectionary has downplayed the literary context in which this hymn was quoted. In fact, if we were to look only at the verses included in the reading for today, we might not even notice that this is really a quotation.

For a better picture of the literary context, preachers should seriously consider adding verses 1–4 to this reading. Those verses not only make it clearer that we are dealing with a quotation, they also help us see that this is not a simple reflection on the Passion. Rather, it is an exhortation to the faithful to have the same kind of faithful attitude Jesus showed in his Passion. The difference is subtle, but important.

The most difficult issue raised by this lesson is deciding how to handle one of its main themes—humility. For years, the Christian tradition has considered the self-effacing kind of humility pictured here to be a virtue. Certainly that is the way the people who composed this hymn and the author who quoted it saw it. For many women today, however, that is not the case. For these women, self-effacing humility is not a virtue at all but rather a means by which women have been kept in their place. Those who preach on this passage will need to be particularly sensitive to the way it will be heard, especially by the women in their congregation.

Matthew 26:14—27:66 (or 27:11–54)

This reading is the Passion Gospel from Matthew. It is not only the controlling lesson for today, it is intended by the lectionary to be the centerpiece of today's liturgy. Two versions are provided for us, a long and a short version. The longer version begins with Judas going to the chief priests and ends with Pilate sealing the tomb. The shorter version begins with the trial before Pilate and concludes with the declaration made by a centurion that Jesus was "God's Son."

Several factors should be taken into account when choosing which version to use. First, if our congregation has well-attended Holy Thursday and Good Friday services, we might be tempted to choose the shorter version that does not include many verses associated with those days. If we want to emphasize the Palm tradition today, we might also be tempted to choose the shorter version of the Passion Gospel. We might also choose the shorter version if we believe our congregation would not tolerate a longer reading.

Choosing the shorter Passion Gospel, however, has some drawbacks that might not be noticed immediately. First, the longer Passion Gospel is the only place where Matthew's version of the Holy Thursday and Good Friday stories appear in the lectionary. If we read only the shorter version these stories will not be heard at all. One option is to read the shorter Passion Gospel now, and on both Holy Thursday and Good Friday use Matthew's versions instead of the assigned readings from John. (Churches who wish to emphasize the footwashing tradition, of course, would want to stay with John.)

Second, the shorter Passion Gospel leaves out some other significant verses as well. These include the prediction of Peter's denial, the scene in Gethsemane, the trial before the Sanhedrin, Peter's denial, the burial of Jesus, and the guard placed at the tomb. None of these appears in the Passion Gospel from John, either. Again, using readings from Matthew on Holy Thursday and Good Friday instead of the readings listed from John would provide opportunity to include most of these verses.

Most importantly, though, the shorter Passion Gospel does not include the women at the cross. Why the lectionary did not go two verses further and include them is not clear, but verses 55 and 56 should be added whenever the shorter version of this reading is used, regardless of whether we are preaching from it.

If, on the other hand, our congregation has no special services for Holy Week, or has only a Holy Thursday service, we might choose instead to use the longer Passion reading. This, too, has its advantages and disadvantages. The major advantage is that Matthew's Passion narrative would receive the attention it deserves. The major disadvantage is the length of the reading. Length can be fairly easily addressed, however. One possibility is to forego preaching and let a dramatic reading of this narrative speak for itself. Another possibility is to shorten the reading by either omitting the verses associated with Holy Thursday (particularly if the congregation will have a Holy Thursday service) or omitting the burial scene in verses 57–66. Both possibilities will still give a more complete rendering of the Passion than the lectionary's shorter version.

Holy Thursday
(Years A, B, and C)

In this set of readings, the lectionary again tries to combine two very different traditions—a Supper tradition and a footwashing tradition. But how the lectionary has chosen to do this may come as a surprise. As one might expect, the lectionary has chosen to feature the Passover in the reading from the Hebrew Bible and Paul's instructions concerning the Supper in 1 Corinthians. But rather than the expected reading from Matthew describing the Last Supper, the lectionary has chosen instead to feature the story of the footwashing from John as the Gospel lesson for today.

This set of readings is also read every year. This not only serves to emphasize these lessons above other lessons, it also means that other biblical reflections on the Supper will not be heard on this special day when the Supper is liturgically highlighted. In order to increase the number of biblical voices heard on Holy Thursday, preachers might consider occasionally using other appropriate readings instead, perhaps Exodus 12:17–20; Deuteronomy 16:1–4; or 1 Corinthians 10:15–17. One might also consider occasionally reading the Supper narrative from the principal Gospel for the year (in this case, Matthew) instead of or along with the reading from John.

Exodus 12:1–4 (5–10), 11–14

Several features are noteworthy about this reading. First, it was chosen for today primarily for the way it relates to the Supper tradition of Matthew, Mark, and Luke, all of whom depict the Last Supper as a Passover meal. This juxtaposition of the institution of Passover and the institution of the Eucharist is very traditional. It can also mislead us, tempting us to see the Eucharist as a "new and improved" Passover. Passover, however, is more than an ancient ritual that has been superseded by the Eucharist, for it is the living context out of which Jesus interpreted his own death and resurrection.

Seen in that light, this reading from Exodus provides some of the historical and theological background we need to understand the events we commemorate on Holy Thursday. This reading explains some of the imagery and symbolism Jesus and his guests would have taken for granted that night. It also reminds us that Jesus remained true to his Jewish heritage even to the very end.

A second feature of this passage is the alternate verses, verses 5–10. These verses contain kosher instructions for the Passover and as such are not essential for Christian congregations. They do provide some of the ancient flavor of Passover and they include the most important Passover symbol, the blood of the lamb on the doorposts. For this reason alone, these alternate verses should be read, particularly if we choose to preach on this reading.

Third, while this lesson is read every year on this day, it is also read again this year for Proper 18A as part of a long series of semi-continuous readings from the life of Moses. Preachers wanting to give this lesson their full attention would do well to preach on it then, when it is not as heavily connected to the Eucharist as it is today.

1 Corinthians 11:23–26

Like the reading from Exodus, this reading was also chosen for its relationship to the tradition of the Supper. In some traditions the words of this reading are even used in the liturgy as a "warrant" for celebrating the Eucharist. In the reading itself, however, Paul is simply relating his understanding of what happened at that last meal Jesus shared with his disciples.

What the lectionary's version of this passage does not tell us is why Paul bothers to explain this in the first place. After all, the Eucharist and the tradition behind it were surely familiar to the congregation at Corinth. We find the reasons for Paul's thoroughness in verses 17–20. There Paul describes his distress at the way the Eucharist was being celebrated in Corinth. Apparently some believers were getting drunk, others were overeating, and the rich were celebrating at the expense of the poor.

Since Paul's distress was his reason for writing this passage, the verses describing that distress (verses 17–22) should be included whenever this lesson is read. This not only gives the congregation important background information, it also helps mitigate some "generic" ways this passage is often used in the liturgy.

If we want to give this passage our full attention, however, we would do better to preach on it at a time other than Holy Thursday. The lectionary does not list such a time, but that does not mean we cannot choose to take it. In fact, to be fair to this well-known passage, we probably should, preach on it at least once in the three-year cycle of the lectionary.

John 13:1–17, 31b–35

With this reading, the lectionary balances the "Supper" emphasis of the first two lessons with the "footwashing" emphasis here in John. Such a balancing act has both advantages and disadvantages. On the one hand, it gives a hearing to both Holy Thursday traditions. On the other hand, it also puts us in the unusual position of never hearing the biblical passages that gave rise to this special day on the day itself.

The most obvious feature about the lectionary's treatment of this passage is the way it has been edited. Verses 18–31a, which recount both Jesus' prediction that a disciple would betray him and Judas' subsequent departure from the Supper, have been omitted. While this omission shortens an admittedly long passage, it also creates the impression that there was no tension at the table that night. This is a false impression, of course, and ought to be countered by restoring the omitted verses, by referring to them in the sermon, or both. Those not intending to preach on this reading should especially consider restoring the omitted verses, if only to restore the drama of this passage as a whole.

In the end, both our use of this reading and the manner of its use will likely be determined by the choice to read or not read Matthew's account of the Last Supper as part of the Passion narrative. If it was read, this reading from John is then an excellent choice for preaching today. That way the congregation will get to hear both Holy Thursday traditions as the lectionary intended. If Matthew's Last Supper account was not read last Sunday, however, it probably should be read now. In doing so, we do not have to give up John's account. His story of the footwashing could be used as part of a footwashing liturgy, as a second Gospel lesson, or (even better) as part of the passing of the peace preceding the Eucharist.

Good Friday
(Years A, B, and C)

Like the readings for Palm/Passion Sunday and Holy Thursday, the readings for today are also yearly readings. In most cases, the lectionary appoints such yearly readings to emphasize those particular passages. That is the intention here as well, particularly for the Passion narrative from John. In fact, the lectionary is deliberately structured to not only emphasize

John's version of the Passion and subsequent resurrection of Jesus, but to make it the high point of the Christian year as well.

Regardless of the lectionary's intention, however, the use of these readings will again depend a great deal on local custom. If a congregation emphasized the Palm tradition last Sunday, these readings might be heard or the Passion narrative from Matthew might be read instead. If a congregation observes a "Seven Last Words from the Cross" tradition, only parts of the Gospel lesson for today might be heard. If a congregation does not have a Good Friday service, these readings are not likely to be heard at all.

The lessons for today are traditional lessons for Good Friday, too. In fact, the tradition associating these lessons with Good Friday reaches back farther than any other associations in the entire lectionary. Because of this, these readings are particularly influenced by ancient theology and methods of biblical interpretation inherited from the early church. Preachers should plan to spend some extra time and effort with these readings in order to hear what each passage says on its own.

Isaiah 52:13—53:12

In this reading, the lectionary has followed an ancient church tradition and once again linked a Servant Song from the book of Isaiah to the Passion of Jesus. In this case, the link is so tight that most Christians find it almost impossible to hear this Servant Song and not think of the Passion.

This powerful link can affect our understanding of this passage in at least two ways. First, it again invites us to equate the Suffering Servant with Jesus. As we have seen before, this is but one of several ways this passage can be interpreted. Taking time to search out Jewish commentaries on this Servant Song or Christian commentaries not based on the lectionary structure could help broaden the scope of our interpretation.

Second, the link between this reading and the Gospel lesson for today also invites us to interpret Isaiah's words primarily through the lens of prophecy/fulfillment. We are meant to see these words primarily as a prediction of the Passion, a foretelling of the events recorded in the Good Friday Gospel lesson appointed for today.

Again, though, the true relationship between this reading and today's Gospel lesson is much more complex than simple prophecy/ fulfillment might imply. In fact, what we have here is another example of how a reading from the Hebrew Scriptures has inspired the Gospel lesson with which it is now linked. Seen in that light, this Isaiah reading is much more than a prediction of the Passion. It was likely the model upon which the Passion narratives themselves (particularly Matthew's) were built.

Hebrews 10:16–25

This is the first of two readings from the book of Hebrews offered by the lectionary for today. Both have long been traditional readings for Lent. Both are indelibly linked to the Passion Gospel for today.

In both cases, the link between these readings and the Passion of Jesus is appropriate. This particular reading is especially appropriate for Good Friday. Not only is it a theological reflection on the benefits believers have received through Christ's death and resurrection, it is also a specifically Christian reflection.

Even so, this reading still calls for some caution on the part of the preacher because of its portrayal of the ancient Jewish sacrificial system. According to Hebrews, Jesus has not only fulfilled the sacrificial system, he has in many ways superseded it. This is one way of viewing the Passion of Jesus. In many respects, it is the lectionary's dominant way of viewing the Passion of Jesus. But it is not the only way. Today, it may not even be the most helpful way, given the ease with which such a view could contribute to an unconscious downgrading of Jewish tradition.

This reading also begins in the middle of a larger discussion of Jesus as the Great High Priest. For the full context, our study of this reading must begin at Hebrews 10:1, where the discussion itself begins. Ideally, that is where the reading should begin, too. Preachers who feel that such a reading would be too long might choose to begin at verse 11. That would also give the congregation a better start on the reading than the lectionary has given them.

Those interested in preaching on this reading might consider that verses 19–25 will appear again next year for Proper 28B. Then it is part of a series of semi-continuous readings from the book of Hebrews. That setting has two advantages. It is less influenced by the church year, and it gives us much more opportunity to reflect on the picture Hebrews gives us of the sacrificial system and its place in the work of Christ.

Hebrews 4:14–16; 5:7–9

This reading is very similar to the reading from Hebrews chapter 10 and raises many of the same issues. For example, this passage has also been edited for inclusion in the lectionary for Good Friday. In this case, instead of the reading's being taken from the middle of a longer passage of scripture, verses from the middle of the scriptural passage have been removed from the reading. Verses 1–6 of chapter 5, which contrast a human high priest with Jesus as High Priest, were no doubt omitted in order to shorten the reading. Those verses are important to the author's train of thought, however, and whenever possible should be restored, particularly if we are going to preach on this reading. If the length of the reading is a concern, verses 4:14–16 are able to stand on their own, even though they will not include the more "Good Friday-like" imagery of 5:7–9.

Like the reading from Hebrews chapter 10, this reading, too, is a Christian reflection on the Passion that is appropriate for today. In some respects, this reading (as it appears in the lectionary) may even be more appropriate because it does not imply quite so much superiority to the Christian "sacrificial" system as its counterpart from chapter 10. If verses 5:1–6 are included, however, care will again need to be taken to represent the ancient Jewish sacrificial system fairly and respectfully.

Like the reading from chapter 10, part of this reading (4:14–16) appears again next year in the series of semi-continuous readings from the book of Hebrews (Proper 23B). There this reading enjoys the same advantages the reading from chapter 10 enjoyed. It is less influenced by the church year and it offers more opportunity for extended reflection on the theology of Hebrews and its use of the sacrificial system to describe the work of Christ.

Verses 5:7–9 also appear twice in the lectionary. They appear here and then again as part of a slightly longer reading (5:5–9) next year on the Fifth Sunday in Lent.

John 18:1—19:42

This reading includes the entire Passion narrative from the Gospel of John, from Jesus' arrest in the Garden of Gethsemane to his burial in the tomb. It is a highly emphasized reading in the lectionary because it not only appears every year on Good Friday, but verses 18:33–37 also appear on the Reign of Christ (Christ the King) Sunday in Year B. It is also clearly meant as a festival reading because it displaces the reading from Matthew that we might have expected this year.

Preachers might want to consider several factors when considering this reading. First, if it is not the local practice to read the Passion narrative from the year's principal Gospel on Passion/Palm Sunday, it might be a good idea to occasionally read that narrative on Good Friday rather than this reading from John. Otherwise none of the synoptic versions of the Passion will be heard.

Second, if we use this passage from John, we should be very clear as to how it differs from the Synoptic version of the Passion. The chronology of John is different. Even the events John records are different.

Once again, the most important issue to be dealt with in regard to this reading, however, is John's use of polemic against those he calls "the Jews." Scholars differ on just whom John means by this term, but one thing we know. "The Jews" does not refer to Jewish people in general because John records that many Jewish people of the time heard Jesus gladly. Knowing this, we should then take care that we neither infer nor imply John's language here to mean "Jewish people," either in Jesus' day or our own.

Holy Saturday
(Years A, B, and C)

This is a unique set of lessons. In many respects, given the lectionary's strong preference for observing this night with an Easter Vigil, it is surprising this set of lessons appears in the lectionary at all. It contains not only some traditional elements we might expect from the lectionary for today, but also some unexpected, yet very worthwhile twists. For example, instead of the expected three lessons, there are five—two readings from the Hebrew Scriptures, two Gospel lessons, and an epistle lesson. Instead of the expected Lenten reading from Romans, Corinthians, or Ephesians, the epistle lesson is from 1 Peter, a book associated far more with Easter than with Holy Week. And while both readings from the Hebrew Bible and the epistle lesson are still linked to the Gospel lessons, none of those links are the kind of prophecy/fulfillment links so characteristic of Holy Week. Instead these lessons are linked together by shared expressions of grief.

Because many congregations now either observe the Easter Vigil (with its own set of readings) or have no Holy Saturday services at all, it is likely this unique set of readings will not ever be heard in worship. This is unfortunate, because it means that members of such congregations will miss a perfect opportunity to reflect on feelings of grief when they are not likely to be personally grieving themselves. Since instituting Holy Saturday services may not be feasible in many cases, preachers might want to consider instead planning ahead and using the reading from either Lamentations or Job on Good Friday rather than the appointed reading from Isaiah.

Job 14:1–14

Choosing to place this lesson on Holy Saturday was one of the lectionary compilers' more inspired decisions. Its unbridled expression of grief is a perfect complement to the Gospel lessons for today. It does not try to prophesy anything. It does not try to make Job a "type" for either Jesus or his grieving disciples. It does not try to proclaim resurrection when resurrection has not yet come. It simply and poignantly gives voice to the cries of all those human hearts still waiting and suffering through that dreadful time between Good Friday and Easter.

Such a lesson could be a challenging and fruitful choice for a sermon. It could be a particularly good springboard for some reflections on faithful grieving. On the other hand, this lesson is so moving, one could also argue that it is probably best not to try and preach on it at all. In that case, a better use of it might be as a dramatic reading, a litany, or even a sermon illustration.

Lamentations 3:1–9, 19–24

Like the reading from Job, this reading is also an inspired choice on the part of the lectionary compilers. It, too, is an impassioned expression of grief that does not try to prophesy or make the writer a "type." It only hints at resurrection.

The most important accomplishment of this reading is the raising of one of the most perplexing issues in the grieving process, the issue of theodicy. The lectionary, in its usual fashion, has edited out the most vivid verses in the reading, but the questions it raises still remain. "Where is God when bad things happen to good people? Does God sometimes cause those bad things to happen, and if so, why?"

Since parts of this reading also appear in Ordinary Time (verses 19–21 on Proper 22C and verses 22–24 on Proper 8B), these questions can and should be dealt with either now or later in subsequent years of the lectionary cycle. Reading this lesson on Holy Saturday, however, raises some additional questions associated with this day in particular. "What was God's role in the crucifixion? Did God really intend the death of Jesus? If so, why would a loving parent God do such a thing to a Son? And if not, why did God allow it to happen?"

These questions are hard but important ones. They deserve to be raised, although the lectionary has not given them a very prominent place. These questions also deserve our best and most careful thinking, even though this is one of the busiest times in the preacher's year.

1 Peter 4:1–8

At first glance, it seems unclear why this reading would appear today, since 1 Peter is more often used during Eastertide, especially in Year A. Upon closer examination, this reading seems to have been chosen for two reasons, the reference to suffering in verse 1 and the somewhat obscure reference in verse 6 to Christ's having preached to the dead. Both references, though, are only tangential to the author's main point—believers are to live according to God's ways, not the ways of the world.

The ties linking this reading to either Holy Saturday or the Gospel lessons for today are so tenuous that it is probably best not to try to pull a Holy Saturday sermon out of such a text. For those who do decide to preach on this reading, a sermon about the way that doing good sometimes leads to suffering could be one possible approach. Another approach might be to extend the reading through verse 11 and concentrate on the author's concrete suggestions for living the Christian life in the midst of a hostile world. Neither approach is particularly Holy Saturday in tone, but both offer ways to use this reading that do not stretch the text beyond what is actually there.

Matthew 27:57–66

This is the first of two possible Gospel lessons for today. It is intended to be the principal Gospel in Year A, B, or C. Here, Matthew records the vigil the women disciples kept at the cross, the burial of Jesus, and the placing of the guard at the tomb.

There are three features of this lesson for preachers to take into account. First, if the longer version of Matthew's Passion narrative was used on Passion/Palm Sunday, these verses have already been heard once this year. This does not mean we should not use this lesson now, but if we do we should be aware of the repetition.

Second, in using this lesson today, the lectionary has once again ignored Matthew's chronology. According to Matthew, Jesus was buried on Friday afternoon, just before the Sabbath began, not on Saturday. This is a minor historical inaccuracy on the part of the lectionary, but scrupulous preachers will want to keep it in the back of their minds, particularly if they are preaching on this text.

Third, this lesson includes an important reference to the women who followed Jesus. The other Gospel lesson for today from John does not. This in itself is a strong argument in favor of choosing this reading from Matthew.

John 19:38–42

This reading presents us with some of the same issues we saw in the reading from Matthew. First, if the Passion narrative from John was read in full on Good Friday, this lesson, too, has already been read this year—in this case, only yesterday. Again, this does not automatically eliminate this lesson for use today, but it does make the Matthew reading more attractive, particularly if only the shorter version of Matthew's Passion narrative was read on Passion/Palm Sunday.

On the other hand, if Matthew's Passion narrative was the one that was read in the Good Friday service, one might then be more inclined to choose this reading from John. This would be particularly true if it was the longer version of Matthew's Passion that was used.

Second, using this lesson today ignores John's chronology as much as the reading from Matthew ignored his. John, too, records that Jesus was buried on Friday, just before the Sabbath (in John's case, the Passover Sabbath) began. Again, this is a minor detail, but one that we will want to keep in the back of our minds.

Third, as we noted earlier, this reading does not mention the women who followed Jesus and stayed with him while he was on the cross. This omission also makes the reading from Matthew more attractive.

E̲ASTE̲R

*I*n the lectionary, the Easter season consists of several parts, readings for the Easter Vigil, two sets of readings for Easter Day, readings for the subsequent Sundays in Easter, readings for Ascension Sunday, and, following a very old tradition in the church, readings for the day of Pentecost as well. Although each set of readings highlights traditional Easter themes, each has its own pattern and flavor.

Readings for the Easter Vigil highlight the story of salvation as found in the pages of the Hebrew Scriptures. The readings begin with the creation account in Genesis. They recall God's promises to Noah, Abraham, and Moses, then close with a restoration prophecy from the book of Zephaniah. Most of these lessons are traditional for Easter and most have been associated with the Vigil for centuries. They are also read each year, except for the resurrection Gospel, which is always taken from the principal Gospel for the year, in this case, Matthew.

The first set of readings for Easter Day highlight scriptural proclamations of the resurrection. There is a restoration prophecy from Jeremiah, a ringing affirmation in Colossians that believers have been "raised with Christ," and two resurrection Gospel lessons—the first from John and the second from Matthew (for those churches that did not read Matthew's account at the Vigil). According to the lectionary, however, the most crucial of these proclamations is the one Peter gives in the reading from Acts.

133

In fact, the lectionary has structured these readings for Easter in such a way that the Acts passage is unavoidable. It always appears as the first reading for Easter Day. If not chosen as the first reading, it automatically becomes the epistle lesson.

The second set of lessons for Easter Day is intended for those occasions when the principal service for Easter is not in the morning. Except for those readings from the Hebrew Bible appointed for the Vigil, these lessons feature the only reading from the Hebrew Scriptures in the entire Easter season that does not also have an alternative reading from the Christian Scriptures. This set of lessons also features the first of three readings this season from the Gospel of Luke.

All readings for the subsequent Sundays in Easter follow similar patterns. The first lesson is always taken from Acts and is designed to highlight the growth of the Christian movement. Except for the readings for Ascension and Pentecost, these readings are all semi-continuous. The epistle lessons are taken from 1 Peter (again with the exception of Ascension and Pentecost) and highlight 1 Peter's baptismal exhortations. For the most part, these epistle lessons, too, are semi-continuous. With only two exceptions from Luke, the Gospel lessons for these Sundays are all from John. From the Second Sunday in Easter to the Fourth, the Gospel lessons highlight appearances of the risen Christ. From the Fifth Sunday to Pentecost, the focus shifts to the "farewell discourses" in John chapters 14—17 in preparation for Ascension and Pentecost.

Although Pentecost has been observed as a festival unto itself in some parts of the church, the set of readings given this day by the lectionary are clearly understood to be Easter readings. The pattern evident in the readings for Pentecost resembles the pattern we saw in the readings for Easter Day. Again, even though there is both a reading from the Hebrew Scriptures (Jeremiah) and an epistle reading (1 Corinthians) listed, the Acts passage is unavoidable. It always appears as the first reading for Pentecost. If not chosen as the first reading, it automatically becomes the epistle lesson. Again, there is also a choice of Gospel lessons, both from John this time.

Since most readings for Easter this year are from Acts, 1 Peter, and John, the most logical place to begin preparation for Easter preaching is to review recent books and commentaries on these particular biblical books. This is especially important for the book of Acts because it plays such a dominant role in the readings appointed for this season.

Preparation for Easter preaching this year should also include a consideration of the way the church year has influenced the choice and positioning of these readings. This is more important than it might appear at first, for in Easter the power of the church year to shape our understanding and interpretation of the texts reaches its zenith.

One example of this influence is the use of John rather than Matthew (the principal Gospel for Year A). There are several reasons for this, all which relate to the church year. John is the favored Easter Gospel because the church year has traditionally considered it a "festival Gospel." John also includes more resurrection appearances than Matthew, and John contains Jesus' "farewell discourses," discourses that could easily be used in the lectionary as preparation for Ascension and Pentecost.

A second example of the church year's influence on the lectionary readings for Easter is the number of times interruptions occur in otherwise semi-continuous readings. These interruptions appear in both the first lessons and the epistle lessons. In the readings from Acts, the semi-continuous readings are interrupted on Ascension Day by a reading that returns us to chapter 1. In 1 Peter, semi-continuous readings are interrupted first by lessons on the Fourth and Fifth Sundays in Easter that are out of canonical order, then by a reading from Ephesians on Ascension Day, and then again by a reading from 1 Corinthians on Pentecost.

The most telling example of the influence of the church year during the Easter season appears in the lectionary's extensive use of Luke-Acts. The Gospel of Luke appears three times, even though the Gospel of John is traditionally the principal Gospel for Easter. Luke appears on Easter evening, the Third Sunday in Easter (often known as Good Shepherd Sunday), and on Pentecost. Again this is largely due to the church year, for Luke is the only Gospel to record events associated with these particular days in the year.

The book of Acts fares better than its Gospel companion. It appears in every set of Easter readings. In fact, readings from the book of Acts have not only replaced the usual readings from the Hebrew Scriptures, but those Acts readings often behave more like controlling lessons than their accompanying Gospel lesson. Again, this is largely due to the church year, in which Acts has long been associated with the Easter season.

In fact, the very structure of the Easter season itself is thoroughly Lukan. Luke is the only Gospel writer to record that fifty days passed between Easter and the coming of the Spirit at Pentecost. Luke is the only Gospel to record that Jesus lingered with his disciples for forty days between his resurrection and ascension. Luke is also the only biblical author to record the events of Pentecost.

Preachers can address the issues created by the church year and its influence on these lessons in various ways. Readings that are not in canonical order can often be easily switched. On those occasions when both the first and Gospel lessons come from the pen of Luke, Luke's heavy influence can also be countered by occasionally choosing to preach on the non-Lukan epistle lesson. Congregations that do not hold an Easter Vigil can also take the readings from the Hebrew Scriptures intended for the Vigil and spread them out over the entire Easter season to be used in addition to other lessons. Congregations that do hold Vigils might choose some completely original Hebrew Scriptures readings. Biblical songs of praise such as 2 Samuel 22:1–20; 1 Chronicles 16:7–13; or 1 Chronicles 29:10–13 would be appropriate, since they are not easily appropriated as "predictions" of the resurrection and they do not appear anywhere else in the lectionary.

In either case, all lessons chosen for a particular Sunday do not need to be read all at one time. Some of the extra readings from the Hebrew Scriptures could serve as calls to worship. Some of the epistle lessons from 1 Peter could be used as responses to prayers of confession. Other readings could be incorporated into prayers or litanies.

Easter Vigil
(Years A, B, and C)

This set of readings comes out of the ancient tradition of preparing new converts to Christianity for their baptism on Easter morning by observing a vigil on the night before. Most readings for the Vigil still reflect this practice. Many are the very same readings used when the tradition of the Vigil first began. As a result, these Vigil readings are very traditional, in some cases even more traditional than the readings we have just seen for Lent.

For the lectionary, these readings mark the high point of the Christian year. To celebrate, the lectionary pulls out all the stops. Instead of the usual three lessons and a psalm, there are twenty-two lessons appointed for the Easter Vigil. Nineteen readings are from the Hebrew Bible—ten principal read-ings and nine psalm readings (two of which come from Isaiah and Exodus). A psalm reading also accompanies the epistle lesson. Of course, there is the expected resurrection Gospel lesson from the principal Gospel for the year, which in this case is Matthew.

No other set of readings in the whole lectionary is quite like the Easter Vigil. The Vigil is the largest set of readings in the entire lectionary. It has the greatest number of readings from the Hebrew Scriptures. It is the only set of readings to have both yearly readings and readings to be read every three years. And, as was noted in the introduction to Easter this year, the Easter Vigil is the only set of readings specifically designed to be read as separate parts of a much larger story.

However, in spite of their high standing in both the lectionary and the tradition, few of these lessons are ever likely to be preached on unless they also happen to appear elsewhere in the lectionary. Readings from the Hebrew Scriptures are especially likely to be slighted in this way. Most Protestant congregations will not even hear these passages read at Eas-ter at all because they do not hold a Vigil. But even congrega-tions who do observe the Easter Vigil will probably not hear these passages preached. If there is a sermon at the Vigil at all, it will more often be drawn from the Gospel or epistle les-son instead.

Whether we preach from them or not, there is one charac-teristic of these readings in particular that should be noted whenever they are used at the Vigil. Like the readings from the Hebrew Scriptures chosen for Lent, readings from the He-brew Bible for the Easter Vigil have also been deliberately cho-sen from the vast number of possible readings in order to high-light the story of sacred history. These readings, too, are selec-tive. They tend to emphasize God's promises to traditional "greats" such as Noah, Abraham, and Moses.

Unlike their Lenten counterparts, however, these readings from the Hebrew Scriptures for the Vigil have not been chosen only to highlight sacred history. They have been chosen also to present the story of sacred history as a long, progressive buildup of God's activity in the world culminating in the coming of Christ.

This version of sacred history comes primarily from Luke. His story, however, is so familiar to us that we often forget that it is not the only version. In fact, the Bible records several ways of understanding sacred history. John, for instance, (whose Gospel is used most during Easter) would not have talked about a progressive buildup of God's activity in history culminating in Christ. In John, God suddenly broke into history through the coming of Christ. Nor would Matthew (the principal Gospel for this year) have talked about a progressive revelation. Instead, Matthew viewed Jesus as the new Moses who came in the fullness of time to call God's people back to the spirit of the Law.

As we have discovered before, addressing this kind of situation is not easy because the lectionary is so thoroughly dependent on Luke. One possible method would be to choose completely different readings from the Hebrew Scriptures that are more consistent with the theology of whichever Gospel is chosen for the Gospel reading. Another option would be to choose readings that highlight baptismal imagery or associations rather than sacred history (Exodus 14:10–31; 15:20–21; Isaiah 55:1–11; or perhaps Exodus 2:1–10).

Genesis 1:1—2:4a

As we might expect, the lectionary begins its Easter rehearsal of sacred history in the very beginning, with the first creation account in Genesis. Surprisingly, the entire account is included, even though it is an exceptionally long reading according to the lectionary's usual standards. Such a long reading is possible only because of the flexible nature of the Vigil itself. When this account appears in the lectionary again, outside the Easter Vigil, only the first few verses are included.

The most important issue regarding the lectionary's use of this passage is the tendency to use it only on festival occasions. It not only appears every year here at the Easter Vigil, verses 1:1–3 also appear this year on Trinity Sunday and verses 1:1–5 appear next year on Baptism of Jesus Sunday.

In all three cases, using this passage exclusively on festivals can subtly influence our understanding of it in two ways. First, festivals give this text a Christological cast it would not ordinarily have. This is especially true in regard to the Vigil when Christological associations are at a yearly high. Not only that, during the Vigil this text is deliberately incorporated into an unapologetically Christological interpretation of Hebrew tradition.

Second, festivals such as Easter also put this reading in constant competition with other readings that have stronger connections to the particular festival at hand. As a result, even though it appears several times in the lectionary, this passage rarely receives the attention it deserves. It is seldom preached on and is rarely heard in its entirety except here at the Vigil when it is just one of several readings.

To do this important passage of scripture justice, we will probably have to remove it from the context of festivals like the Vigil and use it instead on an ordinary Sunday. It is long enough to be used alone or with only one other reading. It could also be used as part of a series of sermons, perhaps one on each day of creation.

Genesis 7:1–5, 11–18; 8:6–11; 9:8–13

Again we have another relatively long reading, by the standards of the lectionary. Like the reading before it, this reading from the life of Noah has also long been associated with the Easter Vigil. In fact, this reading is a perfect Vigil reading. It not only provides a "great narrative" from Genesis that is characteristic of the Vigil, it also provides images often associated with baptism, which is another characteristic of Vigil readings.

This reading is also more highly emphasized than other readings from Genesis. The story of Noah and the flood appears every year here at the Vigil. Parts of it also appear on Proper 4 this year and on the First Sunday in Lent next year.

The most important feature about this reading, however, is once again the way it has been edited by the lectionary. In fact, large pieces of the Noah narrative have been omitted here. Most of these pieces are merely repetitions of verses that already appear in the reading. The omitted verses, however, will appear a few weeks from now as a separate reading on Proper 4. On the other hand, verses 7:19—8:5, which recount details about the flood, the death of those people and animals who were not on the ark, the receding of the waters, and the first appearance of dry land, never appear in the lectionary. This omission is much more crucial, for while these verses are not pleasant to read, omitting them robs the congregation of an important chance to reflect on the "shadow side" of the flood story.

The lectionary is correct, however, that the Easter Vigil is probably not the best time to do that kind of reflection. A more effective occasion for such a sermon would be when the story of Noah is highlighted again on Proper 4 this year. On that day, verses 7:17–24 could then be added to the reading assigned for that day with plenty of opportunity for reflection.

Genesis 22:1–18

This account of Abraham's near-sacrifice of his son, Isaac, is another reading that has long been traditional for the Vigil. In it the church has seen not only an example of faith but also a "type" of the death and resurrection of Jesus. The church has also seen in God's promise to Abraham the beginning point of God's plan to restore creation from its fallen state. Hence this reading's association with the Easter Vigil.

This association, though, obscures one of the most important issues raised by this passage—God's apparent participation in it. Of course, the story ends on a happy note, but the issue still remains. What kind of God would ask such a thing of a father? What kind of God would ask such a thing and not consult the mother? These are important questions that, understandably, are not likely to be addressed at the Vigil. There is not sufficient time or opportunity, given the festive nature of the festival.

The association of this passage with the death and resurrection of Jesus raises similar issues about God's participation in those events, particularly in the death of Jesus. Did God sacrifice Jesus? Did God follow through with the act Abraham was eventually prevented from finishing? If so, what kind of God would ask such a thing from "his" own Son? These questions are not original to the text, but rather are tangential to it. Even so, they, too, are not likely to be addressed at the Vigil.

Fortunately, the lectionary provides opportunities to reflect on both sets of questions. Questions about the near sacrifice of Isaac, for instance, could be explored when this passage appears again this year for Proper 8. It is then part of a series of semi-continuous readings from the life of Abraham. Questions about the death of Jesus could be explored at several points throughout the year, but are probably best explored on Good Friday.

Exodus 14:10–31; 15:20–21

This account of the Exodus is another traditional lesson for the Easter Vigil. It too is a great narrative of faith that has long been seen in the church as a "type" for the death and resurrection of Jesus and as a source of baptismal imagery. The lectionary considers this lesson so important and pivotal that it specifically mandates its reading at the Vigil.

One feature of this lesson is more recent, and that is the inclusion of Miriam in verses 15:20–21. This is one of the few times when the lectionary has taken pains to include a biblical woman. In some respects, the lectionary has even given

Miriam's song precedence over that of her brother, Moses. This alone should commend this reading for regular use at the Vigil.

Again, the preacher should note the way the lectionary has edited this passage. First, the reading opens after the Exodus narrative has already started. Starting the reading at verse 5, or certainly at verse 9, would provide the congregations a better starting point. Second, the first 19 verses of chapter 15 (the song of Moses) have also been omitted from this reading and made into a "psalm" reading. This omission, however, does not appreciably affect the flow of the reading, but to ensure that all verses of this important passage receive proper respect, the "psalm" reading from Exodus 15 should also be read whenever this reading is used.

Preachers who wish to preach on the Exodus would probably do better to wait until parts of this reading reappear this year for Proper 19. That location provides the reading with a natural setting as part of a series of semi-continuous readings from the life of Moses. Since the reading for Proper 19 includes only verses 14:19–31, those who wait might consider expanding the reading for that Sunday to include more verses from the Vigil reading.

Isaiah 55:1–11

With this lesson, readings from the Hebrew Bible shift away from the "patriarchal narratives" that have predominated up to this point. These particular verses, inviting all those who thirst to "come to the waters," are some of the most often repeated verses in the entire Bible. They appear every year here on the Easter Vigil. Verses 1–5 appear again this year for Proper 13. Verses 1–9 appear in Year C during Lent, and verses 10–11 appear not only on Proper 10 this year but also on the Eighth Sunday After Epiphany in Year C.

In each instance, a slightly different part of this passage is emphasized. For the Easter Vigil, the emphasis falls on the theme of repentance and the promise of grace to those who are penitent. In fact, the lectionary has purposely ended this reading right before a reference to a future restoration ("you shall go out in joy") in order to maintain the emphasis on Isaiah's invitation to repentance and grace.

Baruch 3:9–15, 32—4:4

Although it is not as long-standing a Vigil reading as some, this apocryphal lesson has been traditional for the Vigil for some time. In it, Israel is challenged to choose wisdom and return to the "commandments of life." The reading concludes with a hymn celebrating wisdom, "her" part in the creation of the world, and the joy of those who are wise enough to know what is pleasing to God.

Like many other readings for the Vigil, this reading has been edited by the lectionary. The passage from which it was taken was originally intended as a message to exiled Israel that argued that a lack of wisdom had been responsible for their suffering. In the lectionary, however, verses 3:16–31 were omitted in order to emphasize wisdom's call and thus make the reading more general, hence more "appropriate" for the Vigil. This omission is not a crucial one, particularly if the reading is simply read as one of several Vigil readings. Whenever the reading is used as the basis for a sermon, though, the historical context contained in verses 3:16–31 should be restored.

Proverbs 8:1–8, 19–21; 9:4b–6

This reading is the canonical alternate to the reading from Baruch for those churches who do not use the Apocrypha. Like its apocryphal counterpart, it also celebrates wisdom. This reading is also the newest and least traditional of the Vigil readings. In fact, this is its first appearance in a modern lectionary.

Even so, this lesson has been as heavily edited as several of the more traditional narratives. Verses 8:9–20, which elaborate on verses 8:1–8, have been omitted. So have verses 8:22—9:3, which describe wisdom's role at the beginning of creation. The effect of both these omissions is subtle but powerful. The lectionary makes this reading more appropriate for the Vigil by downplaying the general nature of this song and emphasizing wisdom's invitation to come and listen to her life-giving words.

Parts of this song appear two other times in the lectionary. Verses 8:1–4 appear again on Trinity Sunday in Year C. On that Sunday they serve as an introduction to verses 8:22–31, verses the lectionary had omitted during the Vigil. Verses 9:4–6 of the Vigil reading appear again next year as part of the reading for Proper 15. Both occasions offer better preaching opportunities than does the Vigil.

Ezekiel 36:24–28

With this lesson, the lectionary turns again to more traditional Easter Vigil readings. This reading is one of two readings from Ezekiel to be listed for the Vigil. It is also a restoration prophecy, although it is less well known than its counterpart from chapter 37.

As is often the case when restoration prophecies are used as festival readings, the lectionary has purposely omitted from this reading historical references and literary allusions that appear too specific to the historical restoration from the exile in Babylon. References to judgment and the reasons why Israel was in exile in the first place have also been carefully avoided.

If this reading is simply to be read as one of several Vigil readings, it is probably easier to let these historical omissions stand. Those who feel led to preach on this passage, however, should not only add the historical context provided by verses 36:29–36, but also seriously consider preaching on it at a time other than the Vigil. Separated from the Vigil, this reading could even be used as part of a sermon series based on readings chosen from the book of Ezekiel. Such a series could be done near the end of Ordinary Time when the semi-continuous readings from the Hebrew Scriptures have ended. For those who like to plan well into the future, a sermon series from Ezekiel could also be appropriate for Epiphany, since the "glory of God" is a major theme of both.

Ezekiel 37:1–14

This reading is one of the most traditional Vigil readings of all—Ezekiel's vision of the valley of dry bones. It should sound familiar, not only because it is one of the lectionary's favorite passages for the Lent/Easter cycle, but also because it appeared just two weeks ago on the Fifth Sunday of Lent (c.f., Fifth Sunday in Lent, Year A).

At the Easter Vigil, the connections that the tradition has made between this passage and the death and resurrection of Jesus reach their zenith. In fact, those connections are so powerful here at the Vigil that they obscure Ezekiel's original message of hope to an exiled people. Given this effect, it is wise not to attempt a Vigil sermon on this lesson. Instead, the reading would be used more effectively if read simply as another example of God's resurrection power. Those who preached on this passage two weeks ago might choose to omit it altogether now.

Preachers who wish to preach on this passage and passed up the opportunity to do so during Lent will now do best to create their own opportunities once the Easter season is over. Again it might be best to create a sermon series from specially chosen semi-continuous readings from the book of Ezekiel.

Zephaniah 3:14–20

Only two passages from the book of Zephaniah appear in the lectionary. This is the first and it appears both here and on the Third Sunday in Advent, Year C. On both occasions, the lectionary has associated this restoration prophecy with events in the life of Jesus. Here at the Easter Vigil, it is associated with the death and resurrection of Jesus, just as the restoration prophecies from Ezekiel were associated.

It is easy to see why the lectionary chose this reading for Easter. First, as a restoration prophecy, it comes from the part of the Hebrew Bible the lectionary most prefers for a festival. As we have seen before, this is not necessarily the best use of such prophecies. This is particularly true in the case of Zephaniah, whose primary message is one of judgment, not restoration.

Second, while this reading hits an appropriate celebratory note, such a note only partially reflects the original intent of this passage. Like the rest of Zephaniah, this passage is primarily concerned with judgment. In fact, the first 13 verses of this passage are actually an oracle of judgment, but in order to maintain a celebratory Easter note, the lectionary purposely avoided them.

By using this reading in such a way, the lectionary puts us in a bind. If we choose this lesson, we will read a lesson that represents neither the passage nor the book from which it was taken. If we choose to read this lesson, but add verses 1–13, we will have a lesson more representative of Zephaniah, but one that is less appropriate for the Vigil. If we do not choose this lesson, though, we will remove one of the few opportunities the congregation has to hear the words of Zephaniah.

It is not an easy choice. Good arguments can be made for reading the passage as is, adding the preceding verses, or omitting the reading. In most cases, the decision is probably best made on a year-by-year basis, depending on what other readings are planned for the Vigil on any given year.

Romans 6:3–11

With this reading, the lectionary turns again to one of its favorite biblical books, Romans. This lesson is a traditional Vigil lesson, and like many other readings for the Easter Vigil, appears here every year and then again once every three years in the lectionary's cycle. In this case, this same reading from Romans will appear again this year as an epistle lesson for Proper 7.

According to the standards of the lectionary, this is a perfect Vigil reading. It not only uses baptismal imagery characteristic of the Vigil, it also refers to the death and resurrection of Jesus. Both references are appropriate for the Vigil, making this reading one of the best Vigil readings available to us.

This appropriateness also has its downside, though. It overshadows and obscures this reading's original literary and theological context. If the reading is simply read as one Vigil reading among others, this overshadowing may not be a major issue. If we choose to preach on this reading, however, we will need to see that Paul's reasons for writing these words are not lost in all the Easter festivities. This will be especially true if the sermon is to be a baptismal sermon. If we want to concentrate on this passage, we might do better to preach on it when it appears again a few weeks after Pentecost this year.

Matthew 28:1–10

This reading from Matthew is the only Vigil reading that is read every third year rather than yearly. Mark's account of the resurrection will appear in this same place next year and Luke's account in the following year. This structure enables the lectionary to appoint the resurrection account from the principal Gospel for the year each year at the Easter Vigil. In this way, since the account from John is always read as the principal Gospel lesson for Easter morning, all four resurrection accounts appear within the lectionary's three-year cycle.

Such a structure works very well in those congregations who observe an Easter Vigil. It does not work so well, however, in those congregations who do not. In those congregations, there is only one opportunity to read an Easter Gospel, not two. This means that a choice must be made between the account from the principal Gospel for the year (in this case, Matthew) and the account from John. The best, though not perfect solution, is to form a four-year cycle of Easter Gospel readings. This assures that all Four Gospel accounts will be heard, even if it does not fit the lectionary's three-year cycle.

It is especially important that the synoptic accounts such as Matthew's not be slighted, whether there is a Vigil service or not. These accounts contain the most important story of biblical women in the Christian tradition. As such, they should be highlighted whenever possible, particularly if the 1 Corinthians 15 tradition from Paul (which does not mention the women) is also used in any of the Easter services.

This selection from Matthew has many details that differ from the other resurrection accounts. Unique to Matthew are the earthquake, the trembling guards, the women departing with "great joy," and the women meeting Jesus who tells them to go tell the others to meet him in Galilee. Care should be taken, especially when preaching on this passage, not to unintentionally combine Matthew's version of this story with elements from other accounts which are familiar but not actually a part of Matthew itself.

One unique feature of Matthew's account does not appear in the lectionary at all—the report of the guards to the temple authorities and the fabrication both devised to fool "the Jews." Whether to include these verses or not is a tough question. They should probably be included. After all, Matthew did intend them to be a part of his resurrection story. On the other hand, they can too easily aggravate misunderstanding between Christians and Jews. In this respect, the lectionary may have been wise to omit this part of Matthew's story, even if it means that these particular verses may never be heard in public worship.

Easter Day

For Easter Day, the lectionary has given us five lessons—a reading from Acts, an alternate reading from Jeremiah, an epistle lesson from Colossians (with the Acts passage serving as an alternate), and two Easter Gospel lessons, the resurrection story from John and its alternate from Matthew. All five lessons are traditional for this festival. Each has been well associated with Easter for centuries. In fact, these lessons are so associated with Easter that only the lesson from Acts and a few verses from the Colossians reading appear anywhere else in the lectionary.

The principal readings (Acts, Colossians, and John) have all been chosen on the assumption that an Easter Vigil has already taken place and that most if not all of the Vigil lessons have already been read. In many ways the principal readings for today have all been designed to complement and coordinate with the lessons for the Easter Vigil. The reading from Acts connects the Vigil readings from the Hebrew Bible with the lessons from Acts that will characterize the rest of the Easter season. The reading from Colossians complements the Vigil reading from Romans, and the reading from John provides a second, different account of the resurrection for congregations who have already heard an Easter Gospel at the Vigil.

Both alternate lessons, however, better meet the needs of congregations who do not observe an Easter Vigil. The reading from Jeremiah provides such congregations with a reading from the Hebrew Bible they would otherwise not hear during the Easter season. The reading from Matthew provides them with the resurrection account from a synoptic Gospel that they would also not hear, having not heard it at a Vigil.

Acts 10:34–43

We have seen this reading once before this year on Baptism of Jesus Sunday. On that Sunday, the baptismal connections in this passage were emphasized. The lectionary has purposefully downplayed those connections for Easter, but even so, they should not be overlooked. This is especially important if we are going to preach on this reading.

There are several ways we can restore and maintain the important connections this passage has with baptism. Reference can be made to the baptismal imagery of the Easter Vigil. Reference can be made to Easter as a traditional day for celebrating baptisms like those of Cornelius and his family, for whom Peter first preached this sermon. If new members are received or baptized during the service, more concrete, even personal, references are possible.

Today, it is the Easter proclamation in the last half of the passage that is intended to draw our attention. That proclamation is also the primary reason the lectionary chose this reading for the liturgy today. In fact, Peter's declaration that God had raised Jesus from the dead is so important to the lectionary that it gave this lesson special consideration, consideration given to no other lesson in the entire cycle of the lectionary. It not only appointed this lesson to be read every Easter, it assured that it would be read either as the first lesson or the epistle lesson, regardless of whatever other lessons are chosen.

Jeremiah 31:1–6

Except for the Vigil readings, this lesson is one of the few readings from the Hebrew Bible to appear during the Easter season. For congregations that do not observe the Vigil or have an afternoon service on Easter, this may be the only reading from the Hebrew Scripture they will hear until after Pentecost. For this reason alone, it is a tempting lesson to choose for preaching.

Choosing it, however, raises some of the same issues we have seen before regarding the lectionary's use of the Hebrew

Scriptures during festival seasons. First, this lesson is a restoration prophecy, and although it fits the Easter season very nicely, it does not represent Jeremiah. Second, because this prophecy is linked in the lectionary with the resurrection of Jesus, it is easily misunderstood as a prophecy of the resurrection. Third, if we follow the lectionary to the letter, choosing this reading also means choosing against the excellent reading from Colossians.

Given these issues, and given that Jeremiah chapter 31 is well represented elsewhere in the lectionary, it may be best not to use this reading. Instead, these words of Jeremiah might be better used, not as a reading, but as an example of God's restorative power. Parts of this lesson could be used in a call to worship, in a litany, or even in an assurance of pardon in those churches that still have prayers of confession during Easter.

Colossians 3:1–4

As is often the case, the lectionary has been selective about the verses it has included in this reading. Only the first four verses have been taken out of a literary unit that actually continues through verse 17. Those particular verses were selected specifically for their reference to the resurrection. Taken alone, they are intended to be an Easter exhortation to the faithful, and they serve that function beautifully.

The unit as a whole, however, is not about the resurrection per se. It is instead a more general exhortation about the kind of life the author hoped the Colossians would live. Taken in context then, the reference to the resurrection in these first four verses is simply the author's way of emphasizing his larger point. By choosing only these verses, however, the lectionary was able to turn what was originally a general exhortation into a message more appropriate for Easter.

Since this passage does not appear again this year, the best option may be to simply read this passage without comment. It could also be used in an assurance of pardon, an affirmation of faith, or even a charge at the end of the service. The opportunity to preach on this passage in its full context will come in Year C, when verses 3–4 appear in a longer, semi-continuous reading for Proper 13.

John 20:1–18

This reading is the lectionary's intended Gospel lesson for Easter. It appears every year on this festival morning, along with Acts 10:34–43, on the assumption that Matthew 28:1–10 will have already been read at the Easter Vigil.

The lectionary's use of this reading raises two important issues that are of particular interest to women. First, the tradition John records here is significantly different from the one recorded in the synoptic Gospels. In the latter tradition, several women are recorded as the first witnesses to the empty tomb. In Matthew's account, these same women are also said to have been the first disciples to meet the Risen Christ.

John's tradition, on the other hand, is much later. As such, it shows clear evidence that even as early as the time of John, the church was beginning to withdraw from that earlier (and much more scandalous) position. Thus, in John we find the number of women witnesses reduced to only one (Mary Magdalene) and two men (Peter and John) added to the list of witnesses.

Second, if this reading is heard only on Easter, the Easter celebration can easily overshadow the one feature of this reading that affirms women—John's extended account of Mary's conversation with Christ in the garden. This is one of the longest conversations Jesus is recorded to have had with a woman. It is also one of the strongest scriptural arguments for Jesus' having also chosen women as his apostles.

However we use this reading from John, then, it should not be allowed to silence the voices of the women witnesses in synoptic Gospels such as Matthew. This is of particular concern in churches that do not observe the Vigil. In those churches, this resurrection account should probably be used in rotation with the other three resurrection accounts. As mentioned earlier, such a four-year rotation has disadvantages, but most are outweighed by the advantages.

Matthew 28:1–10

(See comments on this passage under the comments for the Easter Vigil, Years A, B, and C.)

Easter Evening

This set of readings follows a different pattern from both the readings for Easter Day and the readings we will see for the rest of the season of Easter. The first reading is a restoration prophecy from Isaiah (a prophecy much like the Easter Day reading from Jeremiah) but there is no reading from Acts. The epistle lesson has been specifically chosen for Easter-like themes, but it is from 1 Corinthians rather than Ephesians (the lectionary's Easter epistle). And, the Gospel lesson records events from the first Easter Day, but those events are later in the day and the record comes from Luke, not Matthew or John (the lectionary's principal Easter Gospels for Year A).

The lectionary specifies these readings for use when the primary service for Easter Day is later in the day. They are not, however, intended as readings for a vesper service. Why the lectionary would consider these readings inappropriate for an Easter vesper service is unclear. They are, in fact, fine vesper readings and preachers should feel free to use them as such if the occasion presents itself.

Since many churches do not hold services later in the day on Easter, however, these readings will probably not be read at all. This is not especially detrimental to either the reading from Isaiah or Luke. Both appear elsewhere in the lectionary. The reading from 1 Corinthians, however, does not. Fortunately, readings very much like it from 1 Corinthians do appear in other years, should this lesson not be read on Easter evening.

Isaiah 25:6–9

This reading is one of the most emphasized readings from the Hebrew Bible in the entire lectionary. It is also a very popular festival lesson. Not only does it appear every year here on Easter evening, it also appears this year for Proper 23 and next year for both Easter Day and All Saints' Day.

The way the lectionary has linked this passage to Easter raises some of the same issues raised by the Jeremiah reading for Easter Day. First, this lesson was chosen for Easter because its restoration images sound so Easter-like. Those images, however, do not represent Isaiah chapters 1—39.

Second, using this reading for Easter removes this prophecy from its original historical context, Israel's exile and restoration. This historical context should not be dismissed. Without it, this reading can too easily be misunderstood as a prophecy of the resurrection instead.

Third, using this reading on Easter also subtly changes the original emphasis of the passage. The Easter celebration shifts attention away from the central image of celebrating the return of the exiles and toward the image of God "swallow[ing] up death forever" instead. The latter is not as central, but it is more Easter-like and thus more attractive for use today.

As with the reading from Jeremiah, it may be best not to use this reading as the lectionary intends and to use it instead as an example of God's restorative power. Again this would probably be best done in a call to worship, a litany, or an assurance of pardon.

1 Corinthians 5:6b–8

Once again, the lectionary has taken a reference to the resurrection originally meant only as an illustration and made it into the primary theme of a reading. As was the case with the Easter reading from Colossians, the resurrection reference here is actually more a literary device than it is a theme. In this case, it is a device Paul used to make his point about the situation among the Corinthians, a situation the lectionary omitted when it cut verses 5:1–6a from this reading.

This again presents the preacher with a dilemma, particularly for those who choose to preach on this passage. In a sermon, the historical context of this passage should probably be addressed in some way. Doing so, however, may take us deeper into the issues present in Corinth than we want for Easter. (There is no doubt why the lectionary edited these historical verses in the first place.) Because of this dilemma, it may be better not to preach on this lesson at all and use it just as the lectionary has given it to us, as a general Easter exhortation to live the Christian life. This may not be a completely accurate reflection of the text, but it could serve as an excellent call to confession, or a charge to the congregation at the end of the service.

Luke 24:13–31

Like the reading from Isaiah 25, this reading too is a popular festival lesson, especially for Easter. It appears every year here on Easter evening and again this year on the Third Sunday in Easter. Verses 24:36–48 appear again next year, also on the Third Sunday in Easter, and verses 24:44–49 appear every year on Ascension Day. Thus, in all three years parts of this lesson will be read at least twice in the Easter season, and often three times.

This particular lesson was chosen not only because it fit so well into the themes of Easter, but also because it fit so well the hour in which these readings are most often used, evening. Like many of the readings for Easter Day and Easter Evening, it assumes that most of the Vigil Lessons have already been used. At the very least, this reading assumes that at least one Easter Gospel has been read as well.

How these readings will be used, then, may depend on which other Easter services have already taken place and which Gospel lessons were used at those services. If, for instance, no Vigil was held and only Matthew's account of the resurrection has been read so far, this may be a good year to substitute John's account of Jesus appearing to Mary Magdalene (John 21:10–18) for this reading. After all, Luke's account of the road to Emmaus will appear again this year in just two more weeks, and his account of Jesus' appearance "behind closed doors" will appear again on Ascension Day. If, on the other hand, an Easter Vigil was held and John's account has already been used, it might be just as well to use this reading from Luke, even it that does mean encouraging the domination of Luke-Acts.

Second Sunday in Easter

These readings are all typical for this part of the Easter season. The first reading is the usual lesson from the book of Acts. It begins a series of three almost continuous readings from Peter's speech on Pentecost. The epistle lesson is from 1 Peter and begins a series of semi-continuous readings that will continue throughout the Easter season. The Gospel lesson is from John and begins a series of readings that recount various appearances of the risen Christ prior to his Ascension.

Acts 2:14a, 22–32

This reading is a perfect example of the lectionary's use of Acts during Easter. First, the reading is again taken from Peter's Pentecost speech. Second, the reading has also been taken out of its original historical and literary setting in order to make it appropriate for Easter. (In this case, verses 14b–21 were omitted because they would have too closely connected this reading to its historical setting in Pentecost.) Preachers should keep this setting in mind, however, particularly if they choose to preach on this reading.

This lesson is also a perfect example of the theology of Luke so prevalent in the Easter season. The use of the Hebrew Scriptures in this reading and the theme of God's foreknowledge and participation in history both reflect Luke's particular interpretation of sacred history. This, too, will be important to keep in mind, particularly if this reading is to become the basis of a sermon.

1 Peter 1:3–9

First Peter is the lectionary's primary epistle for Easter Year A. Readings from 1 Peter span the entire length of not only the season, but the epistle as well. These readings are all semi-continuous and each is specifically designed to emphasize the baptismal exhortation so characteristic of 1 Peter.

This inaugural lesson exemplifies this Easter pattern. Originally, these verses were the first half of the thanksgiving section of 1 Peter. As they appear now, they have been clearly edited in order to make them more appropriate for Easter. For instance, the salutation to this letter (verses 1–2) has been omitted to downplay its epistolary origin. In the same way, the second half of this salutation has been omitted as well to emphasize the more Easter-like verses in the first half.

Both omissions, though, could easily be restored without seriously compromising the Easter themes so important to the lectionary. In fact, adding verses 10–12 in particular might even strengthen the reading. For that reason alone, these verses should probably be added whether the lesson is preached on or simply read in worship.

John 20:19–31

Of the readings for today, only this reading appears on this Sunday every year. It has clearly been chosen for this Second Sunday in Easter for two reasons. One, it records not just one but two post-Easter appearances of the risen Christ. Two, it takes up the resurrection story immediately where the Easter Gospel from John left off last week.

This reading is an excellent lesson for both reading and preaching. It gives us a refreshingly honest picture of the disciples in those first few days following the resurrection. It also gives us an important balance to the more triumphal picture painted by Luke in the reading from Acts. Given the lectionary's usual tendency to minimize less than glowing pictures of the early church, and given the lectionary's tendency to emphasize the history and theology of Luke, the compilers are to be commended for including such a reading.

Third Sunday in Easter

In many respects, this set of readings is very similar to the readings for last Sunday. There is both a reading from Acts and a reading from 1 Peter. Both readings are continuations of semi-continuous readings from the week before. Both readings appear only this once in the three-year cycle of the lectionary.

There is one important difference in these readings, though. Rather than a Gospel lesson from John, there is a reading from Luke instead. This shift is significant. It not only breaks the pattern characteristic of these readings after Easter, it also significantly increases the powerful influence of the author of Luke-Acts.

Acts 2:14a, 36–41

This lesson is the second of three semi-continuous readings from Peter's speech on Pentecost. The lectionary, however, has once again edited this speech to make it more appropriate for Easter. Verse 14 has been used again to introduce this speech as if it was a totally different one from the speech we heard last week. This editing succeeds in make the reading more Easter-like, but it also severely compromises the continuity that should come from semi-continuous readings. Moreover, verses 33–35 have also been omitted from the reading. This, too, makes this reading more Easter-like, but by removing these references to Pentecost and Ascension, the integrity of the text is again compromised.

Fortunately, in this case the problems created by this editing can be addressed fairly easily. First, verse 14, which is not especially necessary to the reading, can simply be dropped. Instead, a brief note connecting this reading to the reading from last week can then be given before this reading is read or preached on.

As was the case last week, preachers should continue to be mindful that we are again seeing the powerful influence of the author of Luke-Acts. This Sunday, however, there is no reading that offers us an effective balance to this Lukan influence. In this case, the most that we can do is to keep this influence in mind whether we are preaching on this reading, the reading from Luke, or the reading from 1 Peter.

1 Peter 1:17–23

This reading is a typical exhortation from the book of 1 Peter. Like the reading from Acts before it, this reading, too, is the second in a series of semi-continuous readings. It has also been edited to make it more appropriate for Easter. In this case, verses 13–16, which would have tied this reading to the one from last week, have been purposefully omitted. Again, this editing makes the reading more Easter-like, but is also obscures the original context and meaning of the passage.

Both those who are planning to preach on this lesson and those who are not might consider adding verses 13–16. This would provide the reading with a more adequate introduction. Those planning to preach on this reading might also consider completing the reading more adequately by adding verses 1:24–25. Both additions make the reading less Easter-like, but in both cases the congregation will be given a better sense of the author's original intent.

Luke 24:13–35

Preachers who used the lessons listed for Easter evening will recognize this reading. It appeared on Easter evening as part of a longer reading from Luke chapter 24. Now it appears as part of the lectionary's pattern of choosing accounts of resurrection appearances for the Sundays after Easter. It also appears on this same Sunday again next year.

There are several features about this reading that preachers will want to take into account. First, the lectionary has turned to Luke in order to have enough resurrection appearances to fill this first part of the Easter season. This means, among other things, that we will be working with a different Gospel today from the one we will see most often during Easter—John. Particularly if we preach on this reading, it will be important to remember we are seeing Luke's unique viewpoint in these particular verses.

Second, it will also be important to again remember how much Luke's viewpoint dominates the readings for today. As we saw in the reading from Acts, this domination can easily lead us into mistaking Luke's viewpoint for *the* Christian viewpoint. Again, Luke is but one early Christian evangelist among many and his words here are best treated as such, even on such a heavily Lukan Sunday as this.

Fourth Sunday in Easter

These readings continue the pattern begun on the Second Sunday in Easter, this time with only minor exceptions. The lesson from Acts continues to be semi-continuous, but now the theme of the reading has shifted slightly to emphasize the growth of the early Christian movement. The lesson from 1 Peter continues to highlight the author's exhortations. The Gospel lesson is once more from John, but due to a tradition unique to this particular Sunday, it does not record the expected resurrection appearance.

In many ways, this Gospel lesson is the most distinctive element of this set of readings. Each year on this Sunday the Gospel lesson is taken from this same speech in John—hence the tradition of calling this Sunday "Good Shepherd Sunday." Such an enticing theme makes it tempting to try to work all the lessons for today into a "shepherd" theme. They are not intended to be used in that way, however, even by the lectionary.

Acts 2:42–47

This reading is another perfect example of the lectionary's use of the book of Acts during Easter. The reading appears only once in the lectionary cycle. It follows immediately upon the reading from last week. It is the second reading in a series designed to show the growth of the early church. It is also a classic statement of Luke's idealistic picture of that church.

This lesson is an inviting one to preach from. It is a powerful reading and excellent sermon material. Those who preach from it, however, should again note the influence of Luke's theology. This influence may not be as strong today as it was last week, when the Gospel lesson was also from the pen of Luke, but it is still very much present.

1 Peter 2:19–25

Like its counterpart from last week, this lesson is another semi-continuous reading from 1 Peter. In this case, however, several verses have been passed over between the reading last week and this one. Many of these verses will appear in the reading from 1 Peter next week. Other verses do not appear in the lectionary at all, even though they contain one of the most powerful metaphors in all of 1 Peter—that of believers being resident aliens while on earth.

In order to include this important metaphor, the reading would have to begin at verse 11. Beginning there, however, can put the preacher in a bind. The resident alien metaphor would receive its proper due, but at the same time, the true context of the verses in this reading would become apparent. In other words, adding verses 11–18 would clarify that the author is not addressing a general audience. He is addressing slaves. The problems of racism raised by this context are legion. They also require a great deal of sensitivity on the part of the preacher, which is probably why the lectionary avoided these verses in the first place.

Such a situation has no perfect solution. If this lesson is to be simply read in worship, it may be wise to just follow the lectionary's lead and begin at verse 19, even though this means missing an important image so characteristic of 1 Peter. If this lesson is to be preached on, however, preachers will have to decide for themselves how much of this problematic historical context they are willing to address, even though choosing not to do so means missing the opportunity to reflect on the less than seemly implications raised by the context of this passage. One thing is certain, however—the context of this reading probably should not be raised unless one is willing to deal with those implications.

John 10:1–10

This reading is one of the most unusual Gospel lessons in the entire season of Easter. On the one hand, it breaks with some of the usual patterns for Easter Gospel lessons. (For example, it does not record a resurrection appearance, nor is it a reading from the farewell discourses of John.) On the other hand, its shepherd theme is very traditional for this Sunday, so traditional that it appears every year in the lectionary's three-year cycle.

The most significant feature of this reading is again John's use of polemic against "those who came before." Once more we will need to be careful and sensitive in our use of such language. In John's world, of course, it meant the leadership of the synagogue. In our world, a more accurate translation would refer to any corrupt religious leaders, including Christian ones.

Fifth Sunday in Easter

These lessons continue the pattern begun on the Second Sunday in Easter, again with some important differences. The first reading, for instance, is again a semi-continuous reading from Acts, but more of Acts has been passed over than was the case previously. The epistle lesson is once more from 1 Peter, but it reverses the semi-continuous reading by coming from an earlier part of the book than the reading last week. The Gospel lesson continues from John, only this time, in preparation for Ascension Day, it has been taken from Jesus' farewell discourse in John 14.

Moreover, none of these lessons is popular with the lectionary. Like most lessons for this part of the Easter season, none of these readings (except a few verses from the Gospel lesson) appear again in the lectionary.

Acts 7:55–60

Like other readings taken from Acts that will follow, this reading was obviously chosen to show the growth of the early church. This the reading accomplishes quite well. In fact, the story of Stephen the deacon has been used for centuries to illustrate the growth of the early church, quite apart from the lectionary.

This particular reading gives only part of Stephen's story, the last and most dramatic part. When the reading begins, even this last part of the story has already been set in motion. In this case, lengthening the reading to include more of the story would be impractical. The account is too long. Even so, preachers should be sure to study the entire Stephen narrative in preparation for preaching. It might also be a good idea to give a brief synopsis of the story before reading this lesson in order to give the congregation a better introduction to it.

Preachers should also remember that Stephen is not the only example of courageous witness that could have been chosen from Luke's account here in Acts. Other examples in the five chapters that were passed over might also have been appropriate. Some of these should probably be chosen from time to time instead of Stephen, just to give the congregation a wider view of the early Christian movement.

1 Peter 2:2–10

To reach this lesson, the lectionary has returned to the beginning of chapter 2. This effectively switches the biblical order of the exhortation we saw last week and the reason for that exhortation, which is in the reading for today. Why the lectionary has done this is unclear. Even so, preachers who want to be strict about such things might consider putting these two readings back in their original biblical order, even though the shift in order does not appreciably affect the meaning of either reading.

The lectionary has also edited this reading to make it more appropriate for Easter. Verse 2:1, in which the author urges his readers to "rid yourselves...of all malice," has been omitted, and (as we found last week) so have the verses that contain 1 Peter's characteristic "resident alien" metaphor. Once again, preachers who want to be strict about such things might consider expanding the reading to include some of these verses, especially those verses that include the famous metaphor, but it is not particularly necessary to do so in this case.

John 14:1–14

With this reading, the lectionary shifts attention from the resurrection appearances in John 20 back to Jesus' farewell speeches in John 14 and 17. This is an important move. It not only draws our focus away from Easter itself, but it also prepares us for Ascension Day next week. In fact, this shift is so important to the lectionary that it occurs on this same Sunday every year.

To make this shift, the lectionary has again played with John's chronology. According to John, these words were spoken before Jesus' arrest, not after his death and resurrection. But because it sounded like a perfect reading in preparation for Ascension, the lectionary has placed it here, after Easter. Preachers should always keep this shift in mind whenever this reading is preached. Mention of it should also be made, even if we simply read this lesson in worship.

Sixth Sunday in Easter

These readings are very similar to the ones used last week. The reading from Acts remains semi-continuous and continues to emphasize the growth of the early Christian movement. The epistle lesson from 1 Peter is once more semi-continuous and once more in proper canonical order. The reading from John continues to prepare us for Ascension Day by providing us another lesson from Jesus' farewell speech in John 14.

Acts 17:22–31

To reach this lesson, the lectionary has again skipped several chapters in the book of Acts. Now we are in the Paul portion of Luke's narrative. This particular lesson highlights Paul's mission to the Gentiles, in this case, the Gentiles in Athens.

No doubt in an effort to shorten the reading, the lectionary has given us only Paul's speech. Both Luke's introduction to the speech and his account of the crowd's reaction to it have been omitted. The introductory verses, 16–21, provide the historical setting for the speech and should be either read or mentioned whenever this lesson is used. Verses 32–33, which record the crowd's reaction, should also be added whether or not this lesson is preached. These verses give a more realistic picture of Paul's work than would be available without them. They also mention another biblical woman.

Like the story of Stephen, this lesson is also a traditional choice for illustrating the growth of the early church. It has often been used to symbolize Paul's work among the Gentiles as well, but it is not the only account that could have been chosen. Other accounts from the life of Paul, such as Acts 17:5–10, might have served the lectionary's purpose just as well and perhaps should be considered from time to time in place of this reading.

1 Peter 3:13–22

This reading is another exhortation from 1 Peter very much like the exhortation we saw this year on the Fourth Sunday in Easter. In fact, many of the same themes in this lesson are the themes of two weeks ago.

Once again, the lectionary has edited the verses that introduce this section of 1 Peter, verses 8–12. No doubt, there was again a concern to keep the reading at an appropriate length for public worship. However, there is no reason these introductory verses should not be included, particularly since they do not add appreciably to the length of the reading. They increase our understanding of it, though, and therefore ought to be included however this reading is used.

To reach this lesson, the lectionary has again passed over parts of 1 Peter. In doing so, the lectionary has avoided the more controversial sections of this reading, i.e., the exhortations to husbands and wives. Since those exhortations are not easily incorporated into any of the Easter readings from 1 Peter, and since similar (but less controversial) exhortations from Ephesians do appear in the lectionary, it is easy to understand the omission of these verses. In this case, it is probably best to follow the lectionary here and leave the readings from Ephesians that we will encounter later on to represent these parts of the Christian Scriptures known as the "household codes."

John 14:15–21

This reading resembles its counterpart from last week. It shares some of the same themes, it appears again (in part) on Pentecost (in this case, Pentecost Year C), and it also comes from the same farewell speech in John 14. In fact, this lesson is really a continuous reading that picks up immediately where the reading from last week left off.

Today, though, the lectionary is even clearer about preparing us for Ascension than it was last week. In this reading, Jesus is not only more direct about having to leave the disciples; he is also more specific about the Spirit he will send to them once he has returned to heaven. Both features make this reading appropriate (in the eyes of the lectionary) for this last Sunday before the Ascension.

As was the case last week, preachers should again keep in mind that the lectionary has once more played with John's chronology here. These words were not originally intended as preparation for Ascension. They were not even originally part of a post-resurrection speech, even though the lectionary has placed them here after Easter. Those who preach on this passage will want to keep this in mind.

Ascension Day
(Years A, B, and C)

These readings differ noticeably from all the readings we have seen so far. The first reading is still from Acts, but the epistle lesson is now from Ephesians and the Gospel lesson is now from Luke (the only Gospel to record the Ascension). These lessons are the only Easter readings not intended for use on a Sunday. All appear elsewhere in the lectionary. All are yearly readings. None are semi-continuous.

These readings are also the only Easter readings that are specifically designed for use on two separate occasions. They can be used, of course, on Ascension Day itself. (This is the primary use intended for them by the lectionary.) They can also be used on the Seventh Sunday of Easter. (This gives churches who do not ordinarily observe Ascension Day an opportunity to celebrate the Ascension on a Sunday.)

These readings are highly influenced by the church year. They are also influenced by the chronology and theology of Luke as well. Such influences are to be expected, given the Lukan character of this festival. Nevertheless, we should still be on our guard here and not take either of these influences for granted. We should also be careful not to treat the influence of the church year and the influence of Luke as if they comprised the only Christian interpretation of these passages of scripture.

Acts 1:1–11

This lesson is as much the centerpiece of this set of readings as the Gospel lesson, for both record the event this festival commemorates. This lesson from Acts is so important to the lectionary that it has been included not only here, but also in a longer version in the readings for the Seventh Sunday of Easter this year. This means that the account of the Ascension as it is recorded in Acts will always be read in Year A, whether or not a congregation holds Ascension Day services or not and regardless of which readings for the Seventh Sunday in Easter are used. No other passage of scripture receives this kind of special treatment, except for the readings from Acts appointed for Easter Day and Pentecost Day.

As is often the case, the lectionary has edited even this well-favored lesson to improve its fit within the lectionary's structure. In this case, verses 12–14, which recount the disciples' return to Galilee and the gathering of the Twelve in the upper room, have been omitted from this reading. Whether this reading is used now, or on the Seventh Sunday in Easter, these verses should definitely be restored. Restoring them completes this account more fully and, even more importantly, includes the women disciples who were also gathered with the others in Jerusalem.

Ephesians 1:15–23

This is one of the lectionary's favorite readings from Ephesians. It not only appears every year on Ascension Day, it also appears this year on the Reign of Christ (or Christ the King) Sunday as well. It can appear on the Seventh Sunday of Easter this year, too, in those churches that choose to use these readings then.

This reading was obviously chosen for its final verses, which refer to the work of the ascended Christ. The original focus of these verses, though, was not the Ascension per se. As we have seen before, the reference to the Ascension here serves more as an illustration than as the main point of the passage. The author's primary point is to express thanks for the Ephesians and to briefly introduce issues he will take up later in the letter. This is important for us to remember, particularly if we choose to preach on this reading.

The reading also begins with the phrase, "For that reason...." This is a clear indication that the lectionary has given us only part of the author's thanksgiving—the last part. We saw the first part at Christmas, but since several months have passed since then, it may be a good idea to go back and look at the initial verses of this letter again. The first part of this thanksgiving is important background for today's reading because it gives us the reason for the author's giving thanks in the first place.

Luke 24:44–53

This reading gives us a second version of the Ascension. Like the other readings for today, it is a yearly reading. It can also be used either today or on the Seventh Sunday in Easter.

Those who preach on this lesson will want to note at least two things about this reading. First, this account of the Ascension differs slightly from the version in Acts. It may be tempting to try and harmonize these accounts, but it may be more fruitful to let the Spirit speak through the differences as these readings interact with one another. Second, with both the first lesson and Gospel lesson coming from the pen of Luke, it will again be important to not take the interpretations we find here as if they are the only interpretations found in the Bible.

Seventh Sunday in Easter

With these lessons, we return to a pattern of lessons similar to the pattern found throughout the Easter season. The reading from Acts is again semi-continuous, the epistle lesson is again a semi-continuous reading from 1 Peter, and the Gospel lesson is once more from a farewell speech in John, this time from chapter 17. These readings also reflect a few post-Ascension characteristics. For instance, the reading from Acts now includes verses 1:12–14 to prepare us for Pentecost. A post-Ascension mood is also evident in the Gospel lesson, as Jesus prays for God to watch over his disciples after he has been taken from them.

Because the lectionary gives the congregation the option of using either these readings or the readings for the Ascension Day, those congregations not holding an Ascension Day service may choose to substitute the readings for Ascension Day today. This may not be the best option, however. These readings seem more appropriate for today than the Ascension readings do. They give the congregation the Ascension story, but unlike the readings for Ascension Day itself, they do not break any of the semi-continuous readings characteristic of the Easter season.

Acts 1:6–14

This reading is almost identical to the Acts reading for Ascension Day. It has also been edited on the assumption that the Ascension Day readings have already been used. Verses 1–5 have been omitted because they seemed to specific to Ascension Day itself, and verses 12–14 have been added because they form an effective bridge to Pentecost. If the Acts reading for Ascension Day has been used, this reading is then appropriately used as it is. If the Ascension Day reading has not been used, this lesson should be lengthened to include verses 1–5. This will give the lesson a better introduction.

1 Peter 4:12–14; 5:6–11

This is the final semi-continuous reading from 1 Peter for this Easter. It appears in the lectionary only once. If the readings for Ascension Day are used this Sunday, it will not appear at all.

To create this reading, the lectionary has spliced together two different passages from two separate chapters of 1 Peter. Omitted is a major portion of chapter 4, which continues the exhortation begun in the first part of this reading. Also missing is an exhortation from chapter 5 that addressed elders in the church.

These verses were clearly omitted to make this reading more appropriate for a general audience and to prevent what the lectionary no doubt considered unnecessary repetition. The omission does not appreciably affect the original meaning of the passage, but it should still be acknowledged in some way whenever this reading is used, perhaps by a brief comment between sections of the reading indicating that verses have been omitted.

John 17:1–11

This reading is another post-Easter lesson from the farewell discourses in John. However, more than two chapters have been omitted between the last reading from John on the Sixth Sunday in Easter and this reading. This is a typical pattern for the Gospel lessons appointed for the Seventh Sunday in Easter. In fact, we will see readings from the 17th chapter of John on this same Sunday in all three years (including the last half of this very reading, which will appear here again next year).

The lectionary has lifted this reading from the middle of the high priestly prayer by Jesus. The reading contains part of Jesus' prayer on behalf of his own work and part of his prayer on behalf of his disciples. Again, this editing does not appreciably affect the original meaning of this passage. That the reading has been edited, however, should be acknowledged, again perhaps by a brief statement indicating that this reading is only part of a much longer prayer.

Day of Pentecost

This set of readings resembles the set of readings we saw on Easter Day this year. There are, for example, five separate readings for Pentecost—three principal readings and two alternates. The reading from Acts, which in this case gives this festival its distinctive flavor, has once again been appointed as both a principal first lesson and an alternate epistle lesson in order to assure that is will always be read regardless of whatever other lessons are chosen. There are again two Gospel lessons, this time both from John.

These lessons resemble this year's readings for Easter Day in other ways, too. Most of these lessons have long been associated with this festival both in the tradition and in the lectionary. All the lessons are linked by one overarching theme—the work of the Holy Spirit. And, although there is no official controlling lesson, both the Acts and the John readings act as controlling lessons.

Acts 2:1–21

With this reading, the lectionary returns us to the beginning of a speech we already heard parts of a few weeks ago on the Second and Third Sundays in Easter. Now that it is Pentecost, we are finally given both the proper historical setting of this speech and Peter's introductory remarks to it.

This reading is the first of two accounts that we will hear today concerning the coming of the Holy Spirit. (The second is found in the reading from John 20.) Perhaps because it gives the historical reason for this festival, and perhaps because of the lectionary's Lukan bias as well, the lectionary has given this account in Acts more prominence than the one in John. In fact, the lectionary is structured in such a way that the reading from Acts will always be read on Pentecost, but the reading from John will be read only every third year and may even be omitted in favor of the alternate reading from John 7.

To redress this emphasis, preachers might consider occasionally making the reading from John the focus of the sermon rather than always turning to the expected reading from Acts. Another strategy might be to focus on both accounts together and let their differences illuminate each other. This strategy would clearly be the more ambitious, but it could also prove to be more fruitful as well.

Numbers 11:24–30

This is one of the most interesting readings for Pentecost, for it records what is in many respects an "Old Testament Pentecost." It deserves better than the alternate reading status it has been given. Not only does this reading provide us an exciting story in its own right, it also gives us some important insights into the work of the Holy Spirit. It demonstrates as well that Pentecost Day was certainly not the first time God's Spirit had been active among the people of God.

Preachers should be very careful, however, not to portray the events recorded here as inferior to those recorded in Acts or John. This "Old Testament Pentecost" is quite capable of standing on its own, and should be allowed to do so. In fact, it may even offer us some instructive illumination to both the reading from Acts and the one from John.

Preachers should also resist the temptation to assume this lesson to be a prediction of the day of Pentecost, for while Pentecost may indeed be a fulfillment of Moses' prayer, the relationship between these two passages is not that direct. A more accurate and more productive approach would be to view both the Numbers and the Acts passages as equally powerful examples of God's Spirit at work.

1 Corinthians 12:3b–13

If used as often as it might be, this reading is one of the most repeated of all the Pentecost Day lessons. It appears as an alternate reading here on Pentecost every third year, verses 1–11 appear on the Second Sunday After Epiphany Year C, and verses 12–31 appear on the Third Sunday After Epiphany Year C. Most importantly, this reading is also from one of the most popular passages from 1 Corinthians, often appearing in litanies, prayers, and special liturgies such as baptisms and ordinations. That may be the best way to use it today, too, particularly if the reading from Numbers is chosen as the first reading.

This lesson has also been edited. It begins in the middle of Paul's thought. It even begins in the middle of a sentence. What is missing are verses 1–3a, which were obviously omitted to avoid what the lectionary considered an awkward reference to the Corinthians' spiritual roots in paganism. Even so, those verses also give this reading a needed historical grounding and should be included in the reading, particularly if it is to be preached on.

In the same way, Paul's reflections on the body have also been cut off in mid-thought. This editing is a bit more awkward than the first, but it is not especially detrimental to our understanding of this reading. Preachers who wish to emphasize this part of the reading may want to extend it in order to complete the thought being expressed there.

John 20:19–23

In this reading we have the second of today's two versions of the coming of the Holy Spirit. John's version differs in some significant ways from the version in Acts 2. First, John's "Pentecost" takes place in the evening of Easter Day, not on the festival of Pentecost fifty days later. Second, the disciples are simply gathered together behind closed doors, with no mention of an upper room. Third, Jesus is clearly portrayed as the giver of the Spirit. There is no rush of mighty wind, no tongues of fire, no charismatic utterances. Jesus simply breathes on the disciples and says, "Receive the Holy Spirit."

It is to the lectionary's credit that it has linked this reading to the one in Acts and not hidden the differences between them. By doing so, the lectionary has invited both passages to speak to us and to each other. This dialogue not only gives us more than one view of the Holy Spirit, it also expands our understanding of both this passage and the passage from Acts. Both should be read together whenever possible.

This is a reading we have already seen once before this Easter season. It appeared as part of a longer reading on the Second Sunday in Easter. On that occasion, of course, the emphasis was on the appearance of the risen Christ. Today, with most of the account of that appearance omitted, the emphasis falls instead on the gift of the Spirit, just as we might expect for Pentecost Sunday.

John 7:37–39

This reading is an alternate to the reading from John 20. Like its counterpart from chapter 20, this lesson appears every three years. Unlike its counterpart, however, it does not appear anywhere else in the lectionary.

This reading was no doubt chosen for two common reasons. It offered a choice to those who might be uncomfortable with repeating verses that were read just over a month ago. It also contains references to the lectionary's main theme for today. Both reasons make this an attractive lesson to the lectionary, even though apparently neither reason was enough to commend this lesson as any more than an alternate. This is particularly true when it is seen next to the commanding lesson from John 20.

This is an interesting lesson, however, and worth considering on occasion for preaching. If this passage is preached on, it presents us with two matters for our consideration. First is the context of this reading in the book of John. Because they have been edited, Jesus' words may sound like a nice little encouraging saying, but they are not. Originally these words were spoken in the midst of controversy to a hostile crowd. Second, preachers should also consider that, in choosing this reading over the reading from John 20, they will lose the opportunity to dialogue with John's version of the Spirit's coming.

THE SEASON AFTER
PENTECOST
(ORDINARY TIME)

*W*ith the season after Pentecost, we again enter Ordinary Time, that time in the cycle of the lectionary when the heavy influence of the church year recedes into the background. During this time, even readings from the Hebrew Bible are left relatively free of the year's usual power over them.

Because the church year is not such an important factor this time of year, one could easily assume that these Sundays are without structure. Nothing could be further from the truth. There is a definite structure to the readings of Ordinary Time, even though that structure is often subtle and easily overlooked.

The season after Pentecost begins with Trinity Sunday, one of the few doctrinal holy days in the *Revised Common Lectionary*. Readings for the following Sundays are assigned according to the weeks of the secular calendar. Each set of readings is assigned to a particular week of the year. Readings for Proper 7, for instance, always fall on the Sunday between June 19 and 25 inclusive. In preparation for the close of the year, readings for Proper 27 and 28 always take on an eschatological tone. Ordinary Time then ends with the Reign of Christ (or Christ the King) Sunday, another doctrinal holy day.

Like Epiphany, the length of the season after Pentecost varies with the date of Easter. In this case, it is the beginning rather than the ending point that is most affected by whether Easter is early or late. Generally, readings for the First Sunday after Trinity begin with the reading assigned to whatever week that Sunday happens to fall within (June 5 to June 11 inclusive, for example). If Easter is as early as March 22, however, readings for this season begin instead by first picking up readings for the end of Epiphany, readings that would not have been read because Epiphany was too short. For example, if the date of Easter causes the Sunday after Trinity to fall between May 24 and May 28, the season after Pentecost begins with the readings for Proper 3, the readings as those for the Eighth Sunday After Epiphany.

This subtle and complicated structure presents us with at least one practical problem. If Easter is late, not all the readings appointed for the first part of this season will be read. If Easter is very late, readings for Propers 3 and 4 will be read (as part of Epiphany), but the beginning of the season after Pentecost will be so shortened that Propers 5, 6, and in some cases even 7, will not.

At first glance, this variability seems insignificant. It is not, however, especially when semi-continuous readings are involved, as in the case of these Sundays following Pentecost. For instance, the semi-continuous readings from the Hebrew Scriptures, which can begin as early as the creation story in Genesis chapter 1, in some years could begin as late as the birth of Isaac. Depending on the date of Easter, semi-continuous readings from Romans could begin as late as chapter 6 and the readings from Matthew as late as chapter 10.

To make the best use of these Epiphany readings will take some advance planning. Such planning should take place well before the season of Epiphany begins. It would also begin with consulting a version of the lectionary that lists every possible reading for the Epiphany season, including those that may not be read in any given year. With all the possibilities laid out, readings for the end of Epiphany and readings for the beginning of the season after Pentecost could then be coordinated and choices made about which readings to use and when to use them.

Readings from the Hebrew Scriptures

The *Revised Common Lectionary* lists two readings from the Hebrew Scriptures for each Sunday in the season after Pentecost. The first reading is semi-continuous. For Year A, these semi-continuous readings come from major narratives in Genesis and Exodus. The second reading is specifically linked to the Gospel lesson for the day and can come from any portion of the Hebrew Bible considered appropriate for that particular

Gospel lesson. Although both are listed, only one reading is intended to be read each Sunday.

With two readings from the Hebrew Scriptures to choose from, it might be tempting to choose whichever lesson strikes our fancy on a particular Sunday. The lectionary, however, intends that the preacher choose either the semi-continuous or paired readings at the beginning of Ordinary Time and stick with that choice throughout the season. This is wise counsel. It respects both the integrity of the semi-continuous readings and the theological structure of the readings that have been paired with the Gospel lesson.

Epistle Lessons

The epistle lessons for the season after Pentecost are all semi-continuous. They take us through Romans, Philippians, and then 1 Thessalonians. The only exceptions to this pattern come on All Saints' Day, Thanksgiving Day, and the final Sunday in the season, the Reign of Christ Sunday.

Gospel lessons

Except for All Saints' and Thanksgiving Days, the Gospel lessons for the season after Pentecost are also semi-continuous. All but one, the reading for Thanksgiving, come from Matthew. In fact, many readings are taken from material that is unique to Matthew and occurs nowhere else.

Trinity Sunday

Even though these are the first readings for this part of Ordinary Time, they are really festival readings. All three are linked by the common trinitarian theme for the day. All but one are well-known readings that have been associated with Trinity Sunday for some time. None is part of the semi-continuous readings characteristic of the rest of this season.

These readings are for the first of four festivals that occur during the season after Pentecost. (The others are the Reign of Christ, All Saints', and Thanksgiving.) These festivals are unique in that they are not based on events in the life of Jesus. Instead, they are doctrinal in nature. This is particularly true for today's festival, which is the only festival in the entire church year specifically dedicated to a church doctrine.

All the lessons chosen for today have been influenced by this festival's highly doctrinal nature. The first reading, for instance, does not fit easily into a trinitarian theme. No reading from the Hebrew Scriptures could fit without its original Jewish integrity being compromised. The epistle and Gospel lessons do come from originally Christian literature, but they, too, fit today's festival in only a tangential way. Both appear today only by virtue of two very brief trinitarian formulae.

Genesis 1:1—2:4a

This account of the seven days of creation is a well-known and often used reading. It appears exclusively on festival occasions—today, every year for the Easter Vigil, and next year on the Baptism of Jesus (verses 1:1–5).

Of all the lessons appointed for today, this is the most unusual. Indeed, it is not clear why this reading was chosen for today at all. It obviously does not contain a strong trinitarian theme. It does not have a particularly strong connection to today's Gospel lesson. It also appeared in the lectionary not long ago on the Easter Vigil.

At first glance, it looks as if the lectionary might have intended this reading to represent the first person of the Trinity. It is an excellent picture of God as Creator. Since none of the other lessons follows through with the rest of the pattern, it may be best to treat this lesson as it is and not try too hard to make it fit today's theme. —

2 Corinthians 13:11–13

This reading was chosen for today primarily on the strength of the trinitarian benediction found in the last verse. The reading has long been traditional for Trinity Sunday and does not appear in the lectionary anywhere else.

The trinitarian benediction, however, is only a small part of this reading. It is not the most important part, either. The exhortations in verses 11–12 are more central to Paul's thought. Today, the temptation will be to highlight that benediction. Care should be taken, though, not to read more into these words than is actually there. This will be particularly important for those who intend to preach on this reading.

Matthew 28:16–30

In many respects, this lesson resembles the reading from 2 Corinthians. It has long been traditional for Trinity Sunday, thanks to the trinitarian benediction in the last verse. It also appears in the lectionary only this once. (Since there are no parallels in either Mark or Luke, it does not even appear in another form.)

Most importantly, the trinitarian benediction is again only a small part of Matthew's intent. He was more interested in the act of commissioning itself and the promise that Jesus would be with his followers "to the end of the age." Once again, care should be exercised so that more is not read into the benediction than Matthew intended.

Equally important is the historical and literary setting of this reading, which is not explicit in the reading itself. By not making the setting more clear, the lectionary has again assumed that everyone who hears this reading will know that it is a post-resurrection event and that it is the conclusion to Matthew's Gospel. Many people will already know this, but we cannot assume that everyone will.

Proper 4[1]

Except for the reading from Genesis, all the readings for today also appeared together on the Ninth Sunday After Epiphany this year. Thus, depending on the date of Easter, these lessons might be read at the end of Epiphany, read here at the beginning of Ordinary Time, or not read at all.

Genesis 6:9–22; 7:24; 8:14–19

This lesson is the first in the lectionary's track of semi-continuous readings from the Hebrew Scripture appointed for Year A. As such, it is a independent reading. It was not linked with the other readings for today when they appeared in Epiphany and it is not intended to be linked in any way with any of them now, including the Gospel reading.

This lesson is also the second time in a row that the lectionary has given us a narrative more often associated with the Easter Vigil—the story of Noah and the Flood. Interestingly, the lectionary had to repeat only five verses (8:14–18) in order to give us this second look. Instead, most of this reading is comprised of repetitive pieces from the Noah narrative that were not used when the story of Noah was read for the Easter Vigil.

Even the editing on this passage resembles the editing done when this passage appeared for the Easter Vigil. Again bits and pieces of a much longer account have been cut and pasted together to form a unified reading. Most importantly, however, the account of the Flood's destruction has again been carefully

---

[1] For Propers 1-3, see pp. 88-94.

avoided, thereby denying congregations the opportunity to re-flect on the "shadow side" of this story.

(For more comments on this narrative and its use in the lectionary see the notes for Genesis 7:1–5, 11–18; 8:6–18; 9:8–13 under Easter Vigil, Years A, B, and C.)

Deuteronomy 11:18–21, 26–28

This is the first of the three lessons for today that also ap-peared on the Ninth Sunday After Epiphany. Unlike the other lessons, however, it is not part of any semi-continuous series. Instead it is intentionally linked to the Gospel lesson for today from Matthew. Both lessons emphasize living the teachings of one's faith, not just hearing them.

As we found on the Ninth Sunday After Epiphany, verses 22–25 have been omitted from this reading, most likely to avoid the troublesome image of God commanding the forcible dis-placement of the Canaanite people from their homeland. Again, it may be tempting to follow the lectionary's lead and omit these verses as "politically incorrect," but doing so, particularly if we are thinking of preaching on this passage, may not always be the wisest move. Sometimes passages like this need to be dealt with openly and forthrightly so that their mythic power might not be driven underground only to arise again in unconscious, unhealthier ways.

For more notes on this passage, see comments for the Ninth Sunday After Epiphany Year A.

Romans 1:16–17; 3:22–28 (29–31)

This lesson begins a long series of semi-continuous readings from Romans. It is also listed for the Ninth Sunday After Epiphany, along with the same readings from Deuteronomy and Matthew. In this case, however, since it is intended to be a semi-continuous reading, it is independent of even the Gospel lesson.

Again, the most significant feature about this reading is the way it has been edited by the lectionary. As we saw when this reading appeared in Epiphany, the most important edit-ing is the almost two chapters of Romans that have been omit-ted within the middle of this reading. Today a second editing issue arises. This lesson is the first in a semi-continuous se-ries, but it does not begin with the opening verses of Romans. Instead, both the salutation and thanksgiving sections of the letter have been omitted. (They both already appeared in Ad-vent this year.) Also missing are Paul's words expressing his desire to visit Rome.

For more notes on this passage, see comments for the Ninth Sunday After Epiphany Year A.

Matthew 7:21–29

In this reading Jesus concludes his Sermon and Matthew records how the crowds were astonished at his teaching. The reading appears only this once, but parts of it appear in other forms, usually the one in Luke. Only verses 28–29 are Matthew's own.

Like the readings from Deuteronomy and Romans today, this lesson is also the same as the lesson from Matthew appointed for the Ninth Sunday After Epiphany. Like the readings from Genesis and Romans, it is also a semi-continuous lesson. In this case, however, it may not feel semi-continuous because the last reading in this series was read way back in Epiphany. Not only that, but several teachings from the Sermon on the Mount have been omitted between that last reading and this one. These omitted verses include sayings on giving good gifts, asking and knocking, the wide and narrow gates, and a tree and its fruits. These teachings do not ever appear in the lectionary in another version.

As noted earlier, the lectionary intends this passage to be a controlling lesson for the reading from Deuteronomy. Preachers who choose to use this link should again take care to treat both the Torah and the teachings of Jesus with the respect called for in their respective passages.

For more notes on this passage, see comments for the Ninth Sunday After Epiphany Year A.

Proper 5

Genesis 12:1–9

With this semi-continuous reading, the lectionary has jumped from the story of Noah to the story of Abraham. In doing so, several chapters in Genesis have been omitted. Of these omitted narratives, only the story of the building of the Tower of Babel appears in the lectionary (Pentecost Year C). Others, such as the accounts of the sons of Noah, never appear at all.

This reading, which recounts God's call to Abraham and Abraham's subsequent journey to Canaan, already appeared in part on the Second Sunday in Lent this year. In that setting, God's call was the primary focal point. Today the reading has been expanded to include not only that call, but also the beginning of Abraham's journey.

Both this reading and the epistle lesson for today offer us one of those rare occasions when independent semi-continuous readings intersect with one another. This reading gives us the beginning of Abraham's story and the epistle lesson gives us some of Paul's theological reflections on that story. This intersection is not an intentional link, but it is a useful one. In fact, it is more useful than those links that have been manufactured by the lectionary. Such an intersection does not impose an interpretive structure on the Bible; it allows the Bible to interpret itself. Those intending to preach on either lesson would be well advised to consider using both as readings.

For more comments on this passage, see notes for Genesis 12:1–4a under the Second Sunday in Lent Year A.

Hosea 5:15—6:6

This lesson is one of only four passages from Hosea to be included in the lectionary. Like the others, it appears only this once. It is, however, the only reading from Hosea that represents the prophet's characteristic theme of judgment as a prelude to grace. The other readings have all been carefully chosen to emphasize grace alone.

This lesson has been linked to the Gospel lesson for today by the general theme of healing. In it, Hosea proclaims that God will come to heal those who are truly penitent. In the reading from Matthew, it is Jesus who comes healing. By connecting these passages, the lectionary encourages us to see the first as a prediction of the second. Of course, as we have seen before, things are rarely that simple. A more accurate and more fruitful approach would be to see both passages as equally valid examples of God's healing power at work.

This lesson also begins in a somewhat awkward place. Who is the "I" mentioned in the first verse? the prophet? God? It is unclear from the reading. Where is the "place" also mentioned in that first verse? That is also unclear. Both ambiguities can be easily remedied by starting the reading at verse 6:1 or even 5:8.

Romans 4:13–25

This reading is only a small part of a larger section on Abraham as an example of justification by faith, a section that encompasses all of chapter 4. Nearly all this material appears in the lectionary at some time or other. The only exception is a short segment on Abraham that addresses circumcision along with a proof text from Psalm 32 that does not appear in the lectionary at all.

Interestingly, this reading is most often associated with Lent. Part of it appeared on the Second Sunday in Lent this year and another part will appear on that same Sunday in Lent next year. In both cases, the season of Lent can exert a powerful influence over both our understanding and interpretation of this passage. Here in the season after Pentecost, of course, Lent's influence is not an issue.

Also of particular interest is the intersection of this lesson with today's lesson from Genesis. As we saw in the notes for that lesson, these two readings are not officially linked, but they do relate to each other in potentially valuable ways. Again, preachers would do well to make use of this rare but fortuitous situation.

For more comments on this lesson, see the notes under the Second Sunday in Lent Year A.

Matthew 9:9–13, 18–26

Almost two chapters of Matthew have been omitted since the reading last week. Most of these verses recount healing stories. There is also a story about Jesus, calming a storm and a teaching about the costs of following Jesus. None of these verses appears in the lectionary in any form.

In the first part of this reading, Jesus calls Matthew. These verses have parallels in both Mark and Luke. The Lukan version never appears in the lectionary, but the version from Mark appears on the Eighth Sunday After Epiphany next year. In the second part of the reading, Jesus heals the daughter of a synagogue ruler. These verses also have parallels in both Mark and Luke. Again, the version from Luke does not appear at all, but the Markan version appears next year (Proper 8 Year B).

Between these two sections of the reading, the lectionary has skipped some verses that recount a dispute between Jesus and religious authorities over fasting and other ritual practices. These verses were obviously omitted in an effort to shorten the reading and to focus attention more clearly on the theme of healing.

Proper 6

Genesis 18:1–15 (21:1–7)

To reach this lesson from the lesson from Genesis last week, the lectionary has again skipped several chapters of narrative. Some of these omitted narratives (Abraham and Lot's choosing to go their separate ways, Abraham's rescuing Lot from being killed by Canaanite kings, and the birth of Ishmael) never appear in the lectionary. The sealing of God's covenant with Abraham appears on Proper 14 in Year C and the establishment of circumcision as the sign of the covenant appears next year on the Second Sunday in Lent.

This reading recounts God's promise that Sarah would bear a son in her old age. The alternate verses also recount the birth of that son, Isaac. This is the only time these verses appear in this form in the lectionary. When this reading appears again in Year C on Proper 11, it is linked to the Gospel lesson for that day and the verses that tell about Sarah are omitted.

Between these two narratives is the story of Abraham's pleading on behalf of Sodom and Gomorrah, which appears in the lectionary on Proper 12 Year C. There are also the destruction of Sodom and Gomorrah, a story about the daughters of Lot, and a story about Abraham and Sarah in Egypt. These never appear in the lectionary, most likely in order to avoid some of the more "unseemly" parts of this section of Genesis. In most cases, this is probably just as well.

Exodus 19:2–8a

In this reading, God instructs Moses to tell the people of Israel that if they keep the commandments they will become a holy nation. Moses gathers the elders and the word is spread among all the people. The lectionary has intentionally linked this reading with the Gospel lesson for today in which Jesus, like Moses, calls his disciples together in an effort to spread his message. The lectionary depicts Moses as a model for Jesus centuries later. This may not be one of the lectionary's most inspired uses of typology, but if we resist the temptation to make Jesus into a "better Moses" it is a biblically appropriate one. In fact, Matthew himself may even have had this passage in mind, or at least one similar to it, when he wrote the verses of the Gospel lesson.

Romans 5:1–8

This reading immediately follows the reading from last week. In it, Paul is building on what he said in that previous reading, even though the figure of Abraham, so prominent last Sunday, does not show up today.

Like its predecessor, this reading also appears in the lectionary several times. It appeared once on the Third Sunday in Lent and verses 1–5 will appear on Trinity Sunday in Year C.

Matthew 9:35—10:8 (9–23)

The lectionary has skipped only a few verses between last week's reading and this one. In those omitted verses, Jesus heals two blind men and a man who could not talk. The crowds are astonished and the religious leaders say he did it by the power of the devil. None of these verses ever appears in the lectionary in any form.

The dispute with the religious authorities is particularly interesting and probably ought to be considered for preaching on occasion. It is a perfect example of the human tendency to demonize those we perceive to be our enemies.

In this reading, Jesus goes about the countryside teaching and healing. Because he observes that "the harvest is plentiful, but the laborers are few," he sends the Twelve out on a missionary journey. He tells them to preach, teach, and heal. The alternate verses include some other instructions as well. This particular reading appears in the lectionary only once, but again parts of it can be found in other versions. Jesus' going about the countryside preaching and his having compassion on the crowds both appear again in Ordinary Time next year in their Markan versions. The statements about the harvest and the sending out of the Twelve appear in their Markan form in Ordinary Time next year and in their Lukan form in Ordinary Time Year C. The listing of the disciples has parallels in both Mark and Luke, but they are never used in the lectionary. The additional instructions found in the alternate verses are all Matthew's own and this is the only time they appear in the lectionary at all.

Proper 7

Genesis 21:8–21

This reading recounting the rivalry between Sarah and Hagar begins immediately where the alternate verses left off last week. It appears in the lectionary only once.

It is to the lectionary's credit that this reading appears at all. Passages such as this are usually ignored by the lectionary, which is often reluctant to show a hero or heroine of the faith in an unflattering light. In this case, both major players in this text are treated a bit irreverently. Sarah comes across as a jealous shrew and Abraham as a spineless husband unwilling to stand up for the mother of his firstborn. Including such a reading may tarnish the image we have of these ancestors in the faith, but it also makes them more real to us, and in the process, provides much better material for a sermon.

This is also an unusual reading in that it includes God's promise to Hagar on behalf of her son. Past lectionary tradition has tended to ignore this part of Abraham's story. Including it gives us a truer picture of the scope of God's promise than would reading the story of Isaac alone.

Jeremiah 20:7–13

In this reading, the lectionary gives us a part of Jeremiah's famous complaint to God. The prophet complains that God has deceived him. He even complains that others are plotting against him. The reading ends, however, just before the most well-known part of the passage where Jeremiah actually curses the day he was born. Because of this, those who are intending to preach from this reading may want to lengthen the reading a bit to get the full impact.

The lectionary has linked this reading with the Gospel lesson. In this case, the link is an unusual one. It is not an example of prophecy/fulfillment nor does it make use of typology. Instead, Jesus' words in Matthew seem to be best understood as a commentary on experiences like those of Jeremiah. A life of faithfulness, Jesus says, does not ensure a life of ease. On the contrary, it may mean a life more like the one Jeremiah knew.

The reading appears in the lectionary only this once.

Romans 6:1–11

The lectionary has skipped almost two chapters between last Sunday's reading and this well-known passage. Most of this material concerns Paul's intricate reasoning about the relationship between law and grace. Some of these skipped verses appear elsewhere in the lectionary. Most do not. This reading, in which Paul admonishes his readers to consider themselves dead to sin but alive in Christ, appears not only here, but verses 3–11 also appear every year as the only Easter Vigil epistle lesson.

An epistle is rarely easy to divide into readings. This is especially true for Romans and particularly true for this chapter. Paul's thought here is almost like a seamless garment and resists being torn into pieces. The lectionary has done a commendable job here, but no decisions about where to begin or end this reading would be completely satisfactory. The most important thing is to resist treating these semi-continuous readings in isolation from one another, regardless of where they begin and end. The entire intent of Paul's words here should always be remembered, even as we work with only part of them at a time.

Matthew 10:24–39

If one includes the alternate verses appointed for the reading last week, this reading begins where last week's reading ended. In the lesson for today, Jesus continues to prepare his disciples for their mission. His words include some of his best-known teachings.

Again this reading appears only once, but several of its Lukan parallels appear in Ordinary Time Year C. These include the saying about having not come to bring peace to the world and the saying that disciples must put loyalty to Jesus above loyalty to family. The saying about the student's not being above his teacher, however, is Matthew's alone.

Proper 8

Genesis 22:1–14

This famous reading about Abraham's near sacrifice of his son Isaac follows closely from the end of last week's reading. Only a less important narrative about Abraham and the king of Egypt has been omitted. That narrative does not appear in the lectionary at all.

This reading appears not only here, but also (as we have already seen) every year in the Easter Vigil. In this case, however, the conclusion of the story in verses 15–18 has been omitted. It is unclear why this omission would be made here and not at the Vigil as well. A concern about passage length? A concern about too much repetition? (After all, the promise to Abraham that concludes this narrative is itself a repetition of earlier passages in Genesis. Some of these repetitions also appear in the lectionary, often more than once.) Whatever the reason for their omission, verses 15–18 could easily be added and probably should be.

For more comments on this passage, refer to the notes from the Easter Vigil.

Jeremiah 28:5–9

This is the second reading in a row from the book of Jeremiah to appear among the readings from the Hebrew Scriptures that have been specifically linked to their respective Gospel lessons. In this case, both passages are linked by a common interest in the role of the prophet. In this reading, Jeremiah's concern is false prophets, whereas Matthew's concern is the proper honor due to those like Jesus, who hold the prophetic office. The link is a bit more tenuous than usual, but still quite viable for preaching.

Again, one of the most significant features of this reading is its lack of historical or literary context. It begins in the middle of a much longer story with little indication about what is going on here or why. Without this context, the reading comes across as somewhat disjointed and confusing. Expanding the reading, perhaps to 28:1–17, would give a more complete picture.

This is the only time this reading appears in the lectionary cycle.

Romans 6:12–23

In this reading, Paul continues his reflections on the meaning of sin and grace in the Christian life. The reading begins immediately where the reading from last week left off. It appears in the lectionary only this once.

Again, the lectionary compilers have been faced with some difficult editorial decisions here. To their credit, they have respected the integrity of Paul's argument by choosing to make this reading continuous with the reading before it. In fact, these two readings are so interconnected it may be wise to always use both whenever they appear.

Matthew 10:40–42

In this short reading, Mark's Jesus continues his instructions before sending the Twelve on their missionary journey. These instructions are continuous to the ones last week. They are concerned about receiving and being received as a minister. The reading in this version appears in the lectionary only this once, but again, parallels to these verses also appear. The Lukan form of verse 40 appears in the reading for Proper 9 Year C and the Markan form of verse 42 appears in that same year as an alternate verse on Transfiguration Sunday.

Proper 9

Genesis 24:34–38, 42–49, 58–67

Between the reading last week and this reading, the lectionary has skipped almost two chapters of Genesis. These chapters include the story of Sarah's death and the beginning of the story we pick up here, the story of Rebekah and Isaac. The part we have missed is the account of Abraham's sending his servant to his homeland to find a suitable wife for Isaac. This beginning account is a fairly long one and was probably omitted because of its length. This is not a problem, however, because most of the information in it is hinted at in the reading itself.

The lectionary has also edited several verses from the middle of this passage. These verses record a wish for Isaac and the payment of the bride price for Rebekah. Again, this omission was undoubtedly done to shorten the reading. Here, too, it does not appreciably affect the reading.

This lesson appears in the lectionary only this once.

Zechariah 9:9–12

This reading about the humble king riding into Jerusalem on a donkey has often been linked to Jesus' triumphal entry into Jerusalem. It still remains in many liturgies. The *Revised Common Lectionary*, however, has shown great restraint and linked it instead to the Gospel lesson for today. That link is not as obvious as the traditional one, but it may prove far more fruitful because it is so unexpected.

This reading is also the only reading in the entire lectionary from Zechariah. It appears only this one time.

Romans 7:15–25a

To reach this lesson, the lectionary has again omitted a sizable number of verses, none of which ever appear in the lectionary. For the most part, this is understandable. Most of the omitted verses either use illustrations that no longer work for modern readers or employ a style of reasoning most would find difficult to follow.

The reading itself is both relevant and understandable, even today. It reflects Paul's struggle to do what he knows is right in spite of his natural inclination to do otherwise. In many respects, it is a cornerstone in Paul's theology. It is also the passage that Martin Luther once said changed his life. Interestingly, this is the only time it appears in the entire lectionary.

Matthew 11:16–19, 25–30

Several verses have been skipped since the reading last week. There was a passage about John the Baptist, an unusual saying about the realm of God coming violently, and a second passage on John the Baptist that described him as the last of the great prophets. Only the first of the passages on the Baptist is ever included in the lectionary. It appeared this year in Advent.

In this reading, which appears in the lectionary only this once, Jesus reflects on his recent encounter with some religious authorities. In the first part of the reading, he talks about the way those authorities had treated John. In the second part, he talks about God's giving wisdom to the unimportant people of the world instead of to its authorities. Both passages have Lukan parallels, none of which are used by the lectionary. The reading concludes with some of Matthew's own material in which Jesus proclaims that his "yoke was easy and his burden light."

Again, one of the most interesting features of this reading is what does not appear—in this case, verses 20–24. These verses contain a string of condemnations against some cities that had not been receptive to Jesus' teaching. Similar condemnations also appear in Luke. Neither appear in the lectionary, however, and it is not hard to understand why. They include some strong words that we are not accustomed to hearing from the lips of Jesus. Even so, we ought not dismiss these uncomfortable words too easily. They not only give us a fuller picture of Jesus' character, they also offer still another biblical counter to the popular misconception that the sin of Sodom and Gomorrah was sexual immorality.

Proper 10

Genesis 25:19–34

Between this reading and the reading for last week, only a few verses have been passed over. These recount the death of Abraham and some genealogy. None ever appear in the lectionary.

This well-known reading appears only once. It is also the only reading in the lectionary that tells us about the rivalry between Jacob and his brother Esau. Passages that record this rivalry do not even appear in later semi-continuous readings from the story of Jacob. Those who preach on this passage, however, would do well to keep these later episodes (such as Jacob stealing Esau's blessing and the brother's eventual reconciliation) in mind.

Isaiah 55:10–13

In this well-known reading, God's word is described as going forth and tenaciously doing its work until it has accomplished the mission for which it had been sent. Unlike most readings during this time of year, this lesson appears in the lectionary several times. We have already seen it once during the Easter Vigil and we will see it there again in both Years B and C. We will also see this reading in Year C on the Eighth Sunday After Epiphany.

Today, these verses have been specifically linked to the parable of the sower found in the Gospel lesson from Matthew. This is a particularly interesting link because, contrary to the picture of God's word in Isaiah, Jesus allows for a number of times when the Word did not take root or accomplish what it had been sent forth to do.

Romans 8:1–11

This reading takes up immediately from where the reading for last week ended. Like the reading before it, it continues Paul's reflections on sin, law, grace, and the life of the Spirit. The lesson is not quite as well known as its predecessor, even though it appears in the lectionary twice—once already this year on the Fifth Sunday in Lent and then again here in Ordinary Time.

Matthew 13:1–9, 18–23

Once again, the lectionary has skipped several passages in Matthew to arrive at this reading. There is a quote from the Hebrew Scriptures about God's chosen servant, Jesus is accused of being the devil, his mother and brothers come for him, and he tells the religious leaders that his only sign to them will be the sign of Jonah. None of this material appears in the lectionary from Matthew, but Mark's version of both the accusation passage and the passage about Jesus' mother and brothers appear next year in Ordinary Time.

In this reading, which appears in the lectionary only this once, we enter a section of Matthew's Gospel characterized by parables. Today, the lectionary gives us both the parable of the sower and its interpretation. Both have parallels in Mark and Luke but neither appears in the lectionary.

Between the parable and its interpretation, Matthew inserted some sayings about teaching in parables and the blessedness of the disciples who hear them. These verses never appear in the lectionary in any form, even though they have parallels in both Mark and Luke. This omission was probably made in order to shorten the passage and to focus attention on the parable of the sower itself. Again, verses like these should not be too easily dismissed. In fact, preachers who choose to include them in the reading may even find they add an important depth to the parable it might not have otherwise.

Proper 11

Genesis 28:10–19a

This lesson recounts Jacob's famous dream about the ladder reaching into heaven. Like other lessons in this section of this series of semi-continuous readings from Genesis, it appears in the lectionary only once.

Several chapters have been omitted since the reading last week. Those chapters contain some important background for the reading today. In a similar way, verses 19b–22, which mention this historical background, have also been omitted. In these omitted verses we find that Jacob is not on just any journey when he has his dream. He has just stolen Esau's blessing and is now fleeing his brother's wrath.

Wisdom 12:13, 16–19

This reading is the first of two readings from the Hebrew Scriptures that have been linked to the Gospel lesson for today. In it, the author defends God's justice and celebrates God's mercy. This is the only time it appears in the lectionary.

The lectionary has linked this reading to today's Gospel lesson in an interesting way. Rather than the usual prophecy/fulfillment, thematic, or typological link, the lectionary has given us a theological link instead. In this case, this reading from the Wisdom of Solomon is meant to serve as theological commentary on the parable of the weeds found in the Gospel lesson. Preachers would do well to make use of such an opportunity while they can.

The lectionary has also edited this reading and omitted verses 14–15. These verses are somewhat obscure, which is no doubt why they were omitted. In this particular situation, what to do with these verses is largely a judgment call. Omitting them does not appreciably affect the reading. Restoring them does not appreciably improve it.

Isaiah 44:6–8

This reading is a canonical alternate to the reading from Wisdom. In it, God asserts divine prerogative by offering a challenge to anyone who would even think of becoming a rival. The reading comes from one of the lectionary's favorite parts of Isaiah, but it appears in the lectionary only this once.

According to the usual pattern in the lectionary, this lesson is supposed to be linked to the Gospel lesson from Matthew. If that is the case, the link is one of the weakest we have seen so far this year.

Romans 8:12–25

This reading is similar to the last two readings from Romans. It is another continuous reading that begins where the reading from last week ended. It is also fairly well known. Unlike its predecessors, though, parts of this lesson appear several times in the lectionary. Not only does it appear here, but verses 12–17 also appear next year on Trinity Sunday and verses 14–17 appear in an alternate reading for Pentecost Sunday Year C.

This reading is also another example of the lectionary's having to make difficult decisions about when to begin and end a reading. Preachers should feel free to either follow the lectionary's divisions or make their own. Those who decide to make their own divisions should remember to keep the meaning of the entire text in mind in doing so. They should also remember that next Sunday's reading from Romans is a continuous reading and will therefore be affected by decisions made today.

Matthew 13:24–30, 36–43

This reading is continuous to the reading from last week and resembles it in several ways. First, it is another parable with an agricultural setting. Second, both the parable and its interpretation are included, with the verses in between omitted. Third, it also appears in the lectionary only this one time.

Two features, however, set this reading apart from its predecessor. One, none of these verses have parallels in either Mark or Luke. They are all Matthew's own material. Two, those verses that have been omitted are not omitted from the lectionary entirely, but appear in the reading from Matthew next Sunday. Acknowledging this displacement is not as imperative here as it is in many other cases, but it would probably help the congregation.

Proper 12

Genesis 29:15–28

This reading continues the lectionary's semi-continuous readings from the life of Jacob and recounts his marriage to Rachel and Leah. Only the story of Jacob meeting Laban has been skipped since the reading last week. This reading appears in the lectionary only this once.

The most notable feature of this reading is the omission of verses 29–30. These verses, which describe Jacob's preference for Rachel, were undoubtedly edited from the reading because they do not reflect very well on the the famous patriarch. Jacob's preference for Rachel, however, is an important (and potentially fruitful) detail, particularly for those choosing to preach on this passage. It not only reveals Jacob for the flawed human being he must have been, but it also reveals the flaws of the patriarchal system under which he and his wives were living.

1 Kings 3:5–12

This lesson recounts the way in which Solomon received his famous wisdom. It appears both here and next year for Proper 15 when it is part of a series of semi-continuous readings.

Two features of this lesson commend themselves to our attention. The first is the link the lectionary has made between this reading and the Gospel lesson for today. The link is with only part of the Gospel lesson, the parable of the hidden treasure and the parable of the pearl of great price. Both offer fruitful commentary on the story of Solomon. The other parables in the Gospel lesson make no such connection.

Second, the lectionary has omitted the concluding verses of this story, verses 13–15. The first two verses are included when this passage appears in the lectionary again next year. The final verse, in which Solomon awakes and realizes the whole episode was a dream, never appears in the lectionary at all. There is no good reason why these verses should not be added to this reading, particularly since they conclude the story while not appreciably adding to its length.

Romans 8:26–39

In this reading, Paul's reflections on the work of grace in the Christian life reach their zenith. The reading resembles its predecessors in several ways. It is the fourth continuous reading from Romans in this series. It is a well-known passage. It also appears in the lectionary more than once. (It appears in full here and in part as an alternate reading next year on Pentecost.)

Matthew 13:31–33, 44–52

This lesson not only continues from where the reading last week ended, it also picks up several verses that had been omitted from that reading. Those verses include two growth parables: the parable of the mustard seed and the parable of the yeast. The first has parallels in both Mark and Luke but only the Markan version also appears in the lectionary (Proper 6 Year B). The second has only a Lukan parallel, which is not included in the lectionary, either. The parables that comprise the remainder of the reading are all Matthew's own. They appear nowhere else in the lectionary. They also conclude this "parable" section of Matthew's Gospel.

Proper 13

Genesis 32:22–31

This reading, too, is a well-known story from the life of Jacob, even though it appears in the lectionary only twice. It is found both here in Ordinary Time Year A and again as a linked reading for Proper 24 in Year C.

The lectionary has omitted several stories in the Jacob narrative since the reading last week. These include the account of the rivalry between Jacob's children, a story about Jacob's flocks increasing faster than the flocks of Laban, and a story about Jacob's tricking Laban out of his best sheep. None of these tales appears in the lectionary at all.

Once again, important and useful background information has been left out by the lectionary. Although the reading itself only hints at it, Jacob again is on the run, this time from Laban. On the night he has his famous dream, he has an angry Laban fast approaching from one side and an equally angry brother on the other. It's no wonder his dreams were disturbed and troubled. It also makes his experience that night more real and accessible to ordinary folks sitting in the pews.

Isaiah 55:1–5

In this lesson, God invites the hungry to come and eat food that will truly satisfy and the thirsty to come and drink water that will never run out. It is another of the few lessons during Ordinary Time that is included in the lectionary more than once. It not only appears here, it also appears every year as part of a longer reading for the Easter Vigil and as part of the reading for the Third Sunday in Lent Year C.

Today the lectionary has linked these verses with the feeding of the five thousand. Unlike the links we have seen the past few weeks, this link is a very strong one. In fact, it is so strong that one might be tempted to see this passage as a prediction of the events recorded in the Gospel lesson. Strictly speaking, it is not. Both passages, however, do speak of God as the source of that which is most satisfying in life.

Romans 9:1–5

This reading is still another continuous reading from Romans. Unlike the other readings in this series, it is not especially well known, and appears in the lectionary only this once.

This is an important reading because it helps counter popular misconceptions about Paul's thoughts on the relationship between law and grace and the relationship between the people of Israel and the people of the church. It is well worth our attention, even if we have not emphasized any readings from Romans up to this point.

Matthew 14:13–21

The lectionary has again skipped several verses between this reading and the one last week. These include a passage on prophets being without honor in their own country and an account of the beheading of John the Baptist. Both passages appear during Ordinary Time next year in their Markan parallels (Propers 9 and 10).

In the reading today, we are given Matthew's version of the feeding of the five thousand. This is the only time this reading appears in the lectionary. However, as is often the case, this same story also appears in similar form in both Mark and Luke. Only the Markan version, however, is included in the lectionary. It appears next year on Proper 11.

Proper 14

Genesis 37:1–4, 12–28

To reach this lesson from the reading last week, the lectionary has skipped nearly five chapters. Some of these omitted stories are ones we would have expected to appear in the lectionary, but they do not. These include the reconciliation of Jacob and Esau, God's changing Jacob's name to Israel, and a confirmation of God's promise to Jacob and his descendants. Most of the other omitted verses contain primarily genealogies and their omission is more understandable.

One omission is particularly noteworthy—the rape of Jacob's daughter Dinah. This passage was obviously omitted because, according to the standards of the lectionary, it was not edifying enough. By any standards, it is certainly not a comfortable passage to read, hear, or preach on. At the same time, omitting this passage and pretending that it does not exist effectively silences this woman who has already clearly suffered enough. Hers is not a pleasant story, but it illustrates the reality many women still face today. That alone is enough reason to not let this passage go by unnoticed.

The reading itself is the first of two readings from the story of Joseph. It recounts Jacob's preference for Joseph, Jacob's giving Joseph a coat of many colors, the jealousy that gift engendered in Joseph's brothers, and their plot to sell him into slavery. It appears only this once.

Again, the most significant feature about this reading is what is not included. Joseph's famous dreams predicting that he would one day rule over his brothers, for instance, are missing. So is the story the brothers told their father when they returned to him without Joseph along with them. Both omissions were undoubtedly made in a effort to shorten the reading. Preachers who would like to spend more time with the Joseph story might consider restoring these omitted verses and dividing this reading into two separate readings. Verses 1–11 could be read this Sunday and 12–36 next Sunday. All the subsequent semi-continuous readings could then be shifted back one Sunday for the remainder of Ordinary Time. Those who are especially interested in Joseph might even consider adding a third reading, perhaps Genesis 41:1–16, 25–40. Such a reading would include another important part of the Joseph story omitted by the lectionary, his interpretation of Pharaoh's dreams.

1 Kings 19:9–18

For this linked reading, the lectionary has taken us again to 1 Kings. In this reading, God appears to the prophet Elijah, who has been hiding in a cave to escape the wrath of Queen Jezebel. These verses appear in the lectionary not only today, but also in part on consecutive Sundays in Year C, once as part of a series of semi-continuous readings and once as a reading linked to the Gospel lesson for the day.

Today the lectionary intends this lesson to be linked to the story of Jesus walking on water and Peter's subsequent failure to do so as well. This is not an especially strong link, but it does have possibilities. Like most of us, both Elijah and Peter had times when their faith needed a boost.

One of the most significant features of this reading, however, is that the lectionary has again omitted verses that might have set the historical and literary context for this lesson. Elijah is not just sitting in the cave, he is hiding there because he is afraid. This is important information, particularly if we are intending to preach on this reading.

Romans 10:5–15

Since the reading from last week, the lectionary has skipped almost an entire chapter in Romans. Most of these verses contain tightly reasoned arguments to bolster Paul's view on law, grace, Israel, and the church. Since most of this reasoning is done in a style of midrash that is not likely to be familiar to many churchgoers, the lectionary has chosen to omit them completely.

In this reading, Paul continues his argument that both Jew and Gentile are justified by faith. This reading begins awkwardly, though, in the middle of that long section of argument that began shortly after the reading last week. It becomes less awkward if efforts are made to connect this reading with the readings preceding it.

Like many readings from this series of semi-continuous lessons from Romans, this reading appears in part elsewhere in the lectionary. In this case, verses 8b–13 will appear again on the First Sunday in Lent Year C.

Matthew 14:22–33

This account of Jesus' walking on the water and Peter's attempt to do the same is a continuous reading. It begins immediately where the reading for last week ended. It is also a well-known and often-preached passage. Given its popularity, one might expect the lectionary to use this reading more than once. Surprisingly, it appears in the lectionary only this one time. Its Markan parallel isn't included at all.

Those who feel inclined to preach on this passage should probably do so now because the opportunity will not present itself again for another three years. Those who have been specifically following the semi-continuous readings from either Genesis or Romans, however, might want to consider instead preaching on Mark's version of this same story next year on Proper 11. The walking on water episode has been omitted from the middle of the reading for that day, but it could easily be restored and probably should be.

Proper 15

Genesis 45:1–15

Almost two chapters in Joseph's story have been omitted since the reading from last week. In fact, so much of the Joseph narrative is missing that it would be difficult to connect this reading with the reading before it unless one were already familiar with Joseph's story. Clearly the lectionary assumes that this is the case. Such an assumption may not be accurate, however, particularly in this age of general biblical illiteracy. Again, preachers may wish to consider creating one or two more lessons from this story and shifting subsequent semi-continuous readings to make room for them.

This reading, which recounts Joseph making himself known to his estranged brothers, also appears in part on the Seventh Sunday After Epiphany Year C.

Isaiah 56:1, 6–8

In this lesson, God speaks through the prophet Isaiah to proclaim a message of radical inclusiveness. Anyone, God says, who does justice and obeys the commandments will be welcomed in Zion. God's house is to be a house of prayer for all nations, not just Israel.

Unfortunately, the lectionary has chosen to omit some of the most radical verses, verses 2–5. In those verses God widens the circle even further by also including both foreigners and eunuchs, people originally excluded from the covenant. These verses are so powerful that they clearly deserve to be restored to the reading even if it is not the primary text for the sermon.

This lesson is also a perfect lesson for pairing with the Gospel lesson for today. Not only does such a link appropriately strengthen the theme of inclusiveness found in both passages, it also counters the common assumption that the Christian concept of God is automatically more inclusive than the picture of God found in the Hebrew Scriptures. In fact, this lesson is an even more straightforward statement of the wideness of God's love than is Jesus' encounter with the Syrophoenician woman.

This is the only time this lesson appears in the entire three-year cycle of the lectionary.

Romans 11:1–2a, 29–32

Between the reading last week and this one, the lectionary has again omitted several verses of Paul's tightly reasoned midrash. His particular concern in those verses was the reason why his own people had rejected Jesus. Given how easily Paul's words could be misinterpreted, this omission is understandable.

In the reading itself, Paul continues his reflections. In the first part of this reading, Paul argues that God did not reject Israel, even though they rejected Jesus. In the last part of the reading, Paul goes on to explain why he believed that was so. Through Israel's act of rejection, he said, God was able to offer salvation to the Gentiles, too. This is only a small part of Paul's reflections, however. The lectionary has omitted many of his words here, verses 2b–28 to be exact, probably for the same reasons it did not give us those earlier verses. Both were seen as too tightly reasoned and too easily misinterpreted. If this reading is merely read, these verses are probably best skipped. If, on the other hand, this reading to be the basis of a sermon, consideration should be given to restoring them, provided, of course, that the preacher is willing to deal with the subtleties involved in these verses from both a Christian *and* a Jewish perspective.

Also missing from this reading is the doxology with which Paul ended his arguments. This doxology is not long and is easily put back into the reading, particularly if verses 2b–28 are not restored as well.

Today is also the only time this reading appears in the lectionary.

Matthew 15: (10–20) 21–28

This lesson begins with alternate verses that recount the end of a discussion Jesus had with some Pharisees about ritual cleanliness. The lesson itself is the story of Jesus' encounter with the Syrophoenician woman. At first, these two passages might seem to be totally unrelated. However, both Matthew (and Mark before him) knew that most observant Jews of the day (and that includes Jesus and most of his followers) would have considered the woman in the story "unclean." Seen in that light, it is clear that both Matthew and Mark have put her story here as an illustration of the teaching Jesus had just finished giving. To receive the full benefit of this reading, then, it is probably best to include the alternate verses. Including the alternate verses is particularly important if this reading is to be the basis of a sermon.

Also, to reach this passage from the passage last week, the lectionary has again skipped several verses of Matthew, all of which appear in their Markan form next year during Ordinary Time (Proper 11 and Proper 17). Like most of the readings in this series, this reading appears in the lectionary only this once. Its Markan parallels, however, also appear. The alternate verses on ritual cleanliness are read next year on Proper 17 and the verses about the Syrophoenician woman appear on Proper 18.

Proper 16

Exodus 1:8—2:10

To reach this lesson, the lectionary has skipped over a great deal of biblical history—Jacob's family settling in Egypt, the death of Jacob, the brothers' anxiety about the possibility that Joseph might now retaliate against them for having sold him into slavery, and Joseph's continued concern for his brothers until his death. Also omitted is the introduction to the book of Exodus, the next volume in the saga of the biblical patriarchs. Since most of this history has never been considered of great importance to the Christian tradition, none of it ever appears in the lectionary.

This reading, which appears only this once, recounts the beginning of the oppression in Egypt, the birth of Moses, and his subsequent rescue from the hands of Pharaoh. It begins a long series of semi-continuous readings from the life of Moses. In fact, this is the longest series of semi-continuous readings from a single First Testament narrative to appear in the lectionary. The reading itself is also unusually long. This not only reflects the fact that Moses is a central character in the Hebrew Bible, it also reveals the lectionary's preference for the figure of Moses as well.

Isaiah 51:1-6

In this reading God again speaks through the prophet Isaiah to proclaim the coming restoration of the exiled people of Israel. This is the only time this lesson appears among the official readings, even though it comes from a part of Isaiah that is very popular with the lectionary.

The oracle from which this reading was taken is a lengthy one, so the lectionary has included only the first part of it. If this lesson is only to be read in worship as one lesson among others, this condensation is not a major problem. Preachers who are preparing a sermon on this reading, however, would do well to study the entire oracle. It includes some wonderfully comforting words about not fearing even those we consider to be our enemies.

According to the structure of the lectionary, this reading is intended to be linked to Peter's confession in the Gospel lesson for today. This is a very weak link at best and preachers are probably better off not emphasizing it. In this case, each reading is more effective on its own.

Romans 12:1-8

Only a few verses separate this reading from the reading last week. If Paul's doxology was added last week, this lesson begins immediately where the reading from last week would have ended.

In today's reading, Paul follows up his doxology with several exhortations to his readers. These exhortations are well known in Christian tradition, largely through their use in the liturgy. In the lectionary, however, they appear only this once.

Matthew 16:13-20

The lectionary has omitted almost two chapters of Matthew between the reading from last week and this one. These verses include the feeding of the four thousand, the demand for a sign, and a warning against the leaven of the Pharisees. All these verses have parallels in either Mark or Luke. Except for two verses from Luke, none of these parallels are included in the lectionary.

This reading, which recounts Peter's famous confession of faith in Caesarea Philippi, appears only this once. It has parallels in both Mark and Luke, but in this case only the Markan parallel is included in the lectionary (next year on Proper 9).

Proper 17

Exodus 3:1–15

Only a chapter or so of Exodus has been omitted between the reading last week and this one, but in this case, this omission is more significant. The lectionary has again chosen to omit verses that show a biblical hero or heroine in a bad light. In this case, the lectionary takes us directly from Moses' infancy to his adult encounter with God at the burning bush, completely bypassing his murder of the Egyptian overseer and his subsequent flight into the wilderness. While this omission is understandable (by its very nature, the lectionary cannot include everything), in this instance such an omission denies the congregation a glimpse into the complexity of Moses' character. Instead, Moses comes across as larger than life and virtually unapproachable to ordinary believers in the pews.

This "larger-than-life" portrait of Moses is further encouraged by the lectionary's cutting off the rest of the conversation between God and Moses that began in verse 4. In these later verses, which never appear in the lectionary anywhere, Moses is shown to be increasingly uncertain about his ability to do what God has asked of him. He gives several excuses, hoping that God might then decide to choose someone else. These verses, too, contribute to our understanding of the "real" Moses. They also contain some rich homiletical material.

Jeremiah 15:15–21

This is another complaint on the part of the prophet Jeremiah. It is similar to the one we saw on Proper 7 of this year. It is included in the lectionary only this once.

Once again the lectionary has omitted some important historical and literary context from a reading. In this case, the missing context is the reason why Jeremiah is suffering in the first place. He is suffering because he has spoken the unpleasant truth about how things were going in Israel and is now being harassed for it. This should probably be shared with the congregation in one way or another, particularly since they will not have had previous readings from Jeremiah that might have acquainted them with his story.

The lectionary has linked this passage with the Passion prediction in today's Gospel lesson. Unlike the link last week, this pairing is very strong, with Jeremiah serving as a "type" for the later figure of Jesus. Both suffer for doing God's will.

Romans 12:9–21

This reading is a continuous reading and completes the exhortations begun in the reading last week. It, too, is often used in liturgies and prayers, but it is not quite as well known as its predecessor. Except for the festival of Visitation, it does not appear in the lectionary again.

Matthew 16:21–28

In this reading, which picks up where the reading from last week left off, Jesus continues the conversation begun by Peter's confession. Again, while this particular lesson appears in the lectionary only this one time, its parallel from Mark appears next year on Proper 19. When it appears then, both the accounts of Peter's confession and the conversation afterward are short enough to appear in the same reading. There is also a parallel to this passage in Luke, but it is not included in the lectionary.

Proper 18

Exodus 12:1–14

In this passage, God gives Moses specific instructions about preparing for that first Passover night. The lectionary obviously intends for it to represent the Passover portion of the Moses narrative. In doing so, the lectionary has omitted a large part of this story, including the confrontation with Pharaoh, the escalation of Pharaoh's oppression, the ten plagues, and most importantly the account of the Passover and Exodus themselves. Also omitted is a very short but significant story about Moses' wife, Zipporah, who breaks a very long tradition by acting as head of the household and circumcising her own son in a ritual to save Moses (Exodus 4:24–26). Not only is this the first and only time in the Hebrew Scriptures that a woman has been recorded as taking on such an important cultic role, it is the second time in his life that Moses has been saved from death by a woman.

Again, preachers might consider creating one or two additional readings in order to include some of these omitted verses. This is a particularly attractive option if additional readings were not added to the highly edited Joseph narrative earlier. Churches that already used most of this reading for Holy Thursday could even substitute one of those new additional readings for this reading, too. Exodus 12:17–39, for example, would be an excellent choice for such a substitution. It includes important pieces of the narrative that otherwise would not be heard, and it does so without repeating verses that have already been included in the lectionary.

Ezekiel 33:7–11

In this lesson, Ezekiel is commissioned to watch over Israel. He is told to warn the wicked in particular. If he doesn't, God says, Ezekiel himself will be held accountable. These verses are from the lectionary's favorite part of the book of Ezekiel. They are also well-known verses in some Christian circles and are often quoted. Even so, this is the only time they appear in the lectionary.

The link the lectionary has made between this passage and the Gospel lesson for today is particularly interesting. Both readings are influenced by the presence of the other. Next to this lesson from Ezekiel, Matthew's words on the proper steps for confronting another person take on a more evangelistic tone. Next to the lesson from Matthew, these words from Ezekiel take on a more down-to-earth, practical tone.

Romans 13:8–14

In this reading, Paul continues his exhortations, this time focusing on "fulfilling the law of love" while we await the coming of Jesus. The last part of this reading may sound familiar. It appeared earlier this year on the First Sunday in Advent (Romans 13:11–14). However, since the focus is not as much on the coming of Christ (as would be the case in Advent), the lectionary has given us more of Paul's general exhortations in this reading than when it appeared earlier in the year.

To reach this reading, the lectionary has skipped an even more familiar passage than the reading itself—Paul's reflections on the relationship between the Christian and worldly authority. Those reflections never appear in the lectionary at all, even though they are often quoted in discussions about the church's role in the political realm. It is not an easy passage to interpret objectively. However, since this passage plays such an important part in the church's political thought, it may be important on occasion to purposely tackle it in a sermon. Recognizing that Paul's thought here often evokes strong emotions, it will also be important for us to be very clear about our own biases regarding the church's role in politics if we do choose to preach on it.

Matthew 18:15–20

The lectionary has also skipped several chapters of text to arrive at this lesson from the lesson last week. Most of these omitted verses have parallels in either Mark, Luke, or both. Many of these parallels are also included in the lectionary. In the case of the story of the Transfiguration, of course, all three parallels appear.

This reading, in which Jesus explains what to do if someone sins against you, is unique to Matthew. It appears in the lectionary only this once.

Proper 19

Exodus 14:19–31

The reading today brings us to the crossing of the Red Sea. On the way, the lectionary has omitted almost two chapters of Exodus. As we saw last week, some of these omitted verses, such as the ones recounting the Passover and Exodus, are important parts of the narrative and should be read if at all possible. Of particular concern today are the verses that introduce this reading. These verses were undoubtedly omitted in an effort to shorten the reading and avoid repeating too many verses that had appeared previously in the Easter Vigil. Without these introductory verses, however, listeners could easily find themselves well into the reading before they become oriented to where they are in the larger Passover/Exodus narrative.

Preachers could give the lesson a better introduction in at least two ways. If this reading was not used in the Easter Vigil, using the Vigil form of this reading (Exodus 14:10–31) would provide the congregation with a much better starting point. If this reading was used for the Vigil, a brief one-sentence introduction to the reading would also serve the same purpose.

Genesis 50:15–21

This lesson is from the very end of the Joseph narrative, when his father, Jacob, has died and Joseph once again needs to reassure his anxious brothers that he has forgiven them. These verses appear in the lectionary only this one time.

In many respects, reading this lesson is like reading the last page of a novel first. If you already know the story, you're fine. If you don't, that last page can be pretty confusing. In choosing this lesson without introducing it with other lessons from the life of Joseph, the lectionary has assumed that everyone hearing it will already know what has happened up to this point. Today, this is not an assumption we can safely make. Even if this lesson is only read and not preached, it is probably best to preface it with a brief summary of why the brothers are so anxious.

Including the historical and literary background to this lesson also strengthens the link the lectionary has made between this passage and the Gospel lesson for today. In the reading from Matthew, Jesus teaches about forgiveness. In this lesson, we see Joseph showing that very same kind of forgiveness to brothers who had once tried to kill him.

Romans 14:1–12

This reading is continuous to the reading from last week. In it, Paul sharpens the focus of his exhortations and concentrates primarily on the community of believers itself. In fact, this reading begins a sizable passage on how best to relate to fellow believers, particularly weaker ones. To fully appreciate Paul's thinking here, the reading should probably be lengthened to also include verse 13, or even better, verses 13–18.

This is the only time this reading appears in the lectionary. It is also the last of these semi-continuous readings from Romans.

Matthew 18:21–25

This lesson is also a continuous lesson and begins where the reading from last week ended. In today's reading, Matthew builds upon the teachings we heard a week ago by turning to the theme of forgiveness. The reading begins with a question by Peter and ends with the parable of the unmerciful servant, which Jesus apparently told in answer to Peter's inquiry. Neither the question nor the parable has parallels in other canonical Gospels. Neither appears in the lectionary except this one time.

Proper 20

Exodus 16:2-15

In this lesson, the people of Israel become hungry as they wander in the desert following their crossing of the Red Sea. God responds to their cries by providing them manna to eat. To reach this part of the story, nearly two chapters of Exodus have been passed over since the reading last week. Most of these verses (the songs of Moses and Miriam) have already appeared in the lectionary for the Easter Vigil. One story never appears in the lectionary at all, an account of Moses' making some brackish water safe to drink.

The lectionary has once again ended a reading before the passage itself has actually finished. In this case, the giving of the manna is included, but the subsequent stories about some people hoarding it and others breaking the Sabbath to go out looking for it are not included in the reading. These are important stories that give us a much fuller picture than would be the case with the verses included in this reading alone.

One possible way to include these stories would be to simply add them by lengthening the reading to include verses 16–31. Such a reading, however, might be considered too long for use in public worship. In that case, another option is to read Exodus 11–31 instead. This restores the omitted verses without making the reading too long. It also avoids some repetition of verses, since verses 2–4 and 9–15 appear not only here but also on Proper 13 next year.

Jonah 3:10—4:11

Even though the story of the whale is more famous, this reading is really the heart of the book of Jonah. In it, God confronts the prophet, who is sulking because the people of Nineveh repented and were not destroyed as he had said they would be. Except for verse 3:10, which appears as part of a longer reading in Epiphany next year, this reading appears in the lectionary only this once.

As was the case last week, the lectionary has again given us a reading from near the end of a much longer narrative. Here, the full story of Jonah may be even less familiar to people in the congregation than the story of Joseph we saw last week. Preachers would do well to briefly summarize Jonah's adventures (particularly his reluctance to go to a "heathen" town such as Nineveh) before reading the lesson. It would certainly help more people appreciate this powerful lesson.

The link between this reading and the parable of the workers in the vineyard is one of the more inspired pairings we have seen this season. Both this lesson and the Gospel lesson teach about God's wonderfully inclusive grace. That in itself would be a useful link. Even more fruitful, however, is the way both passages honestly portray the negative response that grace can sometimes evoke.

Philippians 1:21–30

This is the first of four semi-continuous readings from Philippians. It is a fairly familiar passage, but appears in the lectionary only this once.

In the reading, Paul talks about his conflicting desires to be with Christ while at the same time wanting to be with the Philippians as they suffer for the Gospel. It is one of the most personal greetings Paul was ever known to have sent to any church. However, one would never know this from the lectionary. Again, both the salutation and the thanksgiving that begin this very personal letter have been omitted, in much the same way the salutation and thanksgiving were omitted from Romans earlier. While it is not feasible to restore those verses, it is possible to restore the personal touch Paul intended here by prefacing the reading with a brief comment about this letter and its setting.

Matthew 20:1–16

For this reading, the lectionary has chosen to give us the parable of the workers in the vineyard. Like the reading for last week, this reading too comes from material that is unique to Matthew. It also appears in the lectionary only this once.

Unlike the reading for last week, this reading is not continuous. In fact, the lectionary has skipped a sizable number of verses between this reading and its predecessor. Among these verses are some teachings about divorce, Jesus inviting the children to come to him, and the story of the rich young man. Most of these verses have parallels in both Mark and Luke. The Lukan parallels never appear in the lectionary, but all the parallels from Mark do. They are read next year for Propers 22 and 23.

Proper 21

Exodus 17:1–7

This reading recounts the now famous story of God's bringing water from out of a rock. It is another reading from the story of Moses that has already appeared this year during the Lent/Easter cycle (Third Sunday in Lent). It is a continuous reading that immediately follows the manna story from last week. It is very similar to that story, but is shorter and not quite as fully developed. Therefore the lectionary was able to include it all without having to edit it.

Ezekiel 18:1–4, 25–32

As it stands in the lectionary, this lesson is somewhat vague and enigmatic. In general, these verses challenge the common notion that the sins (or virtues) of the parents are always passed on to the children. That message, however, is not as clear as it might have been because of the way this lesson has been edited. First, important verses were omitted that might have made the writer's message more understandable. In this case, though, the lectionary is not entirely to blame. The eighteenth chapter of Ezekiel is not an easy one to condense. Preachers should feel free to restore to the reading whatever omitted verses make it more understandable to both them and their congregations.

Second, some verses in this reading, particularly 25–32, were specifically chosen in order to give the reading a more general application. Without the intervening verses, however, the last half of the reading seems disjointed and not clearly connected to the earlier verses. Again, preachers should feel free to study the entire chapter and decide for themselves which alterations they might make that would make the reading more understandable.

The lectionary has linked this reading to the parable of the two sons from the Gospel lesson for today. This link lends itself to several possible sermon strategies. If the reading is used as it appears in the lectionary, the sermon could easily focus on the theme of repentance as seen in the figure of the first son. Such a sermon might also reflect on behavior as the evidence of the sincerity of one's faith. If some of the omitted verses have been added, the sermon might then focus more on accepting personal responsibility for one's own actions.

Philippians 2:1–13

This reading begins immediately where last week's reading ended. It is a well-known passage in which Paul extols the humility of Christ as an example to all believers. This is the only time this entire lesson appears in the lectionary. The hymn in verses 5–11, however, appears not only here, but also in all

three years on both Passion/Palm Sunday and on Holy Name
(as an alternate reading).

As noted when this reading first appeared on Passion/Palm
Sunday, the most difficult issue to face the preacher of these
verses is deciding how to handle its humility theme. In fact,
this theme is even more pronounced today, now that verses 1–
4 are also included. Again, preachers will need to be sensitive
to how these words will be heard, especially by women and
others in our society who have traditionally been "kept in their
place" by counsels to practice humility.

See notes on this reading under Passion/Palm Sunday
Year A.

Matthew 21:23–32

In this reading, Jesus and some religious leaders of the
day confront one another over his authority to do the things he
does. In response, Jesus tells a parable about two sons, one
who refuses his father's request and then later changes his
mind and the other who first accepts the request and then later
ignores it. The confrontation is also recorded in both Mark and
Luke but neither parallel appears in the lectionary. The parable of the two sons is Matthew's own. Both are included in
the lectionary only this once.

Because this reading appears very innocently here near
the end of Ordinary Time, it seems at first to be a simple controversy story. It is much more than that, but we would never
know it from the lectionary because too much of the story leading up to this reading has been omitted here. Since the reading last week, Jesus has predicted his death for the third time.
He has talked about coming as "one who serves." He has healed
a blind man, entered Jerusalem on a donkey, cleansed the
temple, and cursed a fig tree. Those are "these things" the
Pharisees confront Jesus about in this passage. They are also
the things that will soon lead to his arrest and execution. Even
though much of this background will appear next year in its
Markan form, it should also be acknowledged here as well,
particularly if this is the passage we choose to preach from
today.

Proper 22

Exodus 20:1–4, 7–9, 12–20

This is another reading that is also associated with the
Lent/Easter cycle. In this case, it does not appear until the

Third Sunday in Lent next year when the Ten Commandments appear again in slightly different form (Exodus 20:1–17).

Between this lesson and the one from last week are three passages that are worth our attention, but are never included in the lectionary. The first is a passage about a battle against the Amalekites. The battle, however, is not as interesting as the events on the sidelines. Moses is on a hillside overseeing the battle. Whenever he holds up his staff, the Israelite soldiers are encouraged and they begin to win against the enemy. Eventually, however, Moses tires. The battle begins to favor the Amalekites until Aaron and Hur (another Israelite) help Moses by holding up his staff with him.

The second noteworthy passage in these intervening verses recounts some counsel Moses' father-in-law gave him about learning to delegate some of his overwhelming responsibilities. Moses listened and appointed several elders to help adjudicate simpler cases. Both this passage and the one before it are perfect readings for sermons reflecting on faithful and authentic leadership.

The third passage recounts what happened at the base of Mount Sinai as Moses prepared to receive the Ten Commandments. This passage is not as meaty as the other two, but it is still worth attention, particularly as a prelude to the official reading for today.

Several verses have been omitted from the reading itself, too, most likely in an effort to shorten the reading. These verses elaborate on both the second and the fourth commandments and differentiate this passage from the version of the Ten Commandments found in Deuteronomy. This alone is a good reason to include them in the reading, even if the lectionary does not.

In a similar way, the lectionary has also omitted the concluding verses of this passage, again no doubt in an effort to shorten it. The lectionary should be commended for including as much of this conclusion as it did and not ending the reading at the last commandment. Even so, adding verse 21 would round out the reading more satisfactorily.

Isaiah 5:1–7

The passage from which this reading was taken is often known as the Vineyard Song. In it, the prophet sings about God having planted a beautiful garden only to find that it has brought forth bitter fruit. His song is a powerful indictment of the corruption Isaiah saw among his people. It is also representative of First Isaiah. In fact, this reading is so representative that it appears in the lectionary again in Year C as one of several semi-continuous readings from the book of Isaiah.

At first, the link the lectionary has made between this reading and today's Gospel lesson seems somewhat superficial. Both readings are about persons having trouble with their vineyards. The connections between these readings, however, are actually much deeper than that, and the lectionary is correct in exploiting them. Not only are both readings about vineyards, both are stinging attacks on corrupt political and religious leadership. Indeed, it is possible that Jesus had Isaiah's song in mind when he told his parable.

Philippians 3:4b–14

In this reading, Paul concludes his exhortations by using himself as an example. He talks about the many reasons he could boast, but does not. Instead, he says, he "presses on toward the goal" to which Christ first called him. This reading appears not only here, but also on the Fifth Sunday in Lent Year C.

To reach this lesson, the lectionary has skipped over several verses between last week's reading and this one. Many of these verses contain personal greetings and refer to events and people contemporary to Paul. These never appear in the lectionary. Other verses, however, are more general in nature. Most of these appear in Advent Year C.

Matthew 21:33–46

Today's reading, the parable of the wicked tenants, is a continuous reading that begins immediately where the reading from last week ended. It appears only this once, although in the Bible it has parallels in both Mark and Luke.

Proper 23

Exodus 32:1–14

Almost twelve chapters separate the reading from last week and this reading, which recounts the making of the golden calf. Most of these omitted chapters contain various laws and regulations about religious places, objects, and rituals. It is not surprising that few of these have been included in the lectionary. The only narratives in these omitted chapters include the story of the confirmation of God's covenant with Israel and the making of the stone tablets bearing the Ten Commandments. The first never appears in the lectionary, undoubtedly because it seemed too ritualistic. The second appeared this year on Transfiguration Sunday.

The major issue about this reading is the way it has been edited by the lectionary. We are told about the calf. We are even told about what Moses and God thought about it up on the mountaintop. (That part of the story appears again on Proper 19 Year C.) We are not told, however, how the story ended. Nowhere in the lectionary do we find that Moses, and eventually God, took vengeance on those who had worshiped the calf, a vengeance even God had at first refused to exact. This is not a minor detail. It reveals an ambivalence about grace and punishment that still bedevils the Judeo-Christian tradition. This part of the story, of course, is not easily incorporated into a reading, but it is certainly worth our reflection, in the study if not in the sermon.

Isaiah 25:1–9

This reading is quite famous, especially the last part (verses 6–9). This is understandable, since these verses appear frequently in the liturgy. They also appear every year on Easter evening and as alternate readings next year on both Easter and All Saints' Day. On those occasions, the emphasis naturally falls on the image of death being swallowed up forever.

Today the emphasis falls instead on the image of the banquet, largely because the lectionary has linked this passage to Jesus' parable of the wedding feast that appears in the Gospel lesson for today. This is a particularly effective pairing since the ethical note in the parable brings out the similar ethical considerations in verses 1–6 of this reading. These considerations are often overlooked when this reading is used on festival occasions, so this emphasis is particularly welcome here.

Philippians 4:1–9

This is the final semi-continuous reading from Philippians and again the lectionary has omitted several verses to arrive at this lesson from the one last week. Most of these verses never appear in the lectionary, except for some very strong words against Paul's opponents in Philippi. Those appear on the Second Sunday in Lent Year C.

In this reading, the mood abruptly shifts to a friendlier, more personal note. It also begins somewhat abruptly, with a "therefore" that is never explained. A smoother beginning would be at verse 2 or even 4.

The reading concludes with a famous exhortation to rejoice and to keep one's mind on what is good. That exhortation appears not only appears here, but twice in Year C, on the Third Sunday in Advent and on Thanksgiving Day.

Matthew 22:1–14

In this reading, the lectionary gives us the parable of the wedding banquet. The reading is a continuous one that appears in the lectionary only this one time. Most verses in it are unique to Matthew, although there is a similar story in Luke 14:16–24 that is never included in the lectionary at all.

Proper 24

Exodus 33:12–23

In this reading, Moses again intercedes before God on behalf of the people of Israel. The lectionary has skipped several verses since the last reading, however, and in so doing most of the historical context for this intercession has been lost. In these omitted verses, the people of Israel prepare to set out for Canaan but God refuses to go with them. They are too "stiff-necked" for God's taste. It is at this point that Moses intercedes, hoping that God will once more relent and take back the threat to abandon the people. Again, this historical context may not be easy to include in the reading, but it is certainly important background information for those who wish to preach from this text and for the congregations who will be hearing these sermons.

This reading appears in the lectionary only this once.

Isaiah 45:1–7

In this prophecy from Second Isaiah, God promises to restore the people of Israel and bring them back from exile. This is to take place, Isaiah says, through the efforts of God's anointed one, Cyrus, even though Cyrus himself might not realize what he is doing.

The historical references in this reading cry out for illumination, particularly the references to Cyrus. Who is this mysterious "anointed" one? Where does he come from and what is his relationship to the people of Israel? Both preacher and congregation will appreciate this reading much more once they know some of its historical background.

The link between this reading and the Gospel lesson today is another of the lectionary's more inspired pairings. Taken by itself, Jesus' admonition to "give therefore to the emperor the things that are the emperor's, and to God the things that are God's," could be understood as an admonition to divide our loyalties appropriately. When paired with this lesson, however, the true intent of Jesus' teaching becomes clearer. Everything belongs to God, even the emperor. God is God of all, even though, like Cyrus, the Roman emperor may not know it.

1 Thessalonians 1:1–10

This lesson inaugurates a series of five continuous and semicontinuous readings from 1 Thessalonians. Unlike the initial readings in both the series of readings from Romans and Ephesians, this lesson includes the salutation and thanksgiving of 1 Thessalonians. In it, Paul greets the Thessalonian believers and commends them for their steadfastness under pressure. The reading is so historically grounded, however, that the lectionary chose to use it only this once.

Matthew 22:15–22

This well-known reading begins immediately where the reading from last week ended. In today's reading, Jesus deflects a potentially dangerous question, "Should godly people pay taxes to an ungodly state?" His deliberately ambiguous answer is so well known that it has been the focus of countless sermons. Surprisingly, however, this is the only time it appears in the lectionary. Not even its parallels in Mark and Luke are included.

Proper 25

Deuteronomy 34:1–12

This reading tells about Moses' receiving permission to see the promised land from afar (even though he is not allowed to enter it), and it recounts the events surrounding the death of Moses. It appears only this once.

It also brings the semi-continuous readings from the life of Moses to an abrupt end. To reach this reading, several chapters in Exodus, the whole book of Numbers, and most of the book of Deuteronomy have been passed over. This is the largest body of biblical material to be skipped in a single series of

semi-continuous readings. Some of this material appears elsewhere in the lectionary, particularly parts of Deuteronomy, but
most of it does not. These sections are comprised primarily of
laws, regulations, genealogies and records—material the
lectionary often omits as unimportant. Ambitious preachers
may want to read it and decide for themselves.

Leviticus 19:1–2, 15–18

In this reading, the lectionary gives us a short compilation
of various Levitical laws. The laws the lectionary has chosen
are primarily ethical laws regarding the way members of the
community are expected to treat one another. The reading also
appeared in a somewhat longer form on the Seventh Sunday
After Epiphany.

Some of the same issues we encountered in Epiphany are
also present today. First, this is the only reading from Leviticus
to be included in the lectionary. Its verses are quite representative of Leviticus as a whole, and for that reason alone they
deserve our attention.

Second, the lectionary has once more omitted verses from
the middle of this reading. In this case, even verses 10–14 have
been omitted. As we saw earlier, some of these omissions (such
as the verses regarding animal sacrifices, for instance) were
obviously made to focus attention on the more general regulations contained in the other verses of the reading. Some of the
omitted verses, however, also contain general laws (such as
the laws regarding Sabbath observance). These verses deserve
to be included in the reading and can easily be added without
adding appreciably to its length.

Today, there is an additional consideration: the way this
reading has been paired with the Gospel lesson from Matthew.
This link is not as strong as the links we have seen the last few
Sundays, but it is an interesting link nonetheless. This is especially true if we manage to avoid the temptation to lift Jesus'
teaching about the Great Commandment above the commandments we find here. In this case, both Jesus and the writer of
Leviticus are teaching us the importance of having love and
respect for those around us.

1 Thessalonians 2:1–8

This is the second in this series of continuous readings from
1 Thessalonians. In this reading, Paul begins the body of this
letter by immediately defending his ministry against critics
who have arisen against him in Thessalonica. Again this read-

ing is so historically oriented that it appears in the lectionary only this once.

Even though it began appropriately at verse 1, this reading ends awkwardly. In fact, it ends right in the middle of Paul's discussion about how hard he had worked not to be a burden to the Thessalonians. Since this discussion follows naturally from the first part of this lesson, it makes sense to add verse 9 to round out the reading.

Matthew 22:34–46

This reading has two very distinct parts—the teaching on which commandment is greatest and a teaching about the "son of David." Matthew's version of these passages appears in the lectionary only this once. Both passages, though, have parallels in Mark and Luke. Both Mark's and Luke's versions of the Great Commandment appear in the lectionary during Ordinary Time in their respective years. This makes the Great Commandment teaching more emphasized than it might appear at first. The teaching on the "son of David," on the other hand, receives no such emphasis.

There is only one passage of Matthew between last week's reading and this one. That passage records the way Jesus answered a trick question about marriage in heaven. It is included in the lectionary during Ordinary Time in Year C (Proper 27).

Proper 26

Joshua 3:7–17

With this reading, we come to the first of two semi-continuous readings from the Joshua narrative. This lesson recounts both the crossing of the river Jordan and God's promise to exalt Joshua in the same way Moses had been exalted. The reading appears only this once, but it is one of the more spectacular portions of the Joshua narrative not associated with a battle. That alone makes it an enticing reading for a sermon.

In moving from the lesson last week to this one, the lectionary has omitted several passages, including the introduction to the book of Joshua. Two of these omitted passages deserve our attention. The first is an account of God's command to Joshua to enter Canaan and conquer it. As we have seen before, the lectionary often omits such passages because they hint at the less comfortable aspects of the conquest of

Canaan. The brutal reality of that conquest, however, should not be so easily ignored if we are to learn its proper lessons.

The second omitted passage that deserves our attention is the story of Rahab, who helped Joshua's spies escape back to camp. This account, too, is not very comfortable, but omitting it effectively silences another biblical woman.

Micah 3:5–12

This diatribe against false prophets is only part of a much longer section in which Micah attacks corrupt leadership of all kinds. Political leaders, economic leaders, military leaders, even the king all come under Micah's judgment.

This broader picture is important to remember, especially when we consider the way this passage has been paired with the Gospel lesson for today. In that lesson, Jesus is pictured as proclaiming a similar diatribe against the Pharisees of his day. Such a link can tempt us to focus exclusively on the Pharisees. Neither Micah nor Jesus, however, would have been satisfied with such a narrow focus.

Except for verse 5, which concludes the reading for the Fourth Sunday in Advent, this reading appears in the lectionary only this once. It is also one of only three passages to be included from Micah.

1 Thessalonians 2:9–13

This is another continuous reading from 1 Thessalonians. It begins where the reading from last week ended, whether that was at verse 8 or 9. In the reading, Paul continues defending his ministry among the Thessalonians. Once again, his words here are so tied to the historical situation in which they were written that the lectionary has chosen to use this reading only once.

Matthew 23:1–12

This reading is continuous to last week's reading from Matthew. It is comprised of several teachings from Jesus that are loosely connected by the theme of authority. He warns against following Pharisees who do not practice what they preach. He expressly forbids his followers to take on titles such as Father or Teacher, and he says that in the realm of God the exalted will be humbled and the humble will be exalted.

This is the only time this particular reading appears in the lectionary, although Mark's version of these same teachings appears next year for Proper 27. Most of these teachings also have parallels in Luke, but they are scattered throughout the Gospel and none are included in the lectionary.

Proper 27

Joshua 24:1–3a, 14–25

To reach this lesson, in which Joshua renews the covenant made at Sinai, the lectionary has omitted most of the book of Joshua. None of these omitted chapters ever appear in the lectionary, except for a very short reading that appears on the Fourth Sunday in Lent Year C. Most of the omitted narratives are battle stories and accounts of how the conquered land was divided up. The most surprising omission, however, is the omission of the famous battle of Jericho. It never appears in the lectionary at all.

Even the reading itself has been edited. Virtually all of Joshua's long rehearsal of sacred history has been been omitted, no doubt in an effort to shorten the reading. The omitted verses, however, can be restored without making the reading impossibly long. Doing so does not appreciably affect the meaning of the text, either. Since additional verses often affect the meaning of the reading, preachers should probably make their decision anew every three years, based on the way they intend to use the reading.

A shortened version of this same lesson also appears as a linked reading next year on Proper 16. Then, even Joshua's dire warnings about what will happen if the people break with God are omitted.

Wisdom 6:12–16

This apocryphal reading is the first of two readings for today from the Hebrew Scriptures. In it, the lectionary gives us a beautiful picture of the wisdom of God.

This lesson, however, is only part of a much longer passage that began with the first verse of chapter 6. Those initial verses never appear in the lectionary, but the concluding verses, which follow immediately after this reading, do. They are today's principal psalm reading.

The lectionary has made an interesting link between this lesson and the parable of the foolish virgins, which appears in the Gospel lesson for today. In many respects, this link is quite appropriate. It offers us one of those few occasions when the

Hebrew Scriptures are used to comment upon a reading from the Christian Scriptures rather than the other way around.

In making this link, though, the lectionary has unintentionally undermined the very eschatological themes it is most interested in today. Ordinarily, the parable of the foolish virgins in very eschatological. Its primary purpose is to encourage preparedness for the coming of Jesus. In the light of this reading, however, the focus of the parable is subtly shifted from being prepared to being wise enough to prepare.

The most interesting and potentially most useful feature about this reading is its exclusive use of feminine imagery. In the Bible, God's wisdom is frequently spoken of in feminine terms, but such language seldom appears in the lectionary. This is a good opportunity to redress this imbalance. Even Protestant congregations, who do not normally make use of the Apocrypha, could find this passage useful for litanies or prayers.

Amos 5:18–24

This well-known reading is the canonical alternative to the reading from Wisdom. It appears in the lectionary only this one time and has clearly been chosen to fit in with the eschatological tone characteristic of lectionary readings for these last few Sundays of the year.

The lectionary has paired this passage with the parable of the foolish virgins in today's Gospel lesson, but the link is a weak one. Both refer to preparing for the coming day of God, but each has a different focus and approach to that preparation. In such a case, it may be best to simply let the two readings illumine each other, taking care not to stretch the meaning of either text in an effort to join them.

1 Thessalonians 4:13–18

This reading is somewhat different from the readings from 1 Thessalonians that have preceded it. First, it is not a continuous but a semi-continuous reading. Several verses of 1 Thessalonians have been skipped between the reading last week and this one. Most of these verses contain more historical references to Paul's relationship with the Thessalonians and do not appear in the lectionary at all. Other verses are of a more general nature and those have been included in the lectionary in Advent Year C.

Second, even though this lesson is semi-continuous, it has been specifically chosen for its eschatological tone. Again, such eschatological themes are often characteristic of these last few Sundays of the year. In many respects, they are the lectionary's way of preparing us for the coming of Advent.

Matthew 25:1–13

With this reading, we come to another lesson that has been specifically chosen for its eschatological tone. No matter which year it is in the lectionary's three-year cycle, the Gospel lessons for Propers 27 and 28 always come from the most eschatological section of their respective Gospels, a section most often known as the "Synoptic Apocalypse."

To arrive at this reading, the lectionary deliberately skipped most of Matthew's "Apocalypse." In fact, the major part of Matthew's version of the Synoptic Apocalypse never appears in the lectionary at all. Instead, the lectionary has chosen to focus on the series of eschatological parables Matthew added to the body of material he had inherited from Mark. Today's reading highlights the parable of the wise and foolish virgins. This parable is Matthew's own and was clearly intended as a warning against being unprepared for Christ's return at the end of time. This is the only time it appears in the lectionary.

Proper 28

Judges 4:1–7

This reading, which appears only this once, is the only reading from the book of Judges to appear in the lectionary. It is also the only story of a biblical woman to be highlighted in this series of semi-continuous readings.

The most significant feature of this lesson is the way it has been edited by the lectionary. Deborah appears in the lectionary, but her story has been cut off in the middle and her song omitted altogether. Not only that, but the story of Jael, whom Deborah predicted would bring victory to Israel, has also been omitted. Both these omissions are understandable because both are violent, especially the story of Jael. Again, however, that must be weighed against the enforced silence of still another biblical woman.

To reach this reading, the lectionary has skipped the opening chapters of the book of Judges. Most of these chapters simply describe Joshua's death, the increasing conquest of Canaan, and the people of Israel's increasing tendency to fall away from the ways of God. None of these are important passages.

More important passages from Judges appear at the end of the book, where the author reflects on the lack of leadership and its effect on the social fabric in Canaan (Judges 21:24–25). These verses have some real homiletical value but can be easily overlooked, particularly since they never appear anywhere in the lectionary.

Zephaniah 1:7, 12–18

In this lesson from the book of Zephaniah, the prophet declares his characteristic message that God's coming day will be a day of judgment. In this respect, the reading resembles the reading from Amos last week, except that religious practice is far less of a concern here. Like its predecessor, though, this reading also has been chosen for its eschatological tone as the lectionary prepares us for Advent.

The eschatological themes of this reading are more evident when seen next to the parable of the talents found in today's Gospel lesson. Both readings picture the coming of God's day in terms of judgment. Both emphasize that on that day all people will be held accountable for their behavior. In fact, both readings call attention to and augment the eschatological themes of the other.

1 Thessalonians 4:13–18

This reading bears a strong resemblance to the reading before it. It too appears in the lectionary only once, and it too has been specifically chosen for its eschatological themes. In the reading, Paul continues his discussion about Resurrection Day and the coming of Christ. He concludes with some specific exhortations on how to wait for that day faithfully.

Matthew 25:14–30

In this reading, the lectionary gives us the second of the two eschatological parables Matthew added to his "Apocalypse." Known as the parable of the ten talents, this lesson, too, was intended by Matthew as a warning against being unprepared for the day of Christ's return. This is the only time this parable appears in the lectionary, even though a similar version of it can also be found in the Gospel of Luke.

Proper 29
(Reign of Christ *or* Christ the King)

Even though these readings are officially appointed for
Proper 29 in Ordinary Time, they are also festival readings.
Each reading has been chosen specifically for its compatibility
with themes characteristic of this day. Each reading is linked
to each of the others by those themes. This is particularly noticeable in the case of the reading from Ezekiel, which is both
the semi-continuous and the paired reading for today.

One interesting feature about these readings is the title
given to them by the lectionary. Christ the King has long been
celebrated at the close of the church year, particularly in more
liturgical communions. In response to the concerns of women,
however, the more favored title for this day is now Reign of
Christ Sunday. This is a significant improvement. It not only
shows an effort on the part of the lectionary compilers to be
more cognizant of women and our issues regarding liturgy, it
also moves the language of the lectionary one step closer toward inclusivity about God as well as the people of God.

Ezekiel 34:11–16, 20–24

This reading has been taken from a much longer passage
on God as the shepherd of Israel. In it, Ezekiel pictures God as
a divine shepherd who will guide the people of Israel to pas-
tures of peace and justice. This is the only time this reading
appears in the lectionary, even though it is taken from one of
the lectionary's most favored parts of Ezekiel.

As we saw earlier, this reading is both semi-continuous and
is paired with the Gospel lesson for today. Those who have been
following the track of semi-continuous readings should treat
this reading as such. In a similar way, those who have been
following the track of paired readings should also treat this
reading as paired as well.

This kind of clear distinction is not easy to maintain, however, particularly for those using this passage as a semi-continuous reading. The shepherd themes in both this reading and
in the Gospel reading are so well matched that it is very difficult not to pair the two unintentionally. This is especially true
if this lesson is simply read alongside the Gospel lesson without at least some elaboration on the distinctions between them.

The lectionary has also omitted several verses from the
middle of this reading. In most cases, the lectionary makes
such omissions in an effort to either focus the reading more

narrowly on the theme for the day or to strengthen a link the lectionary has made with another lesson. In this case, just the opposite appears to be true. The omitted verses, which describe God's frustration with the corrupt leadership of Israel during the time of Ezekiel, could easily have lent themselves to a fusing of the image of God in Ezekiel with the image of Jesus in Matthew. By omitting these verses, the lectionary weakens what is an already powerful link.

Ephesians 1:15–23

This reading comes from the last part of the thanksgiving that begins this letter. In the lectionary, it appears every year on Ascension Day and on All Saints' in Year C. In each case, the emphasis intended by the lectionary shifts as the church year shifts.

Today the emphasis is clearly on the last half of this reading. There God is described as having given Christ authority over all things in both heaven and earth. This is a natural emphasis for the Reign of Christ Sunday. But, as we saw earlier when this same reading appeared on Ascension Day, such a focus may be a legitimate theme in the reading, but is not the primary emphasis of the author. The author's primary concern is to give thanks for the Ephesians and to introduce topics he will take up later in the letter. Among these topics is the cosmic authority of Christ.

Matthew 25:31–46

In this reading the lectionary gives us another parable that is unique to Matthew, the parable of the sheep and goats. This, too, is a natural reading for the Reign of Christ Sunday. These verses not only give us a picture of the "Son of Man" reigning in glory, but also make use of a shepherd theme that is easily linked with the reading from Ezekiel.

Of all the readings for today, this is probably most likely to be chosen as the basis of the sermon. Those who choose to preach on this passage should beware of at least two common temptations. The first is the temptation to make too superficial a link between the Ezekiel passage and this one. The second is the temptation to get so caught up in the "Son of Man" figure that one loses sight of Matthew's message. Falling into either temptation does not help either us or our congregations.

This reading also appears every year in the lectionary on New Year's Day. There, however, the emphasis is not as much on the figure of Jesus as the Great Shepherd. Instead, the figures of the sheep and goats are more prominent to encourage the keeping of resolutions for the new year.

All Saints' Day

Like most sets of festival readings, these lessons have been linked together by a common theme. In this case, the theme emphasizes "the saints," both those who have gone before and those who are present with us now.

At the same time, this set of readings is also unusual, particularly for this time of year. First, it is the only set of readings in Ordinary Time that does not have at least one reading from the Hebrew Scriptures. There are several passages from the Hebrew Bible that could have been chosen, though. There is Isaiah 61:1–11, for instance, or parts of Daniel chapter 7, or even Daniel 3:8–30 (the story of the three youths in the fiery furnace). The last two possible readings do not ever appear in the lectionary, but are sound readings that should be considered on occasion. The reading from Revelation, then, could be used as a psalm reading or as part of the liturgy of the day.

Second, this is only one of two sets of readings in Ordinary Time designed for a festival that usually occurs during the week. In this case, these readings can be used either on All Saints' Day itself or on the First Sunday in November. When used on the Sunday, however, these readings substitute for the readings that ordinarily would have fallen on that Sunday. This interrupts the semi-continuous readings characteristic of Ordinary Time and, in some cases, may require some thought and planning.

Revelation 7:9–17

From the viewpoint of the lectionary, this is a perfect lesson for All Saints'. It not only pictures the "multitude" of the saints in glory, it also pictures them at worship. Even more, there are hundreds of inspiring choir anthems based on these verses as well, which could be used to accompany or even replace the reading itself.

This lesson, however, is only part of a longer section describing the multitude of saints and their worship. The biblical passage from which this reading has been taken continues with John's asking who the multitude might be. He is told that they are the martyrs who "have come out of the great ordeal." These later verses were omitted no doubt in order to make the multitude more inclusive of all the saints, not just those who have been martyred. They need not be included if this lesson is simply to be read, but those who are preaching on this passage might consider adding these extra verses, or at least studying them in preparation for the sermon.

This lesson also appears in the lectionary on the Fourth Sunday of Easter Year C.

1 John 3:1–3

In this reading, the author of 1 John makes several shifts in thought. He begins by reflecting on the love of God that makes us children of God. He then briefly reflects on how the children of God are often misunderstood by the world. He then concludes by reflecting on the future blessings ahead for those children of God who are in Christ.

Like the reading from Revelation, this reading has also been specifically chosen for All Saints'. In this case, the link is more subtle. There are the obvious references to the "children of God" and the references to becoming like Christ at his return. Both references are easily associated with All Saints'. In between, however, are references to being strangers in the world and being misunderstood by it. This is a different slant on the theme that could prove very fruitful for those willing to explore it.

Also like today's reading from Revelation, this reading appears in the lectionary again during the Easter season, in this case on the Third Sunday in Easter next year.

Matthew 5:1–12

With this lesson, the focus shifts from the saints in glory we saw in Revelation to saints in the present. These saints are very down-to-earth. They are the poor in spirit, the humble, those who mourn, those who hunger and thirst for what is right, even those who are reviled and persecuted for righteousness' sake. This, too, is an interesting twist to today's theme that is well worth noting. It not only balances the otherworldly image of sainthood found in Revelation, it also expresses the concept in ways more people can appreciate.

Not surprisingly, this lesson occurs in the lectionary several times. Besides appearing here, it also appeared on the Fourth Sunday After Epiphany. The Lukan version of these same verses appears as well on All Saints' Day in Year C.

Thanksgiving Day

Of all the festival readings in the lectionary, these are the only ones appointed for a day more associated with the secular calendar than the church year. Even so, they still follow the lectionary's usual pattern for festival readings. All three readings are linked by a common theme for the day, in this case the theme of thanksgiving. At least two are fairly well-known readings. None are semi-continuous.

Deuteronomy 8:7–18

In this reading, the people of Israel are about to enter the promised land. Before they do, Moses exhorts the people to not forget God amid the bounty of the land they will soon inhabit.

Such a passage is an appropriate choice for a thanksgiving reading for at least two reasons. It sounds the appropriate thanksgiving theme, and it also combines that theme with an equally appropriate reminder that abundance can often be a hindrance to thanksgiving and gratitude. This makes this reading especially appropriate for North American Christians, who live in lands of abundance where it is often easy to forget or ignore God.

Interestingly, this is the only time this reading occurs in the lectionary.

2 Corinthians 9:6–15

Although it is more often heard during stewardship campaigns, this lesson from 2 Corinthians is another very appropriate choice for a Thanksgiving reading. In this case, however, Paul shifts our focus a bit toward more concrete acts of thanksgiving, such as giving an offering or contributing to charity.

The lectionary, however, has given us only part of the apostle Paul's reflections. Literarily, these verses are part of a much larger passage that includes all of chapters 8 and 9. Historically, they were written as part of an appeal for an offering Paul was collecting for the church in Jerusalem. Again, this is important information for us to be aware of, particularly if we are going to preach on this lesson. At the very least, such background helps connect these high-sounding words to a real-life situation that almost any congregation can relate to.

The reading appears in the lectionary only this once.

Luke 17:11–19

This lesson is another strong reading for Thanksgiving. In it, Jesus heals ten lepers but only one remembers to be grateful once he has his health.

With this reading we return to the theme of gratitude, a theme very much like the one we saw in the reading from Deuteronomy. This should come as no surprise, since that lesson was specifically chosen to illuminate this one.

Why the lectionary chose to abandon Matthew for this festival is not clear, especially since Matthew 6:25–33 appears on Thanksgiving next year. Those who wish to stay with Matthew might consider using this set of lessons for Year C, next year's lessons this year, and the lessons appointed for Year C next year. (The sequence would then be B, C, A)

This lesson can also be found in Year C on Proper 23, when it appears near the end of a long string of semi-continuous readings from the Gospel of Luke. Since this passage can evoke strong emotion, it may be important as well to be clear about where we are coming from whenever we do interpret this passage.

Matthew 18:15–20

The lectionary has skipped several chapters of Matthew. Most of these omitted verses have parallels in either Mark, Luke, or both, and many of these parallels are also included in the lectionary. In the case of the story of the Transfiguration, all three parallels appear.

This reading, in which Jesus explains what to do if someone sins against you, is unique to Matthew. It appears in the lectionary only this once.

INDEX